POPULISTS, PLUNGERS, AND PROGRESSIVES

A SOCIAL HISTORY OF STOCK AND
COMMODITY SPECULATION
1890-1936

BY CEDRIC B. COWING

PRINCETON, NEW JERSEY
PRINCETON UNIVERSITY PRESS
1965

Publication of this book has been
aided by the Ford Foundation program
to support publication, through
university presses, of works in the
humanities and sciences.

Printed in the United States of America by
The William Byrd Press, Inc., Richmond, Va.

WRBS 12.50 | 11.25 | 4/17/79 — Sundra

PREFACE

*H*ow did the 1929 stock market Crash come about? Americans, generally inclined to be moralistic, have found grim satisfaction in the view that the excesses of the "Roaring Twenties" had to be atoned for, that retribution for sin was inevitable. Economists have pointed to the widening gap between productivity and purchasing power in the late twenties and the incubus on foreign trade caused by a high tariff, leading presumably to the accumulation at home of funds vulnerable to speculative uses. Historians, endorsing these opinions, have condemned the isolationist foreign policy that dictated the high tariff and unreasonable German reparations. These familiar explanations fit neatly the decade between Versailles and the Black Friday of October 1929.

There is, however, an important dimension that has been neglected in these analyses. What had been the history of controversy over speculation on the exchanges prior to the twenties? What role did sectional politics play in the discussion? Who were the perennial critics of speculation? Above all, what were the assumptions and predilections that the generation of post-World War I "investors" brought with them to the brokers' offices?

To answer these questions it was necessary to begin with the criticism of commodity futures trading in the late 19th century. From the narrow conflict between agrarians—especially the Populists—and their commercial opponents over the use of the futures contract, emerged a much larger one over speculation on the exchanges in general. Diverse elements combined in the Progressive Era to check speculation, and the controversy spread to many related topics: anti-fraud laws, price-fixing, cooperative marketing, and branch banking.

The narrative concludes with the New Deal legislation of 1934-1936. With the passage of these laws, the epoch of ideological opposition to exchange speculation came to a close.

Scholars are presently examining the relationship of the Populist and Progressive Eras to post-World War I politics and reform; an exploration of the speculation controversy can aid in forming a judgment of these relationships, especially since the heritage of Populism has become controversial in the wake of the McCarthyism of the early 1950s.

While I alone am responsible for the facts and judgments presented herein, I wish to acknowledge the advice and suggestions I have received from several colleagues —Herbert F. Margulies, Merle Curti, and A. Gavan Daws—and from my wife, Sue Brown Cowing. I am also grateful for the kindness shown me by the staffs of the libraries of the Universities of Wisconsin, Minnesota, Missouri, Hawaii, California (Los Angeles), and the State Historical Society of Wisconsin.

CEDRIC B. COWING

September 3, 1964

CONTENTS

POPULISTS, PLUNGERS, AND PROGRESSIVES

CHAPTER 1

AGRARIANS AND COMMODITY

SPECULATORS

*S*PECULATION has had a venerable history in America, as in all capitalist countries, although for a time its effects were ignored by historians. Early in the twentieth century, however, scholars cast a critical eye on the economic records and discovered that colonial merchants and planters seemed to have exercised considerable foresight in anticipating land and bank values and in making their dreams come true. Readers were at first surprised at the implications of this new evidence, which stripped some of the romance from the Founding Fathers, but Americans have never regarded speculation as insidious if it is taken to mean investment of money with the expectation that the property will increase in value.

In the early nineteenth century, speculative interest centered in land. The expectation of increasing land values was a driving force in settling the West, and speculator-controlled legislatures often set the patterns for developing regions. Public antipathy was reserved largely for the absentee speculator who neither improved his land nor contributed to the community.[1] The Civil War, like all wars, increased uncertainty and with it, speculation. In particular the war led to the formal organization of futures trading in provisions and commodities. The Chicago Board of Trade emerged as the major attraction, but organized exchange trading developed in

[1] Paul W. Gates, "The Role of the Land Speculator in Western Development," *Pennsylvania Magazine of History*, 66:314-333 (1942).

St. Louis, New York, New Orleans, Minneapolis, Kansas City, and several other cities in the decade after Appomattox.

The social changes brought by industrialism and accentuated by the war and its aftermath continued to undermine the pre-industrial economic morality. Some parvenus on the exchanges departed spectacularly from the principle of speculating on the economic future and manipulated property to profit from fluctuations; at the same time personal warfare between market titans seemed often to distort intrinsic values. One result of the Civil War had been to hasten the concentration of money in the cities and among the few, and the first rural reactions were Greenbackism, Grangerism, and anti-monopoly. Americans still had the speculative itch to invest in progress but they felt that many of the financiers had not abided by the rules in accumulating wealth so quickly; in the past they had approved of shrewd investment in America's future, but they were beginning to feel the social distance that this process was creating. Americans who felt this way, largely agrarians[2] and those allied with them, longed for the antebellum days when economic control had been more local and therefore more personal.

As yet stock market activity touched only a few, but commodity trading directly affected an increasing number of staple crop producers. The seemingly orthodox futures contract, occasionally used before the Civil War and an outgrowth of earlier "to sail," "to arrive," and "forward delivery" agreements, began to receive unpre-

[2] The term "agrarians" is used throughout this study to apply to the more extreme staple crop growers and their adherents in towns, cities and legislatures. It refers to those who, for various reasons, endorsed the pre-industrial, pro-agriculture rhetoric, who subscribed to what Richard Hofstadter calls the agrarian myth. Their attitude toward the exchanges was markedly moralistic and hostile; they favored the abolition of futures trading and the heavy taxation of speculative gains.

4

cedented attention from speculators. Persons not previously connected with the commodities business had been attracted, and were buying and selling futures contracts in the central markets, especially in Chicago and New York. The number of bushels and bales traded on the exchanges exceeded the annual production from 1872 on and in several years toward the end of the century amounted to sevenfold the annual crop. Prices had moved widely before the war because of weather, economic instability, and imperfect crop information, but it appeared that the new volatility was due to maneuvers by speculators with large purses. Thus "speculator" became more than ever a term of opprobrium; the physiocratic bias against those who produced no primary products was more bitterly asserted as the agrarian population shifted consciously to the defensive. The mysterious and remote commodity speculator seemed more of a parasite to the farmers than the local physician who was holding land for appreciation. Farmers identified the commodity speculator as the villain responsible for erratic price changes in Chicago, Minneapolis, and New York, especially around harvest time. The stage was set; the national crusade against the exchange speculator was about to begin.

The farmers' economic position, worsened by the droughts after 1886, had been declining, and the result was the "Populist Revolt." The futures system came under sharper attack, and Congressional bills to ban futures multiplied along with the outcries from stricken farm areas.[3] Finally in 1892 a composite bill, called the Hatch bill after the chairman, William H. Hatch of Missouri, emerged from the House Agriculture Committee; Senator William Drew Washburn of Minnesota sponsored a very similar measure in the Senate, and the terms

[3] William H. Hatch in U. S. Congress, *Fictitious Dealing in Agricultural Products*. Committee on Agriculture, House of Representatives (52 Cong., 3 sess., Washington, 1892), 4-7.

"Hatch bill" and "Washburn bill" were used interchangeably thereafter. The purpose of these bills was plain: they aimed to tax sales of grain and cotton where the purchaser did not own the commodity, and was selling that which he expected to acquire later. All disputants acknowledged that the tax rate of 10 percent was prohibitive, and that, should the proposal pass, trading on the commodity futures exchanges would decline greatly. It was the desirability of this decline that was in dispute.

Proponents of the bill called many agricultural spokesmen before committees of Congress to substantiate the evils of futures contracts. C. W. Macune of the Farmers' Alliance and Industrial Union explained that his organization was active in all sections of the country except New England, and asserted flatly that farmers were opposed to the existing futures system of trading in commodities. He reiterated that the Hatch bill would not eliminate trading in futures contracts, but would confine it to persons who actually possessed the commodity at the time of option purchase.[4] J. H. Brigham, Master of the National Grange, followed Macune, and testified that labor, farmers, and small communities were behind this bill; they asked only equal treatment under the law and no special favors. He complained that the beleaguered grain brokers had enlisted their powerful press and banking allies in a campaign against the bill. Herbert Myrick, representing the *New England Homestead* and the *American Agriculturalist,* told the legislators that on this issue New England farmers sympathized with their farm brethren in other sections. He condemned futures trading and described his campaign to induce readers to write their Congressmen supporting the bill.

The anti-futures crusaders also received support from many old-timers among the grain and hog merchants. W.

---

[4] *Ibid.,* 249-258. Thirty farm organizations favored the Hatch bill. For Macune's part in Populism, see John D. Hicks, *The Populist Revolt* (Minneapolis, 1931), 106-107.

P. Howard, a member of the St. Louis Merchants Exchange, told how he had been forced out of the hog business because he refused to deal in futures contracts for his customers, and claimed that manipulation rather than supply and demand was controlling the marketplace. How else could hog traders become millionaires when hogs had been selling near cost for ten years? Chicago packers sold high, said Howard, and then "beared" the market so that they could purchase at a much lower price to fulfill their contracts. Although the futures contract method had spread rapidly, there were still brokers of the old school who insisted upon dealing only in actual products. These hold-outs favored the Hatch bill, and some of them circulated pamphlets retailing the evils of board of trade practices.[5]

Even Charles Alfred Pillsbury, the nation's largest miller, spoke for the bill. He had a keen mind, physical strength, and a personality which, combined with his economic position, made him an object of deference among the Congressmen. The miller argued that his interests and those of the Northwest grain growers were identical: both found agricultural prosperity profitable. But, said Pillsbury, neither grower nor miller had as much influence over prices as a few men around the wheat pit in Chicago. Short selling by these few made prices erratic and unstable; opinions based upon supply and demand were worthless in the face of this manipulation. And Pillsbury denied the contention of the futures brokers that the millers needed the futures markets for hedging. He suggested that if there were no futures markets, there would be little speculation, and therefore no need for hedging; the need to hedge was created by speculators who had made markets increasingly unstable over the years. Pillsbury also denied the notion fostered

[5] *Ibid.*, 258-265; 90-93; 145-154; 277-278. See 5, 45, 145, 311, 316, 327, 332, and 335 for other cash grain merchants who opposed the futures method of trading and favored the Hatch bill.

by futures brokers that milling was very profitable and that a millers' syndicate was advocating the Hatch bill solely for its own benefit. The milling industry, he said, had not made expenses in the last ten years and competition had greatly reduced the number of millers.[6]

Were the prevailing low wheat prices caused by bear speculators or by a world-wide oversupply? Several anti-futures witnesses offered facts and figures to show that after 1885 there had been no overproduction, that since then wheat acreage had not even kept pace with the nation's increase in population. Why then was the farmer receiving so little for his crop? Speculation was the obvious answer. The expansion of futures trading in the eighties had made farming chaotic and unprofitable. Previously almost all crops had been marketed without futures—so why had this unfair system become indispensable?

While brokers praised the excess of commodities traded over the amount produced, anti-futures forces made this a prime indictment of the futures method. To them the fact that many times as much grain or cotton was sold in New York, Chicago, and New Orleans as was produced in the nation annually was prima facie evidence of perversion of the market system. To agrarians it seemed as if this tremendous activity, this passing of the same bushel or bale through so many hands, meant less money for the farmer and more money for the brokers and traders. If professional traders in Chicago

[6] Charles B. Kuhlmann, "Charles Alfred Pillsbury," *Dictionary of American Biography* (New York, 1928-1936), XIV, 604-605. Senator Washburn, also an important miller, held essentially the same views. *Congressional Record*, 52 Cong., 2 sess., 6446 (July 20, 1892). Hedging as defined by William L. Clayton of Anderson, Clayton & Company, a large cotton factor, "is the offsetting of a market risk in one transaction by assuming a market risk of the opposite nature in another transaction involving a like amount of the same commodity." Julius B. Baer and Olin Glenn Saxon, *Commodity Exchanges and Futures Trading: Principles and Operating Methods* (New York, 1949 ed.), 202.

8

having no wheat could, for example, offer to sell 10,000 bushels, did not this artificially bear the market by creating an apparently excess supply? The offering of nonexistent quantities of wheat by professionals—at harvest time when the farmer was trying to sell his crop— was, to farm spokesmen, no coincidence; it was a deliberate effort by big speculators to depress the market temporarily in order to buy cheap from the farmer and later sell dear to the miller. Farmers and their allies differed on the amount of collusion involved, but most of them agreed that this was the iniquitous effect of futures contracts. Called "fictitious sales" or "wind wheat," this phenomenon of high exchange sales turnover was to be a major complaint for many years—long after Populism's apogee.

Commodity exchange advocates seemed to take a superior attitude during the committee hearings. They painted a rosy picture of the economy and emphasized the evolution of more efficient business procedures. Futures trading had developed in order to market more evenly crops that were harvested during only a few months of the year. Futures contracts enabled millers and spinners to distribute their purchases over the entire year, instead of being called upon to buy a year's supply at one time; futures also made it possible for growers to get their money more quickly—they did not have to wait until processors were ready to use their crops. Thus the futures contract was a step forward in marketing staple products. To abandon this system or to hamper trading in the contracts would be reactionary, in fact would be sheer primitivism. Moreover, if futures contracts were outlawed, the farmer would not have the constant stream of futures prices from the telegraph to guide him, and he would have to accept what he could get. Prices would vary from county to county, state to state. Chaotic prices would favor the few powerful processors who could then take advantage of the farmer's imperfect knowledge of prices and of his immediate need for cash. The toll of middleman processors would be unknown and uncontrolled, a state of affairs disadvantageous to both grower and consumer.

The exchange men also pointed to another disadvantage if futures were abridged. Without a futures contract market for hedging, price fluctuations would be greater and the farmers would therefore have to assume larger risks; these would be reflected in higher prices to the consumer. Thus, in the eyes of commodity brokers, to revert to the less complex market practices of antebellum days would be not only virtually impossible, but also uneconomic for society.[7] Brokers invoked history to illustrate the folly of tampering with economic processes, and specifically with this marketing device. Because of speculation during the War of 1812, the New York legislature had enacted a law prohibiting short sales. The law was not enforced and was repealed in 1858, in a forcefully worded document that specifically endorsed short selling. The failure of this law, the first attempt to regulate futures in the United States, seemed to indicate that in an increasingly commercial nation such restraints could not be imposed effectively. Commodity brokers also cited a second relevant instance of legal impotence in the face of economic law. In 1864 Secretary of the Treasury Salmon P. Chase wanted to control the price of gold; his object was greater price stability during the Civil War. Therefore on June 17th trading in gold futures was banned; gold could not be sold unless it was in the hands of the seller at the time of sale. Although gold trading was immediately discontinued, the price of gold continued to move erratically lower, and fifteen days later the Chase-sponsored anti-futures law was repealed, like its New York predecessor. Exchange interests said

[7] *Fictitious Dealing*, 186-201, 6-7, and H. H. Aldrich, chairman of the rules of the Chicago Board of Trade, *Fictitious Dealing*, 19-29.

it had thus been demonstrated that, even during war-time, efforts to regulate the economic "Invisible Hand" were harmful or futile.[8]

Although Populist elements viewed commodity spec-ulators as bloated gamblers, virtual robbers who usurped the rewards rightfully belonging to the farmers, ex-change officials drew quite another picture of the typical speculator. They saw him as an inept fellow, inclined to lose as often as he won, a fellow who could be relied upon to pay a large part of the carrying charges while the product was waiting processing. This expense would otherwise fall chiefly on the farmers, who would get cor-respondingly less for their crops. Thus the speculator, while pursuing his own interest in trading, could be called an unwitting philanthropist to the farmer, in-sofar as he absorbed these carrying charges. It was, of course, lamentable that some persons lost heavily at speculation, but brokers viewed the system itself as satis-factory. A continually changing army of speculators carried the nation's major crops—sometimes winning, sometimes losing—but in the aggregate extracting only a small toll for taking the risk in a fluctuating market. Was it not desirable that men with funds should take these chances rather than growers and millers who were less familiar with world-wide market conditions? The brokers' portrait of the speculator was thus free of moral guilt; to them he was simply a specialist who utilized his knowledge to facilitate wider and more con-tinuous distribution of staple products.[9]

Market spokesmen viewed Benjamin P. Hutchinson, Edward Pardridge, and other big plungers as merely un-desirable by-products of an efficient system, men whose

[8] U. S. Congress, *Options and Futures*. Committee on Judiciary. United States Senate (52 Cong., 2 sess., Washington, 1892), 244-248. *Commercial & Financial Chronicle*, 55:42-44 (July 23, 1892).

[9] President Charles Hammill and S. W. Allerton of the Chicago Board of Trade, *Fictitious Dealing*, 156-170, 173-181; Thomas A. Wright, *Options and Futures*, 74-85.

11

power had been exaggerated by sensational journalism. Hutchinson, from Massachusetts, had drifted into pure speculation from the Chicago meat packing business; he dominated the Chicago market in the eighties, and his son was later president of the Chicago Board of Trade. Pardridge, a former dry goods merchant from New York, found his ultimate calling as a "bear" in the Chicago pits, where he held sway from 1890 to 1894.[10] Exchange officials told the lawmakers of their efforts to reduce the type of excess symbolized by these men, but they still believed that speculators as a group performed a useful function.[11] Speculators were needed, the brokers contended, so that farmers and processors could hedge. Hedging, they claimed, was a form of insurance. Growers and processors bought futures contracts to insure themselves against price changes while they were holding the product, and hedging in commodities was particularly important because the period of holding the product was often as long as four or five months. But for every farmer or miller who bought a future and relieved himself of a gamble, there had to be a party on the other end of the transaction—in the modern age of large surpluses and seasonal freight-car shortages, the speculator was inevitable. Who else could assume the risk the farmer abdicated? Surely not the government, the brokers answered; as disciples of laissez-faire they did not think it proper that taxpayers' money be used for such purposes. By using the respectable word "insurance" instead of "hedging," brokers felt they strengthened their case; in fact this whole line of argument made it possible to view the speculator not only as the incidental benefactor of the farmer, as already mentioned, but also as an

[10] Edward A. Duddy, "Benjamin Peters Hutchinson," *Dictionary of American Biography*, IX, 437; Charles H. Taylor, *The Chicago Board of Trade* (Chicago, 1923), II, 925. A bear in market parlance is one who plans his transactions to profit from market declines.

[11] Aldrich in *Fictitious Dealing*, 71-77.

indispensable cog in a system of agricultural insurance.[12]

The exchanges strongly challenged the agrarian charge of fraud implied in the "wind wheat" arguments. Brokers did not see the high ratio of sales to production as harmful; the more hands the product passed through, the more widely distributed was the risk and the more stable the market; large volume meant awakened ambition and quickened enterprise. If trading were confined to actual products, prosperity would disappear.[13] A. J. Sawyer, a Minneapolis grain elevator operator, testified that the farmer was not forced to sell his products within a few weeks of harvest, as the agrarians claimed. He said the farmer could store his grain cheaply in local country elevators and could borrow up to 90 per cent on its value; therefore if the farmer sold at harvest time, it was an act of free choice; if the price rose subsequently and profit accrued to the middleman, the farmer had no cause to complain.[14]

Exchange defenders also exploited a lingering prejudice. Twisting the British lion's tail had been a political device in America since the days of George III, and increased popular government and Irish immigration had kept Anglophobia alive in the nineteenth century. Exchange men warned that passage of the Hatch Bill would drive commodity markets to foreign soil—England or Canada—where America would not benefit from them. Did Americans want to make this sacrifice to the scheming Britons, those absentee landlords of the Mid-

[12] Thomas A. Wright, *Options and Futures*, 74-85.

[13] *Fictitious Dealing*, 156-168. Recent textbooks on speculation and commodity trading emphasize statistical data indicating that commodity prices have fluctuated less and that there has been more evenness in prices through the various months of the year since the advent of futures trading. E.g., Baer and Saxon, 63-69; James S. Schonberg, *The Grain Trade; How It Works* (New York, 1956), 303-309.

[14] *Fictitious Dealing*, 40. The Populist crusade for a sub-treasury plan to facilitate agricultural credit contradicts this testimony that farm credit was available. Cf. Hicks, *The Populist Revolt*, 186-204.

dle West? And who was leading the anti-futures forces? Senator Washburn and Charles Pillsbury, two eminent millers closely associated with the British. These arguments derived some plausibility from the fact that Washburn and Pillsbury had sold their mills to a British syndicate in 1889, but the allegiance and motives of the two men were impugned because of their opposition to futures.[15] Advocates of the trading pits also accused millers of seeking to abolish futures so that they could buy directly from the farmers at their own price. Since there were few millers and many farmers, it was easy to see that impoverished growers would be forced to sell to an "oligopoly." The millers—so ran the argument—would force the farmer to come to him or perish.

Probably the greatest difficulty the exchange forces faced was the task of differentiating between a simple option and a futures contract. Options permitting fulfillment by settlement of differences alone were regarded by the courts as gambling contracts and hence unenforceable, so it was vital that the brokers draw a careful distinction between futures contracts, their principal form of business, and these illegal options. In theory the difference was that a simple option could always be settled by cash, whereas the purchaser of a futures contract *could* demand delivery of the actual product. In practice, however, the distinction was meaningless, because futures contracts were settled just as simple options were —by the payment of differences. In only 3 per cent of the futures trades was there actual delivery; in fact, to demand delivery was to brand oneself a miscreant and led to ostracism by the brokers.

This distinction might have seemed tenuous to the layman, but it was fundamental according to prevailing

[15] See for example, D. B. Smith of the Toledo Board of Trade, *Options and Futures,* 105-118. For documentation of the sale of the mills to British interests, see Kuhlmann, *Dictionary of American Biography,* XIV, 604-605.

legal thought. The right to require delivery, contained in the futures contract, made it possible to say that the seller at the time of the sale intended to make delivery and therefore, his intent being legitimate, the contract was legal and binding. The simple option, on the other hand, was inescapably a wagering contract because the purchaser could offer no intent other than a desire to profit by a price change. The intent to profit, where no goods were exchanged, was held to be socially unjustifiable. Thus it was only the delivery provision in the futures contract that enabled traders to refer to themselves as brokers and speculators rather than gamblers, and decided whether—at least in the legal mind—they were assets or liabilities to society.[16]

This exposition was especially difficult for the exchange interests because there was considerable anti-gambling sentiment at the time; for example, the controversial but profitable Louisiana lottery had recently been outlawed. The market men, therefore, after establishing the legitimacy of their contracts, explained their regulations against trading in simple options. These virtuous declarations were weakened, however, when other testimony revealed that exchange premises were used after official trading hours for dealing in the illegal simple options, and that many of those trafficking in the options were members of the exchanges, augmenting their legitimate business in nefarious fashion. Market defenders had to admit they were unable to police their buildings against such illicit activity.[17]

From this mass of conflicting testimony by growers and brokers, Congressmen had to form opinions about the Hatch bill. Were the farmers and millers right when they claimed that futures markets were harmful and un-

[16] Judge William F. Boyle, *Fictitious Dealing*, 235-247; T. Henry Dewey, *Legislation against Speculation and Gambling in Futures* (New York, 1905), 8ff.
[17] Hammill and Allerton, *Fictitious Dealing*, 156-170, 173-181.

necessary, or did virtue reside in the brokers and speculators who allegedly mediated between producer and
consumer, assuming risks and providing a continuous
market? While the bill was pending, the exchanges com-
municated frequently with their Congressmen. For example, Seth W. Cobb, the representative from St. Louis,
kept in close touch with the Merchants Exchange there.
Cobb, formerly an exchange official himself, kept urging
the exchange to send him more data and arguments to
fight the measure. When the bill passed the House, Cobb
still hoped the Senate Finance Committee would bury it
and, to encourage this, the pro-speculation forces
planned to have flour included in the ban against selling
without ownership. They hoped this stratagem—the ancient parliamentary device of divide and conquer, in this
case directed against the uneasy alliance of growers and
millers—would cause the millers, Washburn, Pillsbury,
et al., to become lukewarm toward the whole bill. Cobb
succeeded in stirring up some resentment against the
millers but there was no split; the bill passed the Senate
anyway.[18]

The nation's press, as always, reflected the views of
its influential readers. In New York City and its financial
outposts many newspapers editorially defended market
practices and decried the "ignorance of rustics." The
Commercial and Financial Chronicle chided the Populists for putting so much faith in a statute, and called the
Hatch bill crude and inopportune. On the other hand,
journals serving smaller areas, especially those west of the
Alleghenies which had many farm readers, perforce
favored the Hatch bill. The *Northwest Miller* claimed
the public was weary of manipulation by Hutchinson
and Pardridge. If the brokers were wise, they would

[18] Seth W. Cobb to George H. Morgan, Secretary of the Merchants Exchange, April 22, July 1, July 6, and July 26, 1892
(photostats from the Merchants Exchange Collection, Missouri
Historical Society).

drive out the rats before the public forced really radical legislation. The *Minneapolis Tribune* also supported the bill, saying that businessmen must find a way to separate legitimate from illegitimate trades. The newspaper cited circulars, put out by brokers themselves, explaining market movements in manipulative terms. The *San Francisco Examiner*, the original Hearst paper, called commodity speculation a vicious occupation that ought to be taxed. The *Examiner* also advocated forcing gamblers to use counters other than wheat, the essential crop for so many farmers.

Even though the big metropolitan dailies, sensitive to their advertisers, supported the commodity brokers editorially, the techniques and proclivities of the journalistic profession itself tended to undermine their pro-business stand. Alert to human interest and the spectacular, newsmen played up the personalities of the marketplace, crafty "Old Hutch," the indomitable Pardridge, John Cudahy, Norman Ream, and other big traders. For weeks in succession financial pages told of "Old Hutch" in control, or, later, Pardridge doing most of the trading while the public looked on. The titans of LaSalle Street put the market up, they put it down; they gave tips to friends and pontificated to admirers. If this drama of financial tangling in the trading pits sold newspapers, it also caused thoughtful readers to question the justice of half a dozen "heavyweights" channeling the flow of commodities through their grasping fingers. The *Chicago Tribune* quoted Leopold Bloom, who had just made $1,000,000 on the Board of Trade, on the art of speculation: "It's a case of gamble, but it's legal and faro isn't."[19] Agrarians cited these lurid tales of exchange "sluggers" to substantiate their charges. Whether such reporting

[19] *Commercial & Financial Chronicle*, 55:42-44 (July 23, 1892); *Fictitious Dealing*, 52-53, and other excerpts from the *Chicago Tribune, Chicago Inter-Ocean, St. Louis Post-Dispatch*, and *St. Louis Globe-Democrat*, 276-279.

was accurate or too sensational, it had an effect, for on this subject most people knew only what they read in the papers.

The floor debates in Congress on the Hatch bill were fully in the nineteenth-century tradition: moralistic platitudes, Jeffersonian clichés, constitutional quibbling, and many allusions to heroes of the past. Senator George G. Vest of Missouri, self-appointed heir to the togas of Hayne and Calhoun, underlined the perils to constitutionalism and states' rights contained in the bill. The emaciated ex-Confederate claimed that it was legislation in favor of the farmer, that it invaded the police powers of the sovereign states. Good Democrats opposed the tariff because it was class legislation; they must likewise oppose this measure, lest they be swallowed up by the plutocratic Republican party. Yielding to popular demand was evil in principle. Vest admitted there were probably some means by which futures could be constitutionally regulated, but he saw no necessity for it; he also resented the prohibitive tax feature, regarding the tax-to-destroy device as an unworthy subterfuge.

John W. Daniel of Virginia, an arch-conservative called "The Lame Lion of Lynchburg" because of his Civil War wounds, concurred with Vest. Section twelve, relating to the licensing of brokers and inspection of their books, was obviously an objectionable invasion of a gentleman's privacy as well as an invasion of states' rights.[20] Edward Douglass White of Louisiana, later to be Chief Justice of the Supreme Court, also criticized the constitutional approach. But as Louisiana was involved in the commercial as well as the agricultural phases of cotton because of New Orleans' futures market, he was not content to attack constitutionality alone. White argued that all political economists except socialists and com-

[20] *Congressional Record,* 52 Cong., 2 sess., 6437-6440; 6448-6450. Richard Coke of Texas also declared that the Hatch bill misused the taxing power.

munists favored futures contracts; he warned the United States not to oppose this consensus. He also submitted a table showing that commodity prices had fluctuated less since futures trading was instituted than before the Civil War when they were not used.

Finally the Southern Senators whose consciences were disturbed by the tax-to-destroy feature of the Hatch bill suggested an alternative: an amendment by James Z. George of Mississippi simply to prohibit futures trading. It was a forthright move that Jeffersonian gentlemen could accept. The George amendment was defeated, however, 51 to 19; Senators from the East and West voted against it.[21]

Few Eastern legislators spoke on the futures question. Aside from a few tributes to the genius of exchange leaders, they were silent—firm in their opposition to regulation of futures trading. Instead it remained for the few Senators from corporation-dominated Western states to voice the objections of business interests. Edward O. Wolcott of Colorado and William M. Stewart of Nevada spoke for the anti's. Wolcott said there was no popular sentiment for the bill except in Minnesota, that there was little mention of it in the campaign literature of 1892. The Colorado Grange was in favor, but this was the only group, said Wolcott, and warned his colleagues not to yield to the Grange against their better judgment. Stewart did not believe that the futures legislation would aid the farmers by checking the decline of farm prices. As a Nevadan, he was a silver champion, and blamed the gold standard rather than futures trading for agricultural woe.[22]

Senators from the Middle Border led the proponents'

[21] *Ibid.*, 934; 990 (January 31, 1893). Dolph of Oregon, Morrill of Vermont and Peffer of Kansas voted with the Southerners. There were ten Southern Senators who favored the George plan of outright abolition but opposed the Hatch bill device of taxing futures contracts.
[22] *Ibid.*, 981.

forces. They knew that the distress that gripped their section was creating the demand for futures regulation and fanning the flames of Populism. Algernon Paddock of Nebraska declared that the futures system made millionaires of the few and paupers of the many. If there had to be speculation, let it be by growers rather than by middlemen. To the Nebraskan, it seemed that the speculator, far from stabilizing prices, merely beclouded and confused the market situation between buyer and seller, so that an outsider—buyer or seller—had difficulty in determining supply and demand. Chance should be replaced by intelligence: knowledge of the business itself, and not knowledge of what some other manipulator intended to do, should govern the marketplace. Paddock here stressed a point that was used by anti-futures advocates for several generations—that speculation had become removed from the realities of economic life, that speculators, like victims of schizophrenia, were content to live in their own world of rumor and secrecy, trying to anticipate each other instead of promoting the nation's business.

Western Senators were not troubled, like their Southern colleagues, by constitutional considerations. Henry Clay Hansbrough of North Dakota, a Republican editor from Devils Lake, believed that the Supreme Court would not probe too deeply into the intent of the tax; he said he was supporting it because the grain growers of his state did. The Western proponents did try, however, to allay the constitutional fears of their Southern colleagues. Senator Washburn, sponsor of the Senate version, cited legal precedents for taxation-to-destroy from jurists Joseph Story and Charles H. Cooley. Senator John H. Mitchell of Oregon argued that if Congress could pass an anti-trust law and a tariff admittedly not for revenue, it could certainly throttle gambling by taxation. If this method failed, he added, then the commerce clause could be used.[23] As committee testimony mounted, however, an ambivalent attitude spread among the Southern and Western proponents. The assurance with which the exchange defenders spoke, the relative cultivation they displayed, and the support they received from the orthodox economists of the day, made thoughtful men— who had been inclined to think only in terms of black and white—examine the grays more carefully.[24] But sometimes agrarian legislators, dismayed by the complex data, reverted to moralistic barrages.

Finally the Hatch bill passed the House, 167 to 46, and the Senate, 40 to 29; all that remained was House concurrence in Senate amendments. This required, however, a suspension of rules, because only a few days remained in the 52nd Congress and the bill was too far down the calendar to reach the floor before adjournment. The vote on suspending the rules, Yea 172, Nay 124, fell short of the required two-thirds by twenty-six votes.[25] Thus the anti-futures bill, representing so much agrarian legislative labor, failed to become law although 80 per cent of the Congress favored it in some form. The gentlemanly constitutionalism—or façade—of some Southerners was a major cause of this denouement. Although they professed to favor futures restriction, they would not accept the method employed. Thus a difference in political approach, even more than the heritage of "the bloody shirt," seemed to keep apart the reformers of the South and West and permitted the East to continue its course without very serious interference.

The Hatch bill votes of 1893 set a pattern for issues of

[23] *Ibid.*, 6881-6883; 6650; 6654; 5832.

[24] H. H. Aldrich cited economists Edward Atkinson and David A. Wells to support his case against tampering with economic law. *Fictitious Dealing*, 71-77.

[25] On January 22, 1894, the House again passed the Hatch bill, 150 to 89. It was reported out of the Senate Agriculture committee but never came to a vote. Carl Parker, "Government Regulation of the Exchanges," *Annals of the American Academy of Political and Social Sciences*, 38:444-457 (September 1911).

21

this kind that changed very little until the 1930's and can therefore be profitably analyzed. Voting was sectional and not according to party.

THE HATCH BILL VOTE BY SECTIONS
OF THE UNITED STATES

		Yea*	Nay*	Absent*	Per Cent Yea
The Speculator Seaboard:	House:	29	31	19	48.3
(Md., Del., Pa., N. J., N. Y., Ct., R. I., Mass.)	Senate:	2	12	2	14.3
Northern New England:	House:	4	0	4	100.0
(Me., N. H., Vt.)	Senate:	6	0	0	100.0
The South:	House:	69	9	25	88.5
(W. Va., Va., N. C., S. C., Ga., Fla., Miss., Ala., La., Ark., Mo., Ky., Tenn.)	Senate:	10	14	2	41.7
East Central Midwest:	House:	57	13	20	81.4
(Ohio, Mich., Ind., Ill., Ia., Wis., Minn.)	Senate:	10	3	1	76.9
Anti-Speculator Tier:	House:	19	0	5	100.0
(N. D., S. D., Nebr., Kans., Tex.)	Senate:	7	2	1	77.7
The West:	House:	5	1	7	83.3
(Wash., Ore., Calif., Ida., Nev., Colo., Mont., Wyo.)	Senate:	9	2	5	80.8
The United States:	House:	183	54	80	77.3
	Senate:	44	33	11	57.3
(The Actual Vote)	House:	167	46		78.4
	Senate:	40	29		58.0

*The Yea and Nay votes listed in the sections include absentee votes that were reported for or against, and those designated here as absent are therefore the remainder that did not vote and reported no preference.

The region between the Potomac and Merrimack Rivers, reflecting its financial centers, opposed futures restriction, although there were some House votes from Western Pennsylvania and New York that were exceptions, and there were many prudent absences. Congressmen from Midwest financial hubs sided with their brethren from the Middle Atlantic states. Northern New England was anti-futures and differed from its southern portion at this time. Later, after World War I, probably because commercial interests came to outweigh agricultural ones, these states swung to a pro-speculation position.

In the South the divergence between Senators and Representatives was very marked. Congressmen, spurred by resentment against urban cotton speculators, strongly favored the bill, while Senators, well-to-do and better insulated from the populace, opposed the bill largely on constitutional grounds. Lawmakers from the West and Southwest, with only a few exceptions, were overwhelmingly against futures. The most vociferous anti-speculator votes came from the tier of states bisected by the 98th meridian. This Great Plains region raised spring wheat, winter wheat, cotton, and corn—cash crops vulnerable to speculators. Although divided on other issues, the area always formed a hostile unit against anything that encouraged economic concentration in the cities.[26]

No law, however well drawn, can be effective if the great majority of the people are indifferent to it and an influential minority is strongly opposed. It is probable, therefore, that if the Hatch bill had become law it would have been ineffective, given the politico-economic arrangements of the nineties. Populism had reached its acme by 1895; William Jennings Bryan submerged it the following year when he lost his "free silver" campaign for the Presidency. Afterward, Senator William A. Peffer, a Kansas Populist, submitted to Congress an account of farmer hard times from 1890 to 1895. In the section on futures contracts the report approved sales for the future by actual growers, and even conceded that it should be permissible to transfer a futures contract that represented the actual product. Fictitious sales, however, not backed by the commodities, should be made a felony.[27]

[26] See Appendix. This region then included North and South Dakota, Nebraska, Kansas, and Texas. The neighboring states of Minnesota, Montana, Iowa, Colorado, New Mexico, and Arkansas showed leanings in the same direction.

[27] U. S. Congress, *Report 787*, Subcommittee on Agricultural Depression, 53 Cong., 3 sess. (Washington, 1895), 31-36, 102. The

Peffer's report turned out to be the final Populist pronouncement.

This first period of anti-speculator agitation came to a close as prosperity returned during 1897. The growers, stirred by agrarian ideology during the depression years, had sought to eradicate the exchange system that had evolved so rapidly after the Civil War, and they had received some support from self-interested millers and from seemingly sympathetic journalists and legislators. But the abatement of agitation was not a permanent victory for the brokers; it was simply an armistice. Senator Peffer's report made it clear that despite voluminous exposition of marketing practices, many farmers and their Congressmen still regarded the privileges and techniques of commodity speculators as unfair.

Report also stated that Eastern farmers controlled more effectively the marketing of their crops and therefore did not have the complaints of Midwest staple crop growers.

CHAPTER 2

FINANCIAL REFORMERS AND

PROGRESSIVES

I

*T*HE rapid expansion and accumulation of wealth during the 1880s and 1890s lent inevitable *nouveau riche* characteristics to the Gilded Age. Sensitive souls on the periphery—in the colleges, churches, and professions—grew outspoken about the vulgarity and hedonism for which quick wealth was responsible. These critics were particularly distressed about gambling. William Buckingham Curtis, an editor and amateur sportsman, wrote an article for the *Forum* condemning its growth. He believed that gambling had never been so prevalent in the United States as it was in 1890. The elements of the population that had formerly wagered on cards and dice had extended their activities to horses, real estate, commodities, and stocks; horse racing papers, for example, had increased from four to forty in a few years. There had been some immediate interest in the games our forefathers bet on—whist, hazard, écarté—but the gambler of the nineties was content to bet on things he never saw, merely for the joy of gambling. Ninety per cent of stock market trading was gambling; puts and calls and commodity margins were pure wagering. Curtis could see no skill in stock speculation or in the lotteries popular in some states. The United States and Australia, according to Curtis, were naturally addicted to gambling. It was, after all, a frontier vice, prevalent where social mobility was great and tradition relatively weak. He warned legislators against trying to ban the impulse by law alone.

"When legislators and moral reformers appreciate the nature of the vice, they may do more than simply change the habit from one form to another."[1] Apparently Curtis was inclined to accept these vices; he did not perceive the more ominous financial possibilities of stock speculation compared, let us say, to racetrack betting.

Americans began to discuss speculation and gambling, and to attempt to distinguish between them, but as we have seen, the attempt was not successful during the agrarian-commercial clashes over the Hatch Anti-Option bill in 1892-1893. In 1895 the Reverend C. H. Hamlin, a Congregationalist missionary, addressed himself to the problem. The moral difference, he declared, depended on the size of the risk: for example, a man who borrowed 10 per cent on his capital was ethical but one who borrowed twenty times his capital was a knave; a risk that was all risk and no work was gambling. Needless risk was wicked; it led ultimately to physical degeneration, for it became an appetite like alcoholism and destroyed the nervous system. The minister bracketed the stock exchange and the bucket shops, which took small sums from the humble, with the racetracks then being legalized in some of the Eastern states.[2]

In spite of the admonitions of genteel reformers, the first agrarian reaction to big city futures traders and stock promoters had expressed itself in extremely repressive state legislation. The California constitution of 1879 forbade futures contracts, and some important grain and cotton states passed anti-futures laws in the next decade. Such crude legal efforts by individual states remained unenforced, and, as happened so often in matters of this

---

[1] William Buckingham Curtis, "Increase in Gambling and its Forms," *Forum*, 12:281-292 (October 1891). For Curtis see *Who Was Who in America, 1897-1942*, (Chicago, 1942) I, 287.

Section I is from the article, "Market Speculation in the Muckraker Era: the Popular Reaction," reprinted here with permission from *The Business History Review*, XXXI (Winter 1957), 403-413.

[2] Reverend C. H. Hamlin, *Arena*, 11:413-416 (February 1895).

type, proved ineffective in reaching interstate organizations centered in the cities. The Hatch Anti-Option bill, like the Interstate Commerce Commission Act, represented a national demand born of frustrated state efforts; the difference was that the former bill was not passed. Although the Hatch measure had foundered in the parliamentary process, resentment against futures trading revived with the general reformist spirit at the turn of the century—this aspect of Populism lingered on. In 1898 Louisiana passed a law banning futures; Massachusetts redefined a gambling contract in 1901; and a near-panic on the exchanges in 1903 produced additional anti-futures laws in some rural states. The nation's courts were called upon more and more to distinguish between a wagering contract, unenforceable in law, and a futures delivery contract, which exchange authorities claimed was legally binding although in 90-97 per cent of the cases no delivery was demanded. The courts, as we have seen, had repeatedly upheld the legality of the futures contract because the wording indicated intent to deliver.[3]

As reformism shifted from the agrarian to the professional classes, from Populism to Progressivism, and as gamblers moved from the commodity pits to stock shares, protests against bucket shops assumed major proportions. The muckraking magazines, with a circulation estimated at three million, added to their list of evils the bucket shops which had appeared in considerable numbers.[4] These establishments catered to small speculators who were reluctant to patronize the legitimate stock and

[3] Carl Parker, "Government Regulation of the Exchanges," *Annals of the American Academy of Political and Social Sciences,* 38:454-457 (September 1911). Additional states that passed laws were: Tennessee (1883); Arkansas, South Carolina, and Texas (1885); Iowa (1886); Michigan (1887); and Missouri (1889); North Carolina (1905); Georgia (1906); Arkansas, Florida Alabama, Mississippi, and Montana (1908).

[4] Cornelius C. Regier, *The Era of the Muckrakers* (Chapel Hill, 1932), 196.

commodity exchanges, or were not aware of them. The bucket shop, or "funeral parlor" in Wall Street parlance, offered this type of patron very low margins, i.e. 3 per cent, and made it possible for him to trade in fractional lots, amounts below the trading minimums of the established exchanges. The shops only pretended to buy and sell in the market; actually they merely booked the transactions and carried the risks of fluctuation themselves. Acting upon the axiom that "the public is always wrong," they assumed they could make a steady profit from the hordes of amateur speculators. Occasionally, of course, when the market entered upon a protracted upward or bull swing, the customers (overwhelmingly bulls) would win and the house would be threatened with collapse. Anticipating such a fiasco, the shops usually closed in haste and their proprietors disappeared, leaving the customers with claims they could not collect.

These shops varied in their pretensions. The crudest captivated their clients with simulated quotes on fictitious stocks, displayed on a revolving tape and a "private wire" system that extended only to the edge of the rug. Such places even accepted the money of children. Other shops went to great length to cast an aura of respectability over their business. They insinuated themselves into Wall Street in order to have the proper mailing address; they provided accurate quotes on real stocks and charged regular commissions. They called themselves bankers and brokers, and did not readily admit that they did not execute orders through the exchanges. Some of these houses had many branches in the cotton and grain belts; their salesmen were able to get much business by promising more than bona fide brokers could, including in some instances the return of money when customers lost and decided to stop trading.[5] It was in

[5] The term "bucket shop" is said to have originated in England ca. 1820. Street urchins made a habit of draining beer kegs discarded from public houses. They would take the dregs to an

these shops that many a boy was first stimulated by the changing values and rapid exchange of money. Larry Livingston learned to read the tape in Connecticut bucket shops. Years later bucket shop proprietors all over the country learned to recognize Livingston on sight, and refused to handle his business. His ability to read the tape always cost them money, and they told him, "bucket shops were for the ever-losing amateur."[6]

When the muckrakers bore down on these bogus concerns they had respectable allies. The New York Stock Exchange and the Chicago Board of Trade were anxious, like the reformers, to shut down shops which drained off much of the business they might otherwise obtain; in fact, in many states the exchanges spearheaded the attack on the shops. By a careful monitoring of their stock quotation service, and later by an agreement with Western Union, the exchanges were able to reduce the bucket shops because few could exist without a constant stream of prices to lure the customers. Inevitably exchange participation in the war on bucket shops provided bucketeers with a defense that had some popular appeal. The operators claimed that their offenses were no worse than those of the exchanges. The markets, like the shops, made no deliveries; they were merely large bucket shops trying to establish themselves as monopolies, and in many ways the client was better off trading at a shop. He could better limit his losses, do business with much less money, and pay smaller commissions. In

---

abandoned shop and imbibe them. This practice came to be called "bucketing" and their rendezvous, a "bucket shop." The idea was transferred to illegal brokers apparently because they too sought to profit from sources too small or too unreliable for legitimate brokers to handle. John Hill, *The Gold Bricks of Speculation* (New York, 1907), 39; Patton Thomas, "Bucket Shop in Speculation," *Munsey's*, 24:68-70 (October 1900).

[6] Edwin S. Lefevre, *Reminiscences of a Stock Operator* (Garden City, 1923), 26-29. Larry Livingston was the pseudonym Lefevre gave Jesse L. Livermore, the famous market bear.

short, these independents resented the idea that their business was unlawful when they could see similar practices amply rewarded within the supposedly legitimate exchange fraternity. The cry of monopoly was a formidable charge in parts of the Midwest and South at this time, and independent shop proprietors could probably count on sympathy from the local citizenry when they were pitted against glib city types in the Board of Trade and its brokers' branches.[7]

The bucket shop articles and exchange campaigns, augmented by agrarians angered by commodity trading, brought results in the form of state legislation. Sympathy for local shoppers was not enough, and in 1905 the grain states of North Dakota and Minnesota prohibited bucket shops and the bucketing of orders. Arkansas and Nebraska followed in 1907, and after the financial panic of that year, additional states sought to eliminate these operators.[8] Thus bucket shops declined during the Progressive Era, owing largely to the publicity compaign the exchanges waged against them. They had, however, a brief renaissance later, when promoters after World War I saw the chance to separate the naïve from their Liberty Bonds.

But aside from the bucket shop crusade, between 1895 and 1907 magazine articles about the exchanges were mild. A *Munsey's* writer was enthusiastic over public participation in the 1899 boom—this time the public was profiting in Wall Street, he declared. He saw Roswell P. Flower, the bullish ex-Governor of New York, as the

[7] Merrill A. Teague, "Bucket Shop Sharks," *Everybody's*, 14: 723-725, 15:33-43, 245-254, 398-408 (June-September 1906). C. C. Christie, "Bucket Shop vs. the Board of Trade," *Everybody's*, 15:707-713 (November 1906). Christie, known as the "Bucket Shop King," operated a large shop in Kansas City, Missouri.

[8] The additional states were: Mississippi, New York, Oklahoma, Rhode Island and Virginia, 1908; Kansas, New Hampshire, Arizona, Iowa and Tennessee, 1909. Parker, "Government Regulation of the Exchanges," 464-467.

daring prophet of a "New Era"; he admired the coura-
geous leaders who could stimulate Americans' faith in
their economic future. Orders to buy were coming from
every hamlet despite the pessimistic fables the old bears
were circulating in the Street. In the *North American
Review* Charles A. Conant, a monetary expert, observed
that stock prices reflected and were related to the direction of new capital; he was not apparently concerned
with the price gyrations caused by manipulators.[9]

In these years *The Independent* devoted the most
space to Wall Street and the articles were generally
more critical than those in other magazines. E. Dana
Durand warned that both consumers and investors
should oppose stock watering, as the practice resulted in
monopoly profits for promoters. Alexander D. Noyes,
financial editor of the *New York Evening Post*, noted
that "wash sales," i.e., the placing of simultaneous buy
and sell orders through the same broker, had become
common. When this practice was discouraged, manipulators found that "matched orders," i.e., buying and
selling through two sets of brokers, was an easy way of
fooling the public and unloading stock.[10] W. R. Givens
in 1905 wrote, "Does Wall Street Speculation Pay?," an
article warning novices of the pitfalls of the Street. He
catalogued the amateur speculator's faults—buying high
and selling low in panic—as taking small profits and big
losses. People were being hurt by losses in the market,
said Givens, and the brokers were quiet about the 80 per
cent who lost. As the gambling spirit gained dominance
in the exchanges, prices were much more susceptible to
sudden decline than to sudden advance. Wall Street, in

[9] H. Allway, "The New Wall Street," *Munsey's*, 21:3-19 (April
1899); Charles A. Conant, "How the Stock Market Reflects Values,"
The North American, 180:347-359 (March 1905).

[10] E. Dana Durand, "Stock Watering," *The Independent*, 54:2238
(September 1902); Alexander D. Noyes, *The Independent*, 58:179-
186 (January 26, 1905). See p. 58 for an explanation of watered
stock.

fact, was a paying proposition only for the broker and the insider, not for the average customer.[11]

A year later an article under the title, "Confessions of a Stock Broker," appeared in *The Independent,* an exposé purporting to be a realistic account of practices at the time. The margin minimum was 10 per cent and the broker made about 1 per cent on relending; 95 per cent of the transactions were on margin, and there was very little short sale business. The three partners in the New York house netted $22,700 apiece in 1904. The anonymous author claimed that the average broker wanted to see his customers prosper and thus stay active, for it meant more commissions for him. But the client usually assumed that he was the exception to the rule, that he could win where his fellows had lost. The more ignorant he was, moreover, the more apt he was to pin his actual faith on the advice of the broker. Most brokers, the article continued, knew they could not accurately foretell the market, so they had learned to let the foolish amateur go his own way. The writer admitted that once in a while a broker attempted to discourage a particularly foolhardy transaction, but he maintained that relations were generally more amicable if the client could not blame the broker for his losses.[12]

A sequel, "Confessions of a Stock Speculator," appeared just at the time of the 1907 panic. The anonymous contributor described his victories and defeats in the Street, and said he had been wiped out for good by the market repercussions of the San Francisco earthquake in 1906. Prior to that his fortunes had fluctuated violently during the peak years of corporate consolidation. Brokers, he believed, were unscrupulous in encouraging business, and financial writers were often well

[11] W. R. Givens, "Does Wall Street Speculation Pay," *The Independent,* 59:494-496 (August 31, 1905).

[12] "Confessions of a Stock Broker," *The Independent,* 61:1465-1469 (December 20, 1906).

rewarded for the seemingly disinterested market advice they offered the public. His conclusions were that tips were calculated to mislead, and that half a dozen giants really controlled the stock market.[13]

But the most sweeping indictment of bankers and brokers emanated from the pen of Thomas William Lawson; his was a sensational exception to the aforementioned mild criticism. A speculator on the Boston Exchange—and with journalistic experience—Lawson gave the readers of *Everybody's Magazine* a lurid picture of financial oligarchy, which he dubbed "The System." The gist of his allegation was that a small group of financiers dominated the nation's banks and corporations, that they used the public's bank deposits to their private advantage, and engaged in "dollar-making" by watering security issues and bribing financial news outlets. Lawson saw the Standard Oil trust—led by William Rockefeller (brother of John D.), and Henry H. Rogers—as the particular center of the System that was strangling American life. Lawson was careful to explain that most contributors to the conspiracy were innocent: they were unwitting tools of a vicious system which had grown up with the trusts. As an example, he cited the fact that banks throughout the United States responded to a stock panic by authorizing the lending of their funds to alleviate the credit stringency in Wall Street. While this was customary banking practice, Lawson contended that it benefited System insiders by enabling them to buy up securities cheap after the public had been "shaken out" by a contrived decline. After arranging a market slump and selling short, the insiders could thus rely on an influx of "other people's money" to finance them for the recovery.[14]

[13] "Confessions of a Stock Speculator," *The Independent*, 62:669-672 (March 21, 1907).
[14] Thomas W. Lawson, *Frenzied Finance* (New York, 1905), 223-225.

Lawson's sensational style, together with his own career as a manipulator, created some doubt as to his credibility. Wall Street used this as a defense against the apostate, but undoubtedly most readers accepted much of what he wrote. It coincided with traditional agrarian beliefs. Some years later, Lawson's fellow-Bostonian, Louis Brandeis, was to give a fuller and more temperate account of what bankers could do with "other people's money." And the Pujo Money Trust Investigation of 1912 confirmed the general validity of Lawson's charges.

In 1912, when the muckraking spirit had waned, Lawson tried to revive his war against the stock exchanges in a number of flamboyant articles in *Everybody's Magazine*. The new series blamed the high cost of living on stock speculation. Ninety-nine per cent of market business was gambling, wrote Lawson. He advocated direct legal action to close the exchanges; he predicted a revolution unless this were done. Lawson charged that gamblers robbed the public of two or three billion dollars a year, that citizens were paying interest on $40 to $60 billion of stocks and bonds that represented counterfeit value. He claimed that Taft, Roosevelt, and Wilson were not even aware of this evil.[15] Eastern reaction to the new Lawson onslaught was negative. The *Cleveland Leader, Hartford Times,* and *New York Sun,* while granting the truth of some of his earlier assertions, all questioned his motives. One of them recalled that a few years before he had urged the public to join him in a crusade against Wall Street by furnishing the funds for a "blind pool."[16]

After he wrote *Frenzied Finance,* Lawson found him-

[15] Thomas W. Lawson, "The Remedy," *Everybody's,* XXVII (October 1912–July 1913).

[16] "Lawson's Remedy," The Literary Digest, 45:548-549 (October 5, 1912); "Dr. Lawson's Panacea," *Current Literature,* 53:647-648 (December 1912). A "blind pool" is one in which the contributors give the manager *carte blanche* to trade as he sees fit.

self *persona non grata* on the exchanges and he shifted
his operations to the Curb where rules at the time were
very lax.[17] On one occasion he put an advertisement in
the newspapers saying, "Don't buy Nevada–Utah Copper until I give the word." Many of the trusting public
did not wait for the word; they bought into the copper
company immediately. A little later Lawson announced
that his investigation had proved the stock to be practically worthless, and of course it declined sharply. This
ruse should have taught some of the gullible a lesson.
By the time of the Pujo hearings, Lawson's reputation
was somewhat tarnished, and in 1916 when he made
his "leak" charges only a few agrarians believed him.
Clearly Lawson's greatest impact was in the earlier
period when his charges were more novel and muckraking was at its height.

The periodicals really glamorized the markets in their
exposés, but only a certain type of operator gained es-
teem from this side effect. The typical broker was pic-
tured as pleasure-seeking and crafty, a nervous dandy
with watery eyes and muddy complexion; he was not
the type that made a good family man, nor the type an
American mother would want her son to become. From
10 A.M. until 3 P.M. on weekdays he shouted and man-
euvered on the exchange floor, but afterward he could
be seen imbibing at one of several clubs. Though he was
generous outside of business hours, he preferred night
life to his family and knew little aside from current
affairs.[18] In this period of bold speculation and financial

---

[17] The Curb was a small outdoor stock exchange.

[18] Robert Stewart, "Metropolitan Types—The Stockbroker"
Munsey's, 21:278-280 (1899); Edwin S. Lefevre, "Pike's Peak or
Bust," *McClure's,* 17:153-163 (June 1901); Earl Sparling, *Mystery
Men of Wall Street* (New York, 1930), Chapter 4 and 105-142.
After some years of this muckraking stereotype, a broker felt the
need to emphasize the diverse intellectual and aesthetic attain-
ments as well as the philanthropies of his fellow exchange members.
William C. Van Antwerp, *The Stock Exchange from Within* (Gar-
den City, 1913), 302-319.

coups, however, the chief interest was centered on the traders themselves, and market leaders became titans in the newspaper accounts and in contemporary literature. Although public debaters might disclaim any concern with personalities, the public was vitally interested in them. Personality was the key. On this basis the great men of the market could be divided into two broad categories, roughly the stereotypes of bull, the optimist whose expectations were on the long or up side—and bear, the pessimist, who favored the short or down side.

The bull was a man most Americans could readily recognize and admire. Active and gregarious, he gave the impression of one who liked to get things done in a hurry. In his public statements he was bold or even defiant, but at the same time he had an advanced sense of public relations. By instinct he knew the right words to use in aligning himself with the people and against its enemies—foreign investors, Wall Street, "the interests," bankers, and brokers. If these gentlemen hoodwinked their admirers now and then, the victims still admired such cleverness. Generally these men were builders as well as traders and they shared great dreams of the future with an appreciative public; if they were from the West—and many were—they could gain additional sympathy in any struggle against Eastern interests, real or fancied. Probably the most famous of this type were Roswell P. Flower, ex-Governor of New York, John W. (Bet-a-Million) Gates of barbed-wire fame, Thomas Lawson, and later, William Crapo Durant, the General Motors boomer. Even Curtis Jadwin and Frank Cowperwood, the fictional financial heroes of Frank Norris and Theodore Dreiser, though they differed in most respects, were alike in their ability to command widespread admiration through boldness and constructive impulses.[19]

[19] Isaac F. Marcosson, "The Passing of the Plunger," *Munsey's*, 49:3-13 (April 1913); Frank Norris, *The Pit* (New York, 1903); Theodore Dreiser, *The Financier* (New York, 1912), *The Titan*

The typical bear type, on the other hand, readily aroused the public's antipathy. Sly and often ascetic, cryptic in utterance, he never bothered to pretend that he had much confidence in the public. He was usually a trader, and perhaps an ex-broker, who lacked the glamor of the bullish doers. Although personally he may have been friendly and generous, the impression he made on the public was the reverse: he seemed aloof, cynical.[20] He did not know how to cover his desire for acquisition with the mantle of the public interest. These men, although they inspired some awe around the Street, were the bogeymen; any inexplicable decline in a stock was ascribed to their handiwork. They were the manipulators whom the public feared and resented. Their dour personalities made it easy for the man in the street to assume that they, more than the others, were the bears, that they gloried in dampening progress and profited from the dissolution of overoptimistic dreams.[21] Perhaps Russell Sage and Hetty Green could serve as extreme examples from the late nineteenth century, but James R. Keene, Jesse L. Livermore, Arthur W. Cutten and Ben E. ("Sell-em") Smith also belong in this list.

The years from 1898 to 1907, the Muckraker Era, found the agrarians still active, but largely at the state level. They were responsible for the continued legislation against futures trading and for the punitive provisions in the various anti-fraud and anti-gambling measures enacted in Western and Southern states. They were aroused by Lawson's charges of a "system" and confused

---

(New York, 1914); Lawson, *Frenzied Finance*, Sparling, *Mystery Men*, 3-44.

[20] Lawson claimed James R. Keene was extremely generous in his philanthropy, *Frenzied Finance*, 80. He was also much interested in his racing stable. Richard D. Wyckoff, *Wall Street Ventures and Adventures, Through Forty Years* (New York, 1930), 144-149.

[21] Sparling, *Mystery Men of Wall Street*, Chap. 4 and 105-142.

by the anti-monopoly defenses of the bucket shopper, C. C. Christie.

The major development of the period, however, was the emergence of the "financial reformers," strong new allies for the agrarians. These were respectable brokers, financiers, and journalists who sought to eliminate fraud and unethical dealers, educate the investing public, and rally the broker fraternity to pride in their calling. The financial reformers succeeded in eliminating most of the bucket shops, and, through the muckraking magazines, warned investors about the shoppers, wash sales, watered stock, and other dubious market practices. They were too wedded to laissez-faire and optimism to consider seriously any talk of regulation, however, and they assumed evolutionary improvement in business ethics. Nevertheless, the Muckraker Era had created a somewhat adverse image of markets and traders in the public mind.

II

In 1907 pressure on the world money supply brought a three-year cycle of business prosperity to a close. This pressure was augmented in the United States by repercussions from manipulative campaigns in the stock market, and revealed a chaotic and uncoordinated banking system; the result was the so-called Bankers' Panic. It came at an inopportune time for the reputations of the nation's bankers and brokers, because lurid articles had been appearing in the press about financial skulduggery on the Street. There was wild talk as the panic subsided; some had plans for a new banking system; others suggested regulation of the stock exchanges.

Under these circumstances, Governor Charles Evans Hughes of New York appointed a committee to investigate stock market practices. He hoped the findings of such a group would temper any extreme proposals that might come before Congress or the state legislature. He named eight committee members: two merchants, two lawyers, one banker, one professor, the state commissioner of banking, and a noted editor, Horace White. The professor was John Bates Clark, a respected economist at Columbia University. The members served without pay and took their own notes, since no stenographer had been provided; during the year 1908 they held a total of seventy-five informal meetings, three per week, in the New York Chamber of Commerce building. The committee planned to conduct interviews privately; in this way they hoped to avoid publicity and obtain confidential information. They explored the situation in other nations and jurisdictions, and in New York found brokers and exchange officers cooperative. At one point the committee split on the policy to be adopted toward stock exchange regulation. Two members, Professor Clark and the banking commissioner, signed a letter to Governor Hughes advising him to take a strong stand in favor of regulation so that New York statutes might set a very high precedent for the nation. They believed that any immediate decline of business caused by regulatory measures would be offset by a gradual strengthening of public faith in New York security markets. Other committee members declined to sign the letter because they feared an immediate adverse reaction.[22]

The committee's report to Governor Hughes, made in June 1909, was conservative in its recommendations. Drawing upon the analogy of deposits on other kinds of goods, the report stated that since margin purchases were legitimate, they should not be banned as some persons had suggested; instead the committee recommended a 20 per cent margin minimum.[23] And the re-

---

[22] *Stock Exchange Regulation,* Committee on Banking & Currency. United States Senate. 63 Cong., 2 sess. (Washington, 1914), 276-294. See also Horace White, "The Hughes Investigation," *Journal of Political Economy,* 17:528-540 (October, 1909).

[23] Ten per cent margin was common during this period. House *Report 1593* (February 28, 1913), 45 (The Pujo Report).

port found that taking the short side of the market was no more reprehensible than choosing the long; it took the orthodox view that short activity dampened bullish excesses. Although the committee admitted that a majority of the transactions on New York exchanges were not of an investment character, it could find no legal way of making a distinction between good and bad. They thought legislation against the gamblers would impair the investment market, and instead put their faith in plenary action by the exchanges themselves.

But in some instances the report was more positive and specific. It suggested a plan for licensing all the tickers operating in the state in order to prevent their use by bucketeers: the installer's name, the subscriber's name, and the number of the ticker were to be duly recorded. The committee believed that if tickers could be thus controlled, no bucket shops could operate, for customers always demanded a constant stream of quotations. It also recommended that New York's anti-bucket shop law of 1908 be strengthened in certain respects: specifically, that New York follow Massachusetts' lead in requiring that only one party be found guilty of intent to settle by payment of differences rather than by the delivery of goods. The New York law requiring that both the client and operator be found guilty of fraudulent intent made convictions much more difficult to obtain than they were in some other states. The committee further suggested that a customer should be able to obtain upon request the name and address of the person to whom he had sold or from whom he was buying stock, thus giving him a better chance to trace a dubious transaction.[24]

The Hughes Committee investigation was greeted

[24] "Report of the Hughes Committee," *Public Papers of Charles Evans Hughes* (Albany, 1910), Appendix I, 288-330.

These last two recommendations became law during Governor William Sulzer's short administration in 1913. See Section III below.

with approval by most periodicals. They noted the committee's staid membership and moderate tone, its affirmation of the legitimacy of futures contracts, discretionary margin rates, and short selling, and its opposition to incorporation for exchanges. Several commentators agreed that the exchanges' boards of governors ought to be spurred by the findings to set their houses in order—specifically by eliminating fraudulent securities from the list, by fighting the bucket shops more diligently, and by sternly punishing any bucketing by members themselves. They saw the evils as primarily moral and thought moral suasion the proper remedy. Speculation was not gambling but simply the legitimate exercise of acumen in the business field, and genuine reform could come only with the gradual growth of an enlightened commercial public and the consequent adoption of higher standards of social ethics. As the fiduciary relation of business to the public became more apparent, there would be a decline in sharp practices.[25]

The Hughes investigation did have some definite results, however. The New York Produce Exchange decided to stop listing mining stocks. During March and April 1910, the New York Stock Exchange enacted rules forbidding trading by messengers, clerks, and others acting in a fiduciary relationship to the brokers; it enlarged its power to inspect the books of members, and tightened its rules to curb manipulation. The exchange also made an agreement with Western Union to control more carefully the stream of ticker quotations, in order

[25] All articles specifically about stock exchange reform were favorable. They were: Franklin Escher, "The Wall Street Investigation," *Harper's Weekly,* 53:II:28 (July 3, 1909); Eugene Meyer, Jr., "The Stock Exchange and the 1907 Panic," *Yale Review,* 18:34-46 (August 1909); Charles A. Conant, "Regulation of the Stock Exchange," *The Atlantic,* 102:307-314 (September 1908); Horace White, "The Hughes Investigation," *Journal of Political Economy,* 17:528-540 (October 1909); John G. Dater, "Stock Exchange Reform," *Munsey's,* 49:129-131 (April 1913); Carl Parker, "Government Regulation of the Exchanges," 471-472.

to keep them from bucketeers. Even before the exchange had acted, Wisconsin passed an act making speculation by those in a fiduciary position a felony; Wyoming, Kentucky, South Carolina, New Jersey, Rhode Island, and Mississippi followed with similar laws.[26] Some years later during the hearings on the Owen bill, Horace White claimed that the exchanges had complied with eight of the twelve recommendations made by the Hughes Committee. Public discussion in 1912 and 1913, however, as well as the Pujo Committee Report, indicated that many people did not regard these changes as adequate to ensure an honest, stable market.[27]

The 1907 panic revived agitation against bucket shops. Although New York's 1908 law had had a wholesome effect, the bucket shop issue appeared for a moment on the national scene in 1909, when Senator Augustus O. Bacon of Georgia tried to attach a tax on bucket shops to the pending Payne-Aldrich Tariff. Before the amendment could be read, Senator Nelson W. Aldrich of Rhode Island moved to have it tabled. The Georgia Senator angrily criticized the lordly behavior of the Rhode Islander, noting that Aldrich seemed to think he had more rights than other Senators. The Aldrich dictatorship prevailed, however, and Bacon's amendment was defeated, 44 to 34. The GOP regulars and Louisiana's two Democratic Senators supported Aldrich; the rest of the Democrats and the nascent insurgents stood with Bacon.[28]

[26] *Stock Exchange Regulation*, 276-294. Parker, "Government Regulation of the Exchanges," 463-472. North Dakota had enacted a law in 1890 against speculation by public officials. Fiduciary relation rules are discussed further in Chapter 4 below.

[27] *New York Times*, February 12, 1914, 2:2.

[28] The insurgents on this vote were: Bristow (R-Kans.); Brown and Burkett (R-Neb.); Chamberlain (R-Ore.); Clapp (R-Minn.); Crawford (R-S. D.); Cummins (R-Ia.); Dolliver (R-Ia.); Jones (R-Wash.); LaFollette (R-Wis.); Nelson (R-Minn.); Newlands (R-Nev.); and Piles (R-Wash.). Beveridge, Borah and Bourne were absent and left no voting preference. The anti-speculator tier

A year later a Kansas Congressman tried to free the commodity markets from the speculators. Representative Charles F. Scott proposed to ban from interstate commerce all matter relating to future contracts in cotton. The Kansan had originally intended to have the bill apply to grains as well, but his colleagues from the Midwest had disagreed on that question. Representative John Lamb of Richmond, Virginia, undertook the defense of the brokers and exchanges. He declared that the Scott proposal was class legislation, a violation of states' rights, and subjected cotton dealers to federal police supervision and espionage. The arguments of Senators George Vest of Missouri and Edward White of Louisiana against the Hatch Anti-Option bill in 1892 Lamb believed to be still valid in 1910. He characterized pressure for the bill as "the echo of the dying wail of Populism"; reformers were misleading the farmers. The latter, he noted, were on Easy Street with the best farm prices since the Civil War. He refused to see any similarity between commodity trading and the outlawed Louisiana Lottery; and he insisted that the distinction between moral and economic issues must be maintained.

Representative Scott had on his side two hundred Congressmen who had signed a petition to consider the Scott bill, and the Farmers' Educational and Co-operative Union, which included farmers in twenty-nine states. Southern legislators reported that the wrath of cotton producers was beginning to rise, that this pressure had closed bucket shops throughout the South and that wire men from the brokerage houses were being driven out of some communities. Hughes of Georgia believed that the New York and New Orleans exchanges were merely a gentleman's ethical substitute for poker; to preserve

---

was 63 per cent in favor of considering the tax; the East was 93 per cent opposed. *Congressional Record*, 61 Cong., 1 sess., v. 44, Pt. 4, 4244-4245 (July 8, 1909). For the voting record of the tier see Appendix B.

equality we must legalize poker, he said, while Beall of Texas observed that the only opponents of the bill were exchange members and speculators. Bartlett of Georgia claimed that the Commissioner of Corporations' 1907 report demonstrated that there was much artificial manipulation in the cotton futures markets. Scott himself thought that cotton trading was the most reprehensible because twenty-eight grades of cotton could be used to fulfill a futures contract; this meant that a legitimate dealer who demanded delivery usually found himself with a grade he could not use. In addition, price differentials from the standard grade were set by exchanges committees, not by government authorities.

Oratory was profuse as legislators excoriated the cotton traders. Edwards of Georgia said the farmers' eyes were fixed on the House of Representatives to see what action would be taken on this bill; the *Atlanta Constitution* believed that the producer had finally decided to cast out the middleman and take his chances on the marketing consequences; and five million farmers were rumored to be organizing for a fight against the middleman. On the momentum of Southern rhetoric, and with farm votes seemingly in the balance, the bill passed 160-41, but it never reached the floor of the Senate.[29] This was the high tide for anti-futures bills in the House; the Senate witnessed futile fights by a minority in ensuing years.

A few years after the Scott bill fiasco, the question of speculation again arose in the reformist 63rd Congress elected with Woodrow Wilson. Senator James P. Clarke of Arkansas announced a rider to the pending Underwood-Simmons Tariff. The rider called for a 50¢ per bale tax on cotton sold by persons who did not own said cotton at the time of sale. The Senator frankly admitted that this was a punitive measure aimed at cotton specula-

[29] *Ibid.*, 61 Cong., 2 sess., v. 45, Pt. 8, 8913ff. (June 24, 1910).

tors; it was supported by the Farmers' Union and the Senate Democratic caucus. Cotton exchange men and their allies fought the rider, and metropolitan newspapers protested. The *Wall Street Journal* wondered if Congress had the power to restrict such transactions; the *New York Sun* called it a tax for votes only, and questioned the business knowledge of the Senate. The *Commercial and Financial Chronicle* thought the rider was on a par with the free silver "heresy"; at last, it concluded, the agrarians had antagonized the Southern business interests. The *San Francisco Chronicle* was the exception; it said it could see the value of stock exchange quotations but regarded futures trading as gambling.[30]

As the summer of 1913 wore on, the debate over the Clarke amendment broadened into a controversy over speculation in general. Senator Albert Baird Cummins, the Iowa Progressive who specialized in railroad matters, urged the reformers to strive for a more inclusive tax on speculators. He offered an amendment providing for a 10 per cent tax on both short sales of stock and commodity futures contracts. Senator Cummins told the Senate why he was making such a sweeping proposal. He said that short selling (of stocks and commodities) was a grave threat to industrial and financial stability, that the exchanges had come to be merely places where bold and unscrupulous men matched wits. Average men could not win, and their moral fiber was often weakened by their market experiences to the point where they were unfit to carry on legitimate business. Cummins said that he was not simply defending Midwestern grain growers but was trying to protect the whole nation from the ominous financial power accumulating in the big cities. He wanted to stop the flow from country banks to New York City because it was providing the credit for

[30] *Commercial & Financial Chronicle,* 97:I:87 (July 12, 1913); "Raking the Cotton Futures Tax," *Literary Digest,* 50:83-84 (July 19, 1913).

gambling. He admitted that his amendment was radical in that it destroyed a business long in operation, but he believed the evil was so great that drastic steps had to be taken.

To buttress his contention that there was excessive speculation in the United States, he quoted the yearly range of stock prices of many American railroads the earnings of which had been very stable during the year. These ranges showed that while earnings fluctuated 5-10 per cent, stock prices moved 30-100 per cent, and the turnover in many issues in a year exceeded the number of shares outstanding. His research indicated that railroad stocks (at that time, 75 per cent of the market) were being manipulated for profit and were not governed by economic conditions on the various roads.[31] Senator George W. Norris of Nebraska endorsed Cummins' proposal because it was comprehensive. He called upon Southern Democrats to cast aside their partisanship and join in the battle against the speculators. After all, the Democratic caucus had passed the Clarke amendment; why not extend it to wheat, corn, and stock?

The Democratic reaction to this call to arms was cool. John Sharp Williams of Mississippi said there was no demand from grain growers for a futures contract tax; he claimed the grievance of the cotton grower was a special case. All the cotton farmer really wanted, according to Williams, was that differentials between grades of cotton deliverable under contract be set by the "spot" (i.e., cash) market rather than by private exchange committees. Senator Joseph Bristow of Kansas challenged Williams' assertion about the grain growers. He stated that the grain growers of the Farmers' Union favored a tax on grain speculation, and the real reason that grain was not included in the Scott bill of 1909 was that the grain exchanges were able to exert enough legislative pressure

[31] *Congressional Record*, 63 Cong., 1 sess., v. 50, Pt. 5, 4036-4037; *New York Times*, September 2, 1913, 6:8.

to have it excluded. Senator Clarke of Arkansas broke in to say that although he approved in principle of the Cummins amendment, he would vote against it because of the tardiness of its presentation.[32]

President Wilson remained aloof from the speculation controversy and from the ensuing discussions of the topic in connection with Senator Owen's bill in 1914. He was said to favor taking the profit out of speculation through taxation, but he did not want such a rider included in the tariff. The Senate defeated Cummins' amendment by a roll call vote of 35 to 16. No Democrat supported it; Western insurgents were the defenders of the faith.[33] Evidently the Democrats were content to confine themselves to equitable cotton grading and ignore the broader speculative problem in grain and securities.

The most authoritative work on speculation continued to be *Speculation on the Stock and Produce Exchanges,* by Henry Crosby Emery. The only son of an intellectual Maine family, Emery graduated from Bowdoin College and went on to Columbia University, where he submitted this dissertation on speculation in 1896.[34] Coming on the eve of the Spanish-American War and the subsequent years of industrial consolidation, the study was timely and stood out as authoritative in its field. As Dr. Emery himself pointed out, most treatises on economic theory slighted speculation and, since Americans were regarded by others as the world's greatest speculators, it was appropriate that an American scholar analyze these markets. Dr. Emery's interpretations were scholarly and quite orthodox. He was firm in his defense of speculation as serving an important economic function. Organized speculation, he believed, provided a world-wide price

[32] *Congressional Record,* 63 Cong., 1 sess., v. 50, Pt. 5, 4386.

[33] *Ibid.,* 4387 (September 6, 1913); *New York Times,* October 1, 1913, 8:3.

[34] Percy W. Bidwell, "Henry Crosby Emery," *Dictionary of American Biography,* VI, 143; Henry Crosby Emery, *Speculation on the Stock and Produce Markets* (New York, 1896).

and directed economic factors into proper channels; it also made for smaller, less extreme price fluctuations. Emery argued that whatever the intention of the speculator, he buys and sells goods whether he actually handles the goods or not—this is in the nature of the transaction itself. In speculation one acquires the right to buy property, and gains or loses the difference between the value of the property at the time of sale and its value at the time of purchase; all speculators may win when there has been an increase in value. Gambling, on the other hand, is taking a chance where one party or the other loses. Emery admitted, however, that some speculative transactions were of a gambling nature.

The economist was particularly critical of the agrarian viewpoint. Speculation, he said, cannot be crushed by legislation without destroying economic conditions. State laws have failed to reduce speculation in stocks and commodities. He denied the argument that prices were at times above or below some objective standard, and claimed that values are determined subjectively in the marketplace. He also rejected the notion that a very high volume of sales in relation to production indicated that speculators were depressing the prices received by farmers. On one hand people blamed speculation for artificially high stock prices and, on the other hand, they blamed speculation for low prices to the farmers. Emery thought speculation usually accompanied high prices rather than low.

In his chapter on "The Evils of Speculation," Emery could find little that was bad. Corners, he thought, were disappearing; the direct loser in corner attempts had always been the speculator anyway, not the consumer. He doubted if there was really much successful short selling because it required so much coolness and skill to go against the tide. The importance of syndicates, or pools as they were popularly known, he believed to be greatly exaggerated, but he did acknowledge that false rumors and purchasable news columns in newspapers were harmful. His chief complaint, and one which he was to reiterate many times, was the moral evil of reckless participation in the market by outsiders. Margins and advertising increased the lure to the outside public. The London Exchange did not permit advertising by its members, said the economist approvingly. Fostering of the gambling spirit was always at the expense of industry. Emery thought the speculating public had increased in numbers but not in intelligence; yet, he went on, it was not possible to eliminate all but the competent since an active market was needed. At what point did the evil of speculation become too great a price to pay for an active market? He could never satisfactorily answer his own question, but in 1896 he went so far as to suggest that the exchange was a quasi-public institution and might therefore be the proper object of corrective legislation. Why was it that Americans were so much slower than the Europeans in trying to solve their economic problems through regulation and supervision?[35]

Seventeen years later, on the eve of the Pujo Report, a second treatise on speculation and the exchanges appeared. *The Value of Organized Speculation* was printed in 1913 as No. 15 in the Hart, Schaffner and Marx Prize Economic Essays. The author, Harrison H. Brace, agreed essentially with Emery's position, but emphasized the evolutionary interpretation so popular at the time. Brace saw the exchange as a newly developed and sensitive tool, one the public had not yet learned to use properly. He anticipated that the proper sort of books, the financial departments in the magazines, and improved trade papers would gradually educate the public to a point where bad practices would disappear. The passing of the plunger was the sign of a wiser public. The long-term trend he believed to be to-

---

[35] *Ibid.*, 7-9, 96-159, 171-191. See pp. 126-130 below for further discussion of speculative competence.

ward more orderly markets, despite temporary aberrations like the trustification stock boom at the turn of the century.

Brace regarded the exchange ideal itself as good. Enlightened self-interest and voluntary associations operating together were the ultimate solution. Taxes, abolition of short selling, or incorporation of the exchanges would do no good. He held that there were many abuses on some of the smaller exchanges which had been incorporated—so incorporation was no panacea. He praised the moderate findings of the Hughes Committee. In any case, Brace concluded, the organized markets could not be destroyed; there was no practical alternative to them. But they could be reformed through popular education. In 1913, in view of the recommendations of the Pujo Committee, these notions were distinctly conservative, but reviewers praised the book as sound and practical.[36] Actually Brace had put into book form a view typical of contemporary financial reformers—namely that there were evils but that evolution would remove them.

Louis Dembitz Brandeis, the controversial Boston corporation lawyer, was the most authoritative writer on the economic aspects of Woodrow Wilson's New Freedom. Brandeis' chief concern was with trustification and the accompanying power it bestowed on investment bankers. In a series of articles in *Harper's Weekly* in 1913, Brandeis offered the public some remedies for the economic concentration that had developed so rapidly after 1898. He called for enforcement of the Sherman Anti-Trust Act, the elimination of interlocking directorates, and the direct sale to the public of some types of securities (to bypass the investment bankers). He

[36] Harrison H. Brace, *The Value of Organized Speculation* (New York, 1913), 200-202, 253-265. *The Independent* said: "a judicious book on practical economics"; the *Nation* said: "common sense in an overstrained era"; the *Springfield Republican*: "broad but a bit tedious," *Book Review Digest* (New York, 1913), 69.

condemned the combinations that had not resulted in improvement of the property but had merely supplied "water" to the promoters and commissions to the underwriters and brokers.[37] While Brandeis did not blame the investment banker directly for speculation, "the People's Attorney" believed that speculation fed the Money Trust by luring the nation's funds to New York City and stimulating stock turnover, which meant larger commissions for the financial men. He noted that the exchange listing requirement of a transfer agent in New York usually caused a corporation to establish a financial office there; this in turn led to a directorship for a banker, thus increasing banker control of industry.

Brandeis, a firm believer in publicity, thought the prospective investor should be given the pertinent facts, not merely sworn statements by company officials. He realized "caveat emptor" was obsolete doctrine, but he also perceived that statutes could not efficiently fix bank rates nor prevent an investor from making a bad bargain.[38] He favored a law similar to the Federal Securities Act finally passed in 1933. Like Easterners in general at this time, he was content to let the citizen act freely provided he was furnished enough material to arrive at his own conclusions. His view therefore differed from the more extreme paternal approach exemplified by the Kansas "blue sky" law and its imitations—these laws aimed to have bureaucrats pass on the merits of the securities before the public was permitted to buy them.[39] Brandeis was criticizing a system, not individuals. Possibly there would have been less speculation had his suggestions been followed, because there would have been fewer mergers with their accompanying excessive stock

[37] Alpheus T. Mason, *Brandeis: A Free Man's Life* (New York, 1946), 412-415.

[38] Louis D. Brandeis, *Other People's Money and How the Bankers Use It* (New York, 1914), 153-155; 101-104.

[39] Mason, *Brandeis,* 408. For a discussion of blue sky laws see Section IV, below.

offerings, a smaller supply of "other people's money" available to investment bankers, and generally less financial concentration in New York City.

Reviewers took the publication of *Other People's Money* in stride. The *Nation* said it was familiar material, that some declarations were too sweeping, but admitted that the book would attract readers who realized the significance of changes in corporate management. Brandeis, the most active mind working on the credit monopoly problem, told what happened to the investors' money, said *Harper's Weekly*. *The Outlook* thought Brandeis went too far in suggesting that private control always meant selfish despotism. The *Boston Transcript* dismissed his thesis as absurd; the *San Francisco Chronicle* called the articles deceptive, and denounced the Trust idea as a myth. The *New York Times* announced that it was weary of the whole subject. On the other hand, the *Washington Star* called the book concrete and forceful. Other critics pooh-poohed the idea of a Money Trust; "How," they asked, "could the nation's financial leaders cheat and conspire and still continue to retain public confidence over the years?"[40]

Brandeis had taken up where the Pujo Committee's recommendations left off. Financial circles were afraid.

III

The report of the famous Pujo Committee lent support to those who had been claiming the existence of a "Money Trust." The report found a monopoly of credit and an interrelation of financial institutions that was detrimental to competitive enterprise.[41] But Samuel Untermyer, a New York lawyer-reformer and the committee's aggressive but persuasive chief counsel, was inter-

[40] *Book Review Digest* (1913), v. 10, 64. Of course, progressives praised the book. Senator LaFollette called it "epoch-making." Mason, *Brandeis*, 416-420.
[41] *Money Trust Investigation, Report 1593* (February 28, 1913).

ested in more than credit monopoly and the monopolistic features of exchange organization. He hoped to extract and publicize the methods of manipulation that he believed were being used to disarrange stock prices.

This proved to be a difficult task. The great J. P. Morgan was the only committee witness willing to agree fully with Untermyer that manipulation was bad. The other witnesses either avoided the name, or justified it in terms of "making a market," publicizing a good stock, or suggested defensively that it was a private right of person or persons so long as exchange procedures were followed. Exchange spokesmen were, of course, wary of this whole line of inquiry. Broker witnesses were careful to make it plain that they knew nothing of manipulative practices at firsthand. New York Stock Exchange President James G. Mabon declared that the governors were doing everything possible to stop it. Mabon, however, was able to cite only one case in which an exchange member was punished for attempting to rig prices. Untermyer reminded him of the many other disciplinary actions taken by the board of governors, suggesting that manipulation was regarded as a very minor offense by the exchange, and other testimony tended to bear out this assumption. Frank K. Sturgis, an exchange governor, told the committee that he could see nothing wrong with orders to buy and sell the same stock provided they came from different brokers, not acting in collusion. He argued further that any manipulative actions not involving the collusion of exchange members were beyond the purview of exchange authority; he refused to be drawn into a discussion of the possible social effects of some of these practices. "Making a market," stimulating trade by buying and selling a stock simultaneously, was simply a form of advertising, he said.[42]

[42] *Money Trust Investigation*, Committee on Banking & Currency. United States House of Representatives. II, 1087; I, 318ff., 806-814; II, 868-879; I, 394-396. Chapin & Company, exchange

Nevertheless Untermyer introduced several other witnesses in order to acquaint the committee with what manipulation by a pool could do. They developed the facts surrounding the infamous pool that operated in Columbus and Hocking Coal and Iron Company stock in 1909-1910. It was established that James R. Keene, a leading Street manipulator, acting as the manager of a syndicate, had bought and sold 124,000 shares of this stock over a period of less than a year; only 70,000 shares were outstanding. Keene operated through the brokerage firm of Popper and Sternbach, where he maintained 59 separate accounts under assorted numbers and symbols. His orders to buy and sell were distributed by Popper and Sternbach to many other brokers, presumably to disguise the source of all the activity. As a result of Keene's operations, Hocking Coal rose from 20 to 90 within a few months, but on January 19, 1910, the stock broke suddenly from 88¾ to about 25. Some insider had been "leaking," selling short against the pool members. Popper and Sternbach promptly went bankrupt. Because he later offered to settle, it was widely assumed that Keene himself had been the guilty short seller, betraying the pool members and violating his agreement with them. Untermyer underscored the fact that, under market rules, the exchange had access to any and all books of the members, yet it had not investigated Popper and Sternbach although this suspicious activity in Hocking Coal stock went on for months. It was an obvious case of matched orders or even wash sales, where one interest was constantly buying and selling similar amounts, to attract gullible outsiders. Even after Keene's sabotage and the collapse of the pool, the exchange took no strong disciplinary action. The story of the Hocking Coal pool

---

brokers, had placed orders to buy 2000 shares with twenty different brokers one morning; as a result, the stock (Rock Island Railroad) rose 30 points for a brief time. The exchange punished Chapin.

must have made quite an impression, however, for many of the Pujo Committee members were Bryan Democrats, quite hostile to Wall Street and its trappings.[43]

The idea that a new and more ethical era was dawning in Wall Street was prevalent from 1911 to 1913; it was consonant with the general political regeneration of those years. Harry Content, veteran broker to the great and near-great, attempted to minimize the impact of the Hocking Coal revelations with the following argument. He told Untermyer that pools of the Keene type had virtually disappeared from the exchanges in the last two years. Big operators were now acting on their own, he said; there had been too much double-crossing under the old syndicate arrangements. Some months later in *Munsey's*, Issac F. Marcosson saw the death of Keene in 1912 as the end of an epoch; the bold, boisterous days of manipulation and pools had passed; normal trading would take over. The Brace book, discussed earlier, was also strongly flavored with the belief that the old days were gone forever, that the public was too wise for that kind of skulduggery. But whether financial people admitted abuses or protested that these were beyond their province, they all opposed legislative remedies.[44] In spite of this attitude, and the fact that the New York Stock Exchange constituted only a subsidiary part of their investigation, the Pujo Committee listed certain recommendations to improve stock exchange ethics and reduce its monopolistic character:

1. Incorporation in the state of location.
2. Complete disclosure by the company at the time of listing on the exchange.

[43] *Ibid.*, I, 708-717; II, 904-908; II, 713-715. Ray Stannard Baker, *Woodrow Wilson: Life and Letters* (Garden City, 1927), IV, 139.

[44] Testimony of Harry Content, *Money Trust Investigation*, I, 318ff. 806ff; II, 868-879. Isaac F. Marcosson, "The Passing of the Plunger."

3. A 20 per cent margin minimum.
4. Prohibition of "wash sales" (buying and selling by the same party).
5. Prohibition of a broker pledging a customer's security for more than the customer owes him.
6. Prohibition of a broker loaning stocks to another broker.
7. Judicial review of the exchange's disciplinary actions.
8. Keeping records available to the Postmaster General.

The Pujo Committee believed that if these suggestions were followed, the exchange would regain public confidence and enter upon a period of unprecedented prosperity.[45]

Following the Pujo findings, Senator Robert L. Owen, a Virginia-born progressive Democrat from Oklahoma, drafted a stock exchange regulation bill. Its purpose was to bring exchanges under state control, and it required incorporation in state of location. It also embodied the other Pujo recommendations listed above. The Postmaster General was empowered to suspend the mailing privileges of, and forbid the dissemination of information about, non-complying exchanges. Samuel Untermyer, who had gained national recognition as counsel for the Pujo Committee, was a central figure in the effort to gain passage of the stock exchange regulation bill, but his conduct and manner offended many people. John G. Milburn, president of the New York Stock Exchange, charged Untermyer with vituperation and demagoguery in his advocacy of Owen's bill; Milburn claimed the lawyer's emotional presentations were below the level proper for Senate committee hearings.[46]

[45] *Money Trust Investigation, Report 1593*, 115-116.
[46] *New York Times*, February 13, 1914, 12:2; April 25, 1914, 18:7. See Chapter 4, Section I below for some Senators' adverse opinions of Untermyer as a result of the Pujo hearings.

The chief grievances of the public against the stock market were manipulation and short selling. Untermyer contended that the exchange apparatus constituted a sort of confidence game, inasmuch as the general public was not habituated to market customs and was not able to evaluate correctly market information and procedure. Moreover, according to Untermyer, exchange officials were obsessed with self-interest and unable to see the wrong in manipulation.[47]

The Senate Committee on Banking and Currency held hearings on the Owen bill but they did not establish the existence of any conspiracy to defraud. The public, however, especially in the Midwest, was unwilling to recognize short selling of stock as legitimate; "short selling is contrary to any moral ethics, which means . . . that it is thievery." The Hughes Committee Report, often cited during this investigation, had held that there was no ethical difference between taking long and short positions in the market. The Pujo findings had also failed to condemn short selling.[48] There was a divergence of view on this economic question; bankers, brokers, economists, and many Senators saw no moral evil in short selling; the agrarian-oriented portions of the public did. Henry Emery, the stock market authority, was probably influential in reaffirming the ideas legislators already had on such matters. Emery declared that all the bills so far presented would do more harm than good, that there were many evils the government could not control. He argued that the Owen bill would drive stocks from the exchange listings, and that it would therefore be wiser to accept the presence of illegitimate deals as the price of an open marketplace. He favored regulatory agreements among brokers rather than legal restrictions on

[47] Samuel Untermyer, "Speculation on the Stock Exchanges and Public Regulation of the Exchanges," *American Economic Review*, 5:sup., 28ff. (March 1915).

[48] *LaFollette's Magazine*, 4:8; (June 28, 1913). *Report 1593*, 116-119.

broker-client relations. Senator Knute Nelson of Minnesota could find little constructive information in Emery's testimony and charged him with too complete a divorce of the economic and moral sides of the problem.[49]

Even the financial centers were disposed to admit some negligence on the part of the exchanges. The *New York Journal of Commerce* told the brokers that they had been careless "or worse" in selling new securities to the public. Warning the Street against trying to thwart public sentiment, the financial paper remarked that "the safer the investor's money is in Wall Street's goods, the greater will be the business on the Stock Exchange."[50] The *New York Evening Mail* thought the exchange ought to take the lead in the reform movement; the *Times* observed that if the exchange's rules were put on a high enough plane, they would have the sanction of public opinion.[51]

The muckrakers and their successors had directed much of their invective toward fraudulent stock issues, and the investment bankers who "made a market" for such issues. Senator LaFollette of Wisconsin had been demanding a physical evaluation of the nation's railroads, in order to determine how much excess capital the public was being required to pay dividends on. During the rapid consolidations of the 1900s many promotional shares were allotted to the financiers, and the public was becoming aware of the fact. Watered stock had become a major complaint against Wall Street.[52] Although exchange authorities did not acknowledge the water, they did recognize that dubious secu-

[49] *Stock Exchange Regulation*, 324-342.

[50] Excerpt from *Journal* of January 29 printed in *LaFollette's Magazine* (March 14, 1914), 3.

[51] "Why the Stock Exchange Fights Incorporation," *Literary Digest*, 50:502-503 (March 8, 1913); *New York Times*, December 27, 1913, 10:3 (editorial).

[52] E. Dana Durand, "Stock Watering," *The Independent*, 54:2238 (September 1902).

rities on their exchanges were creating considerable ill will toward the Street. They suggested, instead of Senator Owen's bill, that Congress enact a law regulating the issue of corporate securities. In this way the public could be protected from spurious stocks and the exchange would remain free of the deadening hand of government supervision. Edward Page, a member of the Hughes Committee in 1908, suggested that the British Companies Act was an excellent model for an American anti-fraud bill, and Senator Gilbert M. Hitchcock of Nebraska thought a national law of this sort would be a sufficient remedy. Samuel Untermyer made it clear, however, that he wanted to do more than control the issuance of securities; he wanted to prevent their manipulation after they were listed on the exchanges. He would not settle for the lesser objective, and continued vociferously to support comprehensive regulation.[53]

Some of the opposition to Senator Owen's bill was to its means rather than its aims. Utilizing the commerce clause, the bill empowered the Postmaster General to ban from interstate mail any information emanating from exchanges that did not comply with the prescribed regulations. Despite assurances from Untermyer, Senator Hitchcock—himself an editor and publisher—feared the precedent of establishing, through a legal device of this kind, the Postmaster General as a censor of information. Senators Joseph L. Bristow of Kansas and Coe I. Crawford of South Dakota concurred, and the *New York Journal of Commerce,* the *New York Post, New York World,* and the *St. Louis Republic* all objected to the power of censorship vested in the cabinet officer. Faced

[53] The board of governors of the exchange endorsed the British Companies Act as a model. *New York Times,* November 25, 1913, 15:1. Page defended watered stock however, claiming that it was a fair way of rewarding the brains involved in an enterprise. *Stock Exchange Regulation,* 298-300.

with serious defection on this point, Senator Owen offered to have the power transferred to the newly created Federal Trade Commission; he was willing to make any reasonable concession to get some form of regulation enacted.[54]

The incorporation requirement was second only to the Postmaster General section in provoking adverse comment. This provision had been suggested and rejected by a majority of the Hughes Committee in 1908, but it had been resurrected as the best means of increasing regulation consonant with the home-rule principles of the Democratic party. Horace White, editor and former member of the Hughes Committee, told the Senators that Congress had no more right to interfere with the exchange than with the Union League Club. On the other hand, the conservative Dr. Emery testified that only the older members regarded the exchange as a private club, that the newer elements realized its public character. He did not favor incorporation, however. James B. Mabon, president of the New York Stock Exchange, believed that if incorporation were brought about by a vote of the majority of exchange members, it would amount to coercion of a minority; this coercion, he held, would be contrary to the spirit of common law. H. H. Boyeson, of the Consolidated Stock Exchange, thought incorporation would impair the disciplinary power of the exchanges' business conduct committees. The *New York Journal of Commerce* and the *New York Tribune* felt the incorporation provision unjust.[55]

Samuel Untermyer was the principal spokesman for the incorporation advocates. He believed that the great power of the exchanges and the opportunity for fraud

[54] *New York Times*, February 12, 1914, 2:2; February 13, 12:2; February 5, 18:1; March 21, 7:6; June 27, 11:6; February 7, 13:5.
[55] "Why the Stock Exchange Fights Incorporation," *Literary Digest*, 50:502-503 (March 8, 1913); *Stock Exchange Regulation*, 276ff.; *New York Times*, February 8, 1914, II: 12:7.

they represented should be regulated by the government. He listed three major reasons for this view:

1. To prevent, detect, and punish fraud through wash sales, manipulation, etc.
2. To secure complete publicity of profits of bankers, brokers, etc. through control of the exchange listing departments, and to prevent unfair delistings.
3. To secure uniformity of corporate regulation. The exchanges should be made instruments for the publicity of corporate affairs; it would gain business thereby and perform a government service.

Surprisingly, H. K. Pomeroy, an ex-president of the exchange, declared in favor of the incorporation scheme. But Senator Knute Nelson of Minnesota, convinced of the power of the exchange lobby in the Senate, was skeptical; the plan would never pass, he said, because if it did, the exchanges would be subject to the law and the exchanges would not like that.[56]

In line with the incorporation provision was another—to subject decisions by the exchanges' disciplinary committees to judicial review. Its proponents said committee testimony had established that disciplinary action was taken almost exclusively against members who violated the exchanges' monopolistic rules, rather than against brokers who were guilty of fraud or bad faith. Judicial review would give the individual exchange member some legal recourse against the power of the exchanges' committees, Untermyer believed, but market representatives feared that judicial review, like the incorporation plan, would sap exchange discipline.[57]

President Wilson's attitude toward the Owen bill was also the subject of dispute. Untermyer claimed that the Library Committee of the New York Stock Exchange—

---

[56] *New York Times,* February 5, 1914, 18:1; February 7, 13:1; *Stock Exchange Regulation,* 328-329.

[57] Untermyer, "Speculation on the Stock Exchanges," 45-48.

its public relations department—was circulating the "canard" that the President opposed the measure; Wilson was for it, said the voluble attorney. A few days after this W. C. Antwerp, counsel for the exchange, forced Untermyer to modify this assertion and retract the statement that the story had originated in the Library Committee. Untermyer conceded that the President had decided to press for only the measures mentioned in the 1912 platform, and stock exchange regulation was not in that platform; the President, however, Untermyer added, was not opposed to regulation. Later the *New York Times* noted that the President was not encouraging the Owen bill.[58]

By the spring of 1914 there were signs that the public had been fatigued by "the battle at Armageddon." The memory of the Pujo Report was beginning to fade. Senator Owen's stock exchange bill, an outgrowth of the Pujo findings, was having trouble in the Senate Banking and Currency Committee. In June the Oklahoma Senator himself filed a report stating that his bill had little prospect of passing—seven of the twelve committee members were definitely opposed to it. Senator John W. Weeks of Massachusetts remarked testily that only one man in the United States, Samuel Untermyer, favored passage; Senator Owen reminded his colleague that he too favored the bill.[59] But the issue of stock exchange regulation was not seriously raised again for twenty years.

In New York State itself there had been a concomitant move to purify stock market practice after publication of the Pujo Report recommendations. In the 1912 election,

[58] *New York Times,* February 5, 1914, 18:1; February 12, 2:2. Professor Arthur S. Link has noted that President Wilson did not favor the stock exchange bill. *Woodrow Wilson and the Progressive Era, 1910-1917* (New York, 1954), 70, n. 39.

[59] Untermyer noted that a majority of the House Banking Committee favored it, and that the Pujo Report had suggested such a bill. Untermyer, "Speculation on the Stock Exchanges," 43-44; *New York Times,* June 26, 1914, 11:2.

William Sulzer, a Democratic progressive of Forty-Eighter stock, was chosen governor. Sulzer had long been a "do-gooder," taking part in national reforms while serving in the Congress from 1895 to 1913. The new governor devoted an important part of his message to the legislature to stock market regulation, reminding them of the Democratic principle of home rule, and suggesting that the state act before Congress did. He began by declaring that the public had a vital interest in honest transactions and that the evils were beyond dispute, citing the conservative Hughes Report of 1909 as substantiation. The governor listed the general complaints against the exchanges: that they were indifferent to the public interest, lax in their rules, and too slow in disciplining members. In his opinion the authority to remedy these wrongs was embraced in the state's police powers.

Governor Sulzer then made specific legislative recommendations which he believed would improve the ethics of the brokerage business. He suggested that a broker be prohibited from acting as an agent for a customer while at the same time participating as a principal whose interest was opposed to that of the customer. Another suggestion was that a broker be banned from doing business after he was bankrupt; a third, that rules about orders given "at the market" be tightened so that the broker could not use them for personal advantage. The governor also favored making the issuance of erroneous information a criminal offense. He reaffirmed the Hughes Committee recommendation that the bucket shop law be strengthened. He also asked that written permission be required from customers before a broker could use their hypothecated securities; by 1913 there was a definite awareness of the power invested in brokers by virtue of the hypothecated securities under their control.[60]

[60] *The Public Papers of William Sulzer* (Albany, 1914), 55-69; *New York Times*, August 22, 1913, 12:3. Professor Frank Freidel is skeptical of "Plain Bill" Sulzer's progressivism, suggesting that

Sulzer's program drew sympathetic comment from some magazines. The *Nation* noted that patronage of the exchanges had been narrowing to a group of immensely wealthy men who were making prices go up or down by brute force, and to a group indulgent toward these new Fisks and Goulds. The people at large had lost their faith in the market; maybe the present reform would restore respectability. John G. Dater, in *Munsey's*, was inclined to blame the exchange itself for its predicament; it should have recognized and admitted its public character earlier. If it had adhered more readily to all the reforms recommended by the Hughes Committee, the exchange's popular reputation as a huge gambling hall might have declined. The writer, however, was cool toward a proposed raising of the state stock transfer tax from 2 to 4 per cent, on the ground that it might drive the exchange business over to New Jersey. Nor did he decry short selling; it was an economic function sanctioned by common law; it was simply unfortunate that inexperienced market amateurs were only aware of the long side.[61]

Governor Sulzer was so zealous in his reformism that he rapidly alienated the Tammany members of his own party. His desire for open primaries and stock exchange reform made him an "impossible governor" to the political stalwarts. Charles F. Murphy, the boss of Tammany, discovered after diligent research that Governor Sulzer had not returned some $40,000 that friends had donated for his 1912 gubernatorial campaign. Tammany construed this as a violation of the campaign expenditures act, and, supplementing it by corollary charges, used it as a basis for impeaching the crusading governor. One of

---

his career prior to 1912 was unsavory. *Franklin D. Roosevelt: The Apprenticeship* (New York, 1951), 178.

[61] "Reforming the Stock Exchange," *Nation,* 96:165 (February 13, 1913); John G. Dater, "Stock Market Uncertainties," *Munsey's,* 49:131-132 (April 1913).

the allegations was that the governor had used part of the left-over campaign money for flyers in the stock market, and that one of the purposes behind his stock exchange reform was to affect stock prices in his own favor. Progressive circles were incensed at the brazen Tammany effort to crucify the New York governor, but with GOP legislators indifferent, Tammany succeeded in impeaching and removing Sulzer from office in October of 1913.[62] Of the many stock exchange reforms proposed by Sulzer only a few were passed by the recalcitrant legislature. In the nation's greatest financial state, exchange reform came late and left early.[63]

After the demise of the Sulzer program, and while the Owen bill was foundering on the rocks of mismanagement, the fight against commodity speculators was stirring anew. Less than a year after the defeat of Cummins' amendment to the Underwood Tariff, wheat farmers of the Old Northwest gathered in a convention wearing buttons reading, "We Want an Honest Market." They complained that the Chambers of Commerce were thwarting the marketing efforts of farmers' cooperatives, that the commercial interests were seeking to preserve broker parasites. They also charged dishonest grading of

[62] Gregory Mason, "Sulzer and the Invisible Government," *Outlook*, 105:356-361 (October 18, 1913); "Impeachment—An Unusual Process," *Review of Reviews*, 48:259-272 (September 1913).

[63] The bucket shop law of 1908 was changed to the Massachusetts version as recommended by the Hughes Committee in 1909; manipulation of securities was made a felony; brokers were required to give clients memos promptly about the previous owner of a purchased security; grain dealers were required to have licenses. New York Stock Exchange brokers had to deal with those of the Consolidated Exchange. Another Sulzer law required that the broker get permission from the customer to hypothecate his stocks. This was an attempt by Sulzer to restrict brokers' use of their clients' funds; in operation it was nugatory, for the exchange discovered it could comply with the law by having each customer sign a statement of permission as a condition to doing business. *Papers of Sulzer*, 113-114; *New York Times*, August 22, 1913, 12:3, September 1, 4:8.

grain and reasserted their demand for the abolition of options.[64]

Senator Ellison Durant Smith of South Carolina, the Senate cotton expert, had been working on a cotton measure affecting speculators; it was enacted in 1914 and perfected in 1916. This law, the Cotton Futures Act, was much less drastic than the Clarke and Cummins proposals of 1913; it merely set government grading standards for cotton and reduced the number of grades deliverable under a futures contract from twenty-seven to eight. "Cotton Ed" Smith believed that his law would make the futures contract more useful to spinners, while at the same time narrowing the orbit of outside cotton speculators. The cotton exchanges fought the bill, believing that it would diminish their speculative business. Because, like the Owen bill, Smith's act employed the legal device of forbidding the reporting of information from non-complying exchanges, it too was open to the charge of censorship, and roll call votes were therefore avoided.[65]

The national and state moves for stock exchange regulation during the Progressive Era were, as we have seen, largely failures. Aside from some minor rules adopted by the exchanges following the Hughes Report, practices changed little and the markets did not officially acknowledge the public character of their activities. The "newer elements," the financial reformers who realized the importance of public confidence in the markets, were not yet strong enough to replace the legalistic exclusiveness of the older statesmen. That part of the New Freedom emphasizing decentralization and home rule was singularly ill-adapted to the stock exchange situation, because New York, where the most important exchanges were located, benefited so much from them that it was

[64] "Wanted: An Honest Market," *LaFollette's Magazine* (March 28, 1914), 3.
[65] *New York Times,* March 28, 1914, 15:1.

unlikely to take drastic steps which would drive them across the river to New Jersey. The other states, which wanted to curb the markets, found their legislative devices impotent in the face of the interstate character of the exchanges' facilities. Even more than the railroads, the stock exchanges seemed to be a federal problem.

IV

As we have seen, the Spanish-American War and the Rooseveltian prosperity that followed had increased the number of charlatans who were preying upon the financially unsophisticated. Particularly in the West, questionable mining and oil stocks were peddled to the humble who saw a chance to make a killing. But the panic of 1907 stirred some citizens against the pirates who had been operating under the cloak of prosperity. Reformers wanted stock exchange regulation, a federal banking system free from banker control, and legislation to protect the public from fraudulent stocks and bonds. The last demand finally resulted in the passage of the first blue sky law in Kansas in 1911. Laws of this type came to be called "blue sky" because their purpose was to prevent fast-talking swindlers from selling a piece of sky to the gullible.[66]

Kansas enacted its law after a concerted campaign against fraudulent stock. The state legislature rejected that old caveat, "let the buyer beware," and instead designated a commission to pass on the soundness of all securities sold in the state. In addition to requiring full disclosure, licenses, and monthly reports from brokers, the commission was empowered to determine whether the security seeking a permit "promises a fair return." The Jayhawkers aimed to regulate the security business in the same way that they were regulating banking. Ini-

[66] In 1910 Rhode Island amended its constitution to require that financial statements be filed with the Secretary of State. Jacob Murray Edelman, *Security Regulation in the 48 States* (Washington, 1942), 1-5.

tially the standards set by the commission were so high that less than 100 out of 1500 applicants were granted permission to sell their securities in Kansas the first year. Three-fourths of the applications were rejected as fraudulent propositions and another 12½ per cent were declared to be too risky. Yet Walter R. Stubbs, the progressive Republican governor, was enthusiastic over the measure, stating that every state and the federal government ought to have such a law. He estimated that the statute had saved Kansas a million dollars in the first year, and rid the state of thirty-seven dishonest dealers.

The "Kansas Idea" caught fire in a number of Southern and Western states, and almost every state asked for a copy of the new law. Arizona, Louisiana, and South Carolina enacted similar laws in 1912; twenty other states followed in 1913. Governor Robert D. Carey of Wyoming called the Kansas law "splendid" and observed that too often big names on prospectuses lured the ignorant; he asked that his state follow the Kansas example. But the triumph of the "Kansas Idea" was not universal even in progressive regions. In 1912 the Oregon voters rejected a proposed blue sky measure; in 1914 Washington defeated a similar proposition: Yes, 142,017; No, 147, 298.[67] Generally speaking, the former Populist strongholds acted more swiftly and were more inclined to imitate the severity of Kansas. In Arizona and Idaho, where fraudulent mining stock was abundant, penalties were especially harsh. The Kansas, Arizona, Idaho, North Dakota, Missouri, and Tennessee acts all called for a maximum of ten years imprisonment and a large fine; these states were also slow in modifying the laws later.[68]

The commercial East was hostile to the Kansas statute

[67] Clarence A. Dykstra, "Blue Sky Legislation," *American Political Science Review*, 7:230-234 (May 1913); *Governors' Conference Proceedings*, 1911, 245-247; 1913, 384.

[68] Robert R. Reed and Lester H. Washburn, *Blue Sky Laws* (New York, 1921), 1-155.

and its imitators. Opponents, led by the Investment Bankers Association, charged that the blue sky laws were foolish, crude, and unconstitutional, and complained of the nuisance and expense of having to conform to different laws in different states. But they were especially vehement in denouncing the "fair return" discretion given to state security commissioners under the Kansas plan. If state commissions would permit no really risky securities to be sold, how could new and hazardous businesses raise money? They feared these laws would impede the flow of capital to legitimate small enterprises; paternalism was the epithet they used most frequently to condemn the Kansas principle.[69] The financiers opposed a blue sky movement in New York on the ground that a law to protect Western villagers from the impositions of traveling peddlers did not apply to regions where commerce was more complicated. In a similar vein, Massachusetts legislators reported that since securities were traded almost exclusively through bankers and established brokers, the Kansas type of statute was too paternalistic for the Bay State.[70] The East did not pass any general security laws until after World War I, and those they did ultimately enact were less severe.

The Investment Bankers Association did not want the commissioners to pass on the probable fair return on the offerings of its members. Accordingly, the bankers tried to have securities traded on the major exchanges automatically exempted from compliance with the detailed blue sky requirements. They wanted the states to concern themselves solely with fraud and not to interfere with the flow of risk capital. Their tactic was persistently to challenge the harsh provisions in the courts, hoping for favorable decisions that would weaken the statutes.

[69] George W. Hodges, *Blue Sky Bill,* Committee on Foreign & Interstate Commerce. United States House of Representatives. 67 Cong., 2 sess. (Washington, 1922), 53-55.

[70] "Blue Sky Laws," *The Nation,* 96:343-345 (April 3, 1913); Dykstra, "Blue Sky Legislation," 230-234.

In this they were fairly successful; they got the stiff Michigan and Iowa acts declared unconstitutional.[71] Between 1913 and 1916 many states amended and modified their laws—some discovered they had acted in haste. The United States Supreme Court, in *Hall* vs. *Geiger-Jones* (1916), invalidated many sections of earlier statutes, thereby speeding the process. Between 1911 and 1920—by the latter year most states had enacted some type of law to meet this problem—more and more exemptions were made for reputable listed stocks.[72]

The Eastern commercial states reluctantly yielded to the trend to the extent of passing stock fraud laws after World War I. These acts were much weaker than the Western blue sky statutes because they were punitive rather than preventive; they did not provide for regulation but merely increased the penalties for persons convicted of stock swindling under extant fraud laws. Operating after the fact, these acts required very diligent law enforcement agencies to be effective. Needless to say, enforcement did not meet this standard; there were few prosecutions because of the expense and difficulty of proving a case.[73] Nor were publicity provisions adequate. Wisconsin found that its citizens went right ahead investing in shady companies even when information indicating their fraudulent nature was readily available. Hegekirk N. Duff, president of the National Association of Security Commissioners, thought federal regulation was needed because "the gullibility of the American public is the same to-day as it was in the days of Phineas T. Barnum, while their penchant to get rich quick is the same now as in the reign of the Mississippi Bubble and Dr. Thompson's eye water."

Finally many state security commissions, like the in-

[71] *New York Times,* April 26, 1914, IX, 15:5.
[72] Edelman, *Security Regulation,* 8-10.
[73] Edward E. Denison, "Fleecing the Public of its Liberty Bonds," *The Progressive,* June 1922, 91.

vestment bankers, arrived at the conclusion that a federal law was needed to standardize the multitude of state codes on this subject. Congressman Edward E. Denison, a Yale-trained lawyer from a southern Illinois Democratic district, took the lead. He drew up a bill that would facilitate state laws but would at the same time leave states free to exercise their individual preferences in most matters; it would have no effect in the few states without blue sky laws.[74] Thus, like the proposed Owen stock exchange bill of 1914, Denison's measure was a Wilsonian compromise between decentralization and the need for federal control of interstate commerce. Congressman Denison had the support of the National Association of Security Commissioners, but he realized that the cooperation of the investment bankers was also needed. In a conference of interested groups—bankers, businessmen, and security commissioners—exemptions to the proposed law were worked out; the result had the endorsement of all groups concerned, and only Western mining and oil interests opposed such moderate legislation.[75] Government and foreign government securities, railroad and other public utility stocks, and charitable institution shares were all exempted from the operation of the proposed law. Knowing the general prejudice against bureaucracy both among businessmen and yeoman Democrats, Denison stressed the point that the Attorney General would enforce the law and that no special bureau would be created to administer it.

Although swindlers became bold again after World War I, taking an estimated $500,000,000 from the public

[74] *Blue Sky Bill,* 116, 50-57, 15-40. In 1922 six states—Connecticut, Colorado, Delaware, Nevada, Pennsylvania, and Washington—had neither blue sky nor stock fraud laws.

[75] *Ibid.,* 9-15. The National Better Business Committee of the Associated Advertising Clubs of the World also endorsed the bill, 192. *Blue Sky Laws,* Subcommittee of Committee on Foreign & Interstate Commerce. 68 Cong., 1 sess. (Washington, 1923), 200-201.

through fraudulent shares, Congress never got around to enacting the Denison bill. Even with widespread support, the measure languished in Congress from 1922 to 1925.[76] National blue sky legislation did not finally arrive until the Federal Securities Act of 1933. The Democratic platform of 1932 had devoted a plank to the "Truth in Securities" idea, promising to protect the investor from misrepresentation. The findings of Congressional investigations after the Crash made this again a live issue. The 1933 act, which pertained almost exclusively to new security issues, was much more stringent and comprehensive than the Denison versions of the twenties.[77]

What had begun in Kansas as an attempt to protect the citizen from speculative securities culminated in laws that simply made information about certain concerns more accurate and complete. Brokers and investment bankers had brought enough pressure on the state legislatures of the West to ensure that only the smaller, unlisted stock issues would be regulated or eliminated by the various state codes. The original Western idea of a security commission to pass on the soundness of a proposed stock issue was modified in favor of one that concerned itself only with flagrant fraud in connection with little-known shares. We may conclude, however, that these state laws in the aggregate increased the protection of the prospective investor and, through their various registration requirements, provided him with more information upon which to base his investment decisions. The laws did not directly affect speculation on the major exchanges because their shares were generally exempt, but the ethics of the whole profession were raised by the elimination of many dishonest dealers and practices.

[76] *Report on H. R. 34.* Committee on Foreign & Interstate Commerce. United States House of Representatives. 69 Cong., 1 sess., 5ff. (December 22, 1925); *Blue Sky Bill,* 2-3.
[77] See Chapter 6 below, pp. 232-235.

Strong agrarian prejudices, expressed in the early blue sky laws in some Western states, yielded to compromises with the "evil" broker and promoter elements. Like the extreme anti-futures laws of agricultural states between 1870 and 1900, they could not stand up against the pressure of legal opinion and the invasion of commercial mores. If public opinion can be measured by laws enacted, only a few states such as Kansas, North Dakota, Idaho, Arizona, Missouri, Montana, and Tennessee seem to have been strongly infected with the anti-Wall Street virus in this matter, and even this wrath was probably aimed at door-to-door salesmen of oil and mining shares rather than at the whole system of security trading.

Progressivism reached its apogee in the United States between 1907 and 1914—between the Bankers' Panic and the outbreak of World War I. Woodrow Wilson and the Congress elected with him in 1912 put on the books many of the reforms that had been discussed for a decade. Progressivism took different political labels—Democrat, Republican, Progressive, Socialist—but was truly a national movement for reform in politics, economics, and social welfare.

The agrarians reacted sharply to the Bankers' Panic, but they continued to play only a subsidiary role in reform. In the Bacon and Clarke amendments to tariff bills, they attempted frontal assaults on their enemies, the bucket shoppers and futures markets, but were unsuccessful, despite the general reformist tide. And they used much rhetoric against the central bank idea contemplated by Senator Aldrich and the Eastern Republicans. At the state level they were more important, contributing heavily to the severity of Western and Southern blue sky laws. The financial reformers retained control, however, and dominated the period. Already worried about their public images, they moved quickly in the wake of the Bankers' Panic to promote reforms from within financial circles. These men subscribed to the Hughes

Committee recommendations, to most of Sulzer's proposals, and to some of those suggested by the Pujo Committee. In arguing with the agrarians, they resisted such remedies as incorporation or federal regulation and emphasized the upward trend in ethics.

In addition to the financial reformers and the agrarians, a third reform element among the anti-speculators gradually became discernible in these years: the "progressives." Unlike the agrarians, they did not believe that stock and commodity trading mechanisms could be eradicated by statute. But neither did they agree with the financial reformers that anti-fraud laws, publicity and education, self-government by financiers, or evolutionary morality was enough to ensure fair trading. The "progressives" were more and more to emphasize taxation of speculative gains and comprehensive regulation, state and federal. Powers bestowed on the Interstate Commerce Commission by the Hepburn Act, the newly created Federal Trade Commission, and the Federal Reserve System were encouraging developments; they suggested that the "progressive" solution was destined in the long run to triumph in the exchange field also. But in 1914 the progressives were still inconspicuous and held only a few tents in the reform camp.[78]

[78] Cf. Robert H. Wiebe, *Businessmen and Reform: A Study of the Progressive Movement* (Cambridge, Mass., 1962), whose three categories (1) country bankers; (2) Midwest city bankers; and (3) Eastern magnates, are closely related to agrarians, progressives, and financial reformers and standpatters. Wiebe argues that the moderate Midwestern group was thrown into disarray by the 1907 Panic and lost its leadership to the Eastern magnates who proved to be intransigent in the face of the rising reformist tide. The "progressive" viewpoint came largely from Congress in these years and they at least conciliated the Midwesterners sufficiently to get the Federal Reserve System compromise through, although it was opposed on the right by the Eastern magnates and on the left by country bankers.

CHAPTER 3

WORLD WAR I AND THE GROWTH

OF SPECULATION

I

*E*VEN as Senator Owen and Samuel Untermyer argued their case against stock speculators and for regulation, world conditions were working against them. After the archduke's assassination in July 1914, and the initial panic liquidation caused by Allied stockholders selling to raise money for the war, the prospects of war seemed bullish. Speculation could not be restrained even when the formal markets were shut; inevitably there were some ready to take advantage of war-caused shortages in materials and commodities.[1] When the markets reopened, they were swamped with buy orders. The speculators realized that the United States' role as neutral supplier to the belligerents was bound to be profitable.

As the war infected more and more of the world during 1915 and 1916, speculation flourished in the United States. General Motors rose from $55 to $114, and American Woolen from $12 to $50, but these were the most spectacular; the trading was always somewhat selective.[2] Margin purchases and brokers' loans jumped to new highs. The large brokerage firms with many branch offices, often referred to as "wire houses," showed particularly big increases. Call loan rates were high; in fact

---

[1] The international credit situation and the concomitant change-over to the Federal Reserve System caused the stock market to close its doors for about four months following the outbreak of the war. "Re-Opening of the Stock Exchange," *The Nation*, 99:387-388 (September 24, 1914).

[2] *Literary Digest*, 62:120 (July 12, 1919). These price ranges cover July 1914 to April 1917.

at the end of 1916 banks were beginning to discriminate in accepting stocks as collateral. E. F. Hutton and
Company, for example, was carrying over twice the
amount of margined stock it had previously carried. Brokers and bankers alike feared sudden price breaks, yet
there were few demands for regulation of the stock markets. The war boom was, indeed, stifling reform.

As 1916 ended, however, the public was suddenly and
forcibly reminded of Wall Street. At 5 p.m. Wednesday,
December 20th, President Wilson released for publication in the morning press his offer to mediate between
the Allies and the Central Powers. The "peace scare"
selling that followed confirmed the bankers' worst fears;
in three days over three billions in stock values were
erased. As the over-bought markets reeled under the
President's announcement, several Congressmen were re-
liably informed that certain financial wires had carried the
gist of the President's diplomatic note as early as 1 p.m.
Wednesday, four hours before the authorized release
time. Immediately a cry went up throughout the nation.
The press demanded to know who was responsible for this
important leak and who had profited by the advance information. While Congress was pondering a resolution
to investigate, Thomas L. Lawson of Boston, financial
huckster and reformer, and the author of *Frenzied Finance,* made extravagant statements implying that high
government officials and Congressmen had profited in
the markets through advance knowledge of the President's message. The public was indignant, discussion
was well flavored with partisanship, and the GOP minority in Congress was hopeful that wrongdoing could be
fastened on the Wilson Administration and the Democratic majority. With only a few weeks remaining before
adjournment on March 4th, the fight to get the investigation under way was intense.

In the middle of January Congress passed the resolution for an inquiry. A central point in the controversy

was the credibility of Lawson; some thought Congress should not dignify his charges by acknowledging them, but the majority believed that the nature of the charges was too serious and well publicized to ignore. The nation's press seemed to support the view that Lawson should "put up or shut up," should tell what he knew under oath, and that the alleged leak should be carefully explored. The *Detroit Free Press* scored previous Congressional investigations for "white-washing"; it called for a real probe, claiming "There is a lack of moral sense in Washington." The *Boston Traveler, Indianapolis News,* and *Washington Times* thought that Lawson's charges must be answered or public doubts would linger. Even the *New York World,* a strong Democratic organ, urged the investigation, although it observed that most legislators were undoubtedly honest. The *Albany Argus* reminded its readers that speculation by those in government might occur again if adequate measures were not taken. Meanwhile a rumor was being circulated to the effect that Bernard M. Baruch sold 15,000 shares of U. S. Steel short when he obtained advance information on the peace note. Later another rumor had it that Lawson suggested Samuel Untermyer as counsel for the investigating committee. Both stories were subsequently refuted.

Seven days before Congress adjourned the unanimous report of the so-called leak investigation was made public. The committee could find no corroboration for Lawson's charges that administration officials or Congressmen had speculated on the "peace scare." Secretary of the Treasury William McAdoo, whom Lawson had impugned, was given a clean bill of health. The report did, however, contain pertinent information on the leak itself and make some observations about current speculative practices. It confirmed that there had been a leak, through two newspaper correspondents who were receiving small retainers from brokerage houses to report just such situations. The brokers had wired the tip to their correspondents; it was then carried as a rumor by the nationwide Dow-Jones ticker service. Thus the essence of President Wilson's message was known in brokers' offices some time before the market closed on Wednesday, and before it was carried by the regular news services.[3]

Committee Congressmen indicated their disapproval of the ethics of the newspapermen, and suggested Press Gallery rules against reporters who accepted retainers on the side from brokers. In addition, the report took cognizance of the motives of brokers themselves. It noted that E. F. Hutton, and other comparable firms carrying large blocks of margined stock for their customers, were in a particularly advantageous position to sell short on advance tips of this kind, and to profit from a peace scare which meant losses to a large number of their clients who were "long." The committee questioned the system of hypothecation that made it possible for a broker to use or to lend margined stock against the interests of the customer. The Hughes and Pujo committee reports had previously criticized the exchanges for permitting members to use their clients' deposits so freely. Not until 1932, during the Great Depression, did the New York Stock Exchange itself see the wisdom of restricting in this respect what a broker could do with his clients' partially paid-for securities.[4]

For obvious reasons speculation in foodstuffs attracted even more attention and indignation than did leaks in the stock market. Inflation had arrived; food and rents were rising much more rapidly than wages, and the pinch was felt particularly in farm areas and small towns. The Midwest—already stirred by its Equity, Nonpartisan League, and Progressive party—was in the forefront of the demand for controlling the prices of neces-

---

[3] *Congressional Record*, 64 Cong., 2 sess., v. 54, Pt. 5, 4439-4442; Pt. 1, 801-808, Pt. 2, 1273-1289.
[4] See Chapter 6, Section I, below.

sities, especially the prices of what the farmer had to buy. And wheat, the staff of life to much of the world, was peculiarly vulnerable to speculators at this time because the shipping shortage made the wheat crops of Argentina, Australia, and India—short crops anyway—virtually unobtainable to the Allies.[5]

Germany's resumption of unrestricted submarine warfare at the beginning of 1917 accentuated the talk of food shortage, and the United States' declaration of war in April capped the speculative frenzy in commodities. When the Chicago Board of Trade was forced to close the trading in May futures on May 11th, wheat had reached $3.25 a bushel.[6]

Several days later, during the debate on the heterogeneous Espionage bill, Senator Charles Thomas of Colorado, a Democrat, opened the struggle to circumscribe the speculator in the interest of the war effort. He proposed an amendment empowering the President to close any exchange for the duration of the war. Many Senators expressed approval of the amendment's aims but urged Senator Thomas to wait until the administration's Food Control bill came up; they thought the Thomas amendment was an inappropriate rider and decried the starvation talk that was taking hold of the country. On the other hand, Senator James K. Vardaman of Mississippi challenged the motives of his colleagues; he observed that the exchanges' friends always sought delay, claiming that immediate action would disorganize business. Senator Robert M. LaFollette of Wisconsin concurred. Thomas, in his remarks to the Senate, took note of the disorganized trading that had forced the Chicago Board of Trade to close its doors. He cited letters from constituents, who argued that current daily fluctuations were

[5] Herbert Hoover, "America's Grain Trade," an address at the Conference of Representatives of the Grain Trade of the United States, April 30–May 1, 1918.

[6] "Our War Profiteers, the Food Speculators," *Literary Digest*, 54:1583-1584 (May 26, 1917).

not justified by the economic facts and urged the curtailment of commodity trading.

Senator Thomas P. Gore of Oklahoma offered a moderate substitute which gave the President power to prevent unfair manipulation and prescribe trading rules. Senator William S. Kenyon of Iowa, although supporting the Gore version, warned the Senate that food speculators were making socialists almost as fast as the government was making soldiers. The Senate defeated the Thomas amendment, 48 to 25. The majority of the faithful twenty-five were from the Great Plains area, the rest from Southern populistic regions. The Gore substitute was not acted upon.[7]

In hearings on the Food Control bill, anti-speculators were outspoken. They offered to acquiesce in the proposed price-fixing of wheat and the delegation of great powers to Food Administrator Herbert Hoover if the government would put a stop to futures trading. Ex-Congressman John E. Kelly of Pierre, South Dakota, wanted the government to own the grain elevators and advance the farmers cash on crops stored in them; in this way the farmer would be enabled to hold his crop until he could get a favorable price in the regular market place. Kelly would not demand the abolition of the exchanges if gambling profits were destroyed. Benjamin Drake, of the Equity Co-operative Exchange of St. Paul, wanted futures trading stopped permanently. Hedging, he observed, constituted less than 10 per cent of grain trading. Therefore the main business in Chicago, and to a lesser extent in Minneapolis, was gambling in commodities. Democratic Congressmen complained about Hoover's proposed powers and suspected him of a lack of sympathy with the farmers. They wanted laws, not men to guide the wartime food administration.[8]

[7] *Congressional Record,* 65 Cong., 1 sess., v. 55, Pt. 3, 2241-2261 (May 14, 1917).

[8] *Food Production, Consumption, and Distribution,* Committee

80

A month later Senator Thomas tested anti-speculator sentiment again, during the debate on the Food Control bill. President Wilson had already chosen Hoover as Food Administrator and this bill gave him sweeping powers over the allocation and marketing of the nation's crops. In offering his amendment, the Colorado Democrat scored the non-productive role of the growing cities and condemned the spirit of speculation that seemed to pervade them. He observed that there was "an element in human nature which takes advantage of a situation for profit regardless of social consequences," and that the successful could somehow prevent the application of this law to themselves. A query by Senator Kenneth Mc-Kellar of Tennessee revealed, however, the usual difference between Southern agrarians and Midwest progressives as to the remedy. McKellar wanted an absolute ban. Thomas replied that he had no faith in legislative fiat by itself; that the only way to reach the problem was to control the speculative machinery.

Senator Knute Nelson of Minnesota introduced a substitute for the Thomas amendment; it was similar to the one Gore had offered in May. Nelson's version empowered the President to warn traders who were guilty of irregularities, and to close the exchange if the offending individuals persisted in their unethical activity. The idea was to curtail wartime speculation without stopping trading.[9] Senator Nelson had received many letters urging haste in enacting the Food Control bill; only one claimed that the food shortage was a myth created by "roll-top desk" farmers. The millers of Minneapolis were particularly anxious for passage, arguing that the high

---

on Agriculture. United States House of Representatives. 65 Cong., 1 sess. (Washington, 1917), 422-430, 449-450, 473-476. The recently enacted Federal Warehouse Act was not meeting the farmers' storage needs, judging from this testimony.

[9] *Congressional Record*, 65 Cong., 1 sess., v. 55, Pt. 4, 4268-4272, Pt. 3, 3221.

grain costs were damaging the milling industry. A. C. Loring of the Pillsbury Mills categorically denied that the millers themselves were responsible for the prevailing high grain prices. The Senator's correspondents said nothing specific about the respective merits of the Thomas and Nelson amendments, but C. W. Harrington of the Van Dusen–Harrington Mills reminded the Senator that even former Senator James H. Kyle, the South Dakota Populist, had stressed the value of speculation during the Anti-Option bill debates of 1892-1893; and James MacMillan of the Cargill Elevator Company suggested to the Minnesotan that he was "under misapprehension" if he sought to regulate or close the exchanges.[10] Judging from Senator Nelson's mail, Minnesotans were virtually unanimous in their demand for food control, but offered no opinions on whether exchange trading should continue or not. In these circumstances the Senator may have felt safe in heeding the wishes of millers like Harrington and MacMillan who wanted the exchanges to remain open.

As Senator Thomas pointed out, the warning system made it possible for exchanges to stay open if only the traders noticed by the President desisted from their practices, and he might not notice many of them, anyway! The Nelson version, moreover, was weak, because it did not include provisions (pork) and lacked the phraseology to prevent clandestine trading in a street or building not designated as an exchange. James P. Kirby of Arkansas and McKellar hoped that the Thomas version would obviate the necessity of a food dictator, an office abhorrent to Southern Jeffersonians. Senator James Thompson of Kansas entered several letters to indicate that food speculation loomed large in the minds of his

[10] Senator Knute Nelson's Papers, Minnesota Historical Society. Andrew Dunn, Winnebago, Minn., to Hon. Knute Nelson, May 3, 1917; A. C. Loring to Nelson, May 18, 1917; C. W. Harrington to Nelson, May 11, May 22, 1917. James MacMillan, Minneapolis to Nelson, May 23, May 31, 1917.

constituents. Senator LaFollette called upon his colleagues to perfect the Thomas version if they approved its motives. When the roll call finally came, however, the Senate rejected Thomas' amendment, 33 to 15, and approved Nelson's, 37 to 17. Only the staunchest anti-speculators held out for the more stringent Thomas version. Senators Jones and Poindexter of Washington and Kenyon of Iowa were among the insurgents who deserted to the Nelson camp.[11]

The debate over the Food Control bill itself lasted several weeks in the Senate. The House had passed it 365 to 7 without debate, but the Senate was disturbed about constitutional matters: how far could the Constitution be stretched in a war emergency? Assistant Secretary of Agriculture Carl Vrooman was among those who campaigned hard for the bill. He claimed that speculators maintained a paid lobby in Washington to work against it, and noted that food prices were lower in countries which had instituted controls.[12]

Many newspapers editorially excoriated food speculators and endorsed the administration's Food Control bill. The *Indianapolis News* told speculators to look to themselves before casting aspersions on the loyalty of others. The *New Orleans Item* scored those who were patriotic only when it cost them nothing, while the *New York Sun* classed speculators with spies and traitors. The *Springfield* (Mass.) *Republican* and the *St. Louis Post-Dispatch* suggested joint United States–Canada action to prevent evasion by American speculators in Canada. The *Christian Science Monitor* hoped the Food Control Act would bring food prices down 30 per cent. The *New York Tribune* wanted the middleman conscripted. The *Newark News* and the *Richmond Times-Dispatch*

[11] *Congressional Record*, 65 Cong., 1 sess., v. 55, Pt. 3, 3226, 3229 (June 2, 1917).
[12] *The Nation*, 105:55 (July 19, 1917); "Mr. Hoover Fights the Food Pirates," *Literary Digest*, 54:1975-1976 (June 30, 1917).

brushed aside the constitutional aspect; they were for it because the people wanted it and it was necessary for victory. Many other papers approved of the bill.

A minority of newspapers, however, disapproved the measure on the ground that it was too sweeping, that circumstances did not call for so extreme a bill. The *St. Louis Times* claimed that the bill Prussianized food management; the *San Antonio Light* had the same fear, as did the *Louisville Post,* which added that it was unworkable. The *New York Sun* predicted the Food Control Act would produce results opposite from those intended, i.e., high prices and low production. Noting that William Jennings Bryan and Samuel Gompers favored it, the *Sun* called the act the product of ignorance and demagoguery.

One very controversial provision fixed the price of wheat, and the bill as a whole gave rise to the complaint that the Food Administrator had been given the power to interfere with the personal habits of the farmer. In the end, however, Congress overwhelmingly approved it. The wheat provision meant, of course, that there would be no trading in wheat futures until the end of the war, and actually it was not until July 15, 1920, that the Chicago Board of Trade resumed wheat trading.[13] The act did not include the lesser grains—rye, corn, oats, etc., and futures trading continued in these products.

The government policy was that such trading should continue, in order to keep intact the private marketing machinery which would again take over all trading at the end of the war. The erratic behavior of prices in some of these subsidiary commodities, however, soon led to a demand for control. Conferences of the rye, rice, and bean trades, and some others, resulted in the adoption of stricter trading rules for wartime, while a conference of

[13] *Congressional Record,* 65 Cong., 1 sess., v. 55, Pt. 5, 5382; Federal Trade Commission *Report on the Grain Trade* (Washington, 1920-1926), II, i-iii.

those in the lesser grains ratified a proposal to report all the transactions of customers, to limit their holdings to 200,000 bushels and to set daily fluctuation limits.[14]

Unfortunately, different market conditions for wheat and cotton during the war served to continue and to accentuate the Midwest-South reform division already evident in the New Freedom years. Wheat was food, and essential, first for the American role of "breadbasket" for the Allies, and later for feeding the American doughboys in France. Therefore Congressmen from the Republican wheat-growing Midwest, to stabilize wheat and to reduce the speculative interest, generally approved the fixing of what at $2.20 a bushel in August 1917; this price was at first satisfactory to growers because it was some three times greater than the average prewar price. By the summer of 1918, however, $2.20 per bushel looked much less attractive to wheat growers, as other items, uncontrolled, had risen considerably. President Wilson vetoed a raise to $2.50 for the new crop and again proclaimed $2.20 as the government price for wheat; it was estimated that at the time wheat would bring $5 a bushel in the open market. Senator Gore, a vigorous opponent of price fixing, called this veto "a crime against wheat."

In marked contrast to this was the condition of cotton. Cotton prices had risen more slowly than wheat prices after the war began in Europe, and Senator Caraway of Arkansas complained that cotton growers were being left behind in the wartime prosperity. When cotton prospects finally improved, the President was under political pressure from Southern Congressmen to refrain from controlling the price of raw cotton; this he managed to do, although in May 1918, the government set prices for finished cotton goods. Southern newspapers and the Cotton States Official Advisory Marketing Board, spon-

[14] Frank Macy Surface, *The Grain Trade during the War, being a History of the Food Administration Grain Corporation* (New York, 1928), 212, 224-226.

sored by the Farmers' Union, kept the President and Congress constantly aware of Southern sentiment against price fixing.

There were several reasons why raw cotton prices were never set during World War I. In the first place, Wilson was in principle opposed to price-fixing and had yielded to it only when convinced it was absolutely necessary, as in the case of wheat. In the second place, at the time of the controversy, cotton, unlike wheat, was in ample supply and the Treasury's funds would have been dissipated in maintaining the proposed price. Nevertheless, the allegedly preferential treatment given cotton by the Wilson Administration provided the GOP with a major partisan issue for the 1918 Congressional elections. This charge of cotton favoritism proved to be effective in the Midwest, where the Republicans gained five Senate seats and 21 of 23 new seats in the House, to capture control of Congress. The GOP victory at the polls was widely interpreted as a repudiation of Wilson's wartime leadership and postwar peace plans, but actually it was the result of Republican exploitation of this sectional issue. Its significance here is that the election left scars that would further impede understanding between agrarians and progressives in trying to limit the activities of stock and commodity speculators.[15]

During the war the progressives had urged greater government controls. They wanted the guarantees and stabilization afforded wheat growers extended to other crops. Congressman John M. Baer, a North Dakota Nonpartisan Leaguer, hoped for the continuation of price-fixing after the war was over. He commended Food Administrator Hoover for eliminating "useless" middle-

[15] Seward W. Livermore, "The Sectional Issue in the 1918 Congressional Elections," *Mississippi Valley Historical Review*, XXXV: 29-60 (June 1948); Dewey W. Grantham, Jr., *Hoke Smith and the Politics of the New South* (Baton Rouge, 1958), 315, 324-326; Josephus Daniels, *The Wilson Era: The Years of the War and After, 1917-1923* (Chapel Hill, 1946), 244-246.

men, and declared "The war has brought democracy to the farmer and worker." Senator Arthur Capper of Kansas kept up a running fire against food speculators; he wanted punishment meted out to them as if they were errant bankers. But William Allen White proved only a mediocre prophet when his *Emporia Gazette* predicted that the socialistic devices used during the war would remain forever—that there would be no turning back.[16]

II

By the time the marketing machinery for commodities had been completely restored to private hands, serious adjustments in supply and demand were taking place. When trading in wheat was resumed in July 1920, the futures immediately began to sag, and the decline gained momentum as the end of the year approached. Legislators from the wheat regions emitted anguished cries, and many candidates in the fall elections castigated the Federal Reserve Board, claiming it was under the influence of commodity speculators. Parley P. Christensen of Utah entered the Presidential race as the candidate of a new party, the Farmer-Labor, which amalgamated many elements of economic unrest.[17]

The consequences of the 1920-1921 credit contraction were so harsh that even Congressmen elected on a tide of "normalcy" had to take note. Wheat had always loomed fairly large in Republican politics, especially in the Senate—so Congress passed resolutions and held hearings to discover what relation the return to normalcy bore to the devastating price decline in wheat. The major product of this politically inspired inquiry was the seven-volume study of the grain trade by the Federal

[16] *LaFollette's Magazine,* 10:7 (June 1918), and 11:93 (June 1919); "Mr. Hoover Fights the Food Pirates," *Literary Digest,* 54:1975-1977 (June 1917).

[17] *New York Times,* October 11, 1920, 14:8, October 20, 12:4; William Hard, "Christensen and Back of Him," *New Republic,* 23:273-276 (August 4, 1920).

Trade Commission, which was printed in full by 1926.[18]
The findings indicated simply that commercial commodity dealers had quickly and accurately anticipated
the lower prices that would come about when the crops
of India, Australia, Argentina, and Europe were again
available in the American market. The farmer could not
or would not adjust himself as quickly to altered market
conditions, and therefore found himself overextended
and forced to accept ruinously low prices.

Political pressure on the Republican party was intense
for several years. The American Farm Bureau Federation, a powerful organization that had appeared on the
national scene during the war years, wanted some modifications of commodity exchange practices to relieve the
farmer. Some Senators, from states where the farm problem weighed heavily, got together and agreed to work
for agricultural reform; they came to be known as the
Farm Bloc, and one of their announced aims was to obtain passage of a law regulating grain futures. Commodity trading during the 1920 deflation had caused the res-
urrection of so much populistic sentiment that action in
this sphere seemed necessary.[19]

Congress held hearings on proposed commodity exchange remedies; they bore some resemblance to those
of 1892-1893 and 1909 but were, on the whole, less extreme. The Farm Bureau Federation, dominated by the
more affluent, commerce-oriented farmers, did not
want to antagonize small town businessmen by threatening to destroy the marketing machinery.[20] The Farmers'
Union, on the other hand, was more radical, and in-

[18] *New York Times,* August 21, 1921, 21:4; Federal Trade
Commission, *Report on the Grain Trade* (Washington, 1920-1926),
7 vols.

[19] Henry R. Mussey, "The Farmers and Congress," *The Nation,*
112:12-13 (January 5, 1921); Saloutos and Hicks, *Agricultural
Discontent,* 321-325; Arthur Capper, *The Agricultural Bloc* (New
York, 1922), 89-91, 157.

[20] Grant McConnell, *The Decline of Agrarian Democracy*
(Berkeley, 1953), 54ff.

cluded in its membership more marginal farmers of the trans-Missouri West who were not very familiar with commercial techniques. C. H. Hyde, an Oklahoma member, observed that the farmers of the Southwest hedged very seldom and were generally opposed to the futures marketing system. He suggested a revision so that hedging would not be necessary: the government could take over the middleman function and stabilize prices, exacting only a small profit for this service. Hyde thought the price the farmer was receiving bore little relation to the price the consumer paid. Charles S. Barrett, president of the Farmers' Union, bitterly attacked speculators as frock-coated parasites who employed glib counselors to convince the public that black was white. He traced the use of railroad stocks as counters in the stock-jobbing between the Civil War and World War I, and blamed the speculators for all the panics since 1819. In fact, he said, people had come to accept the inherent dishonesty of speculation.

One witness mentioned the demoralizing effect of the existence of futures markets upon managers of farmers' cooperative elevators. He said that managers entered the market ostensibly to hedge their elevator holdings but were lured into futures speculation. Representative J. N. Tincher of Kansas, co-sponsor of the leading exchange bill, was distressed over the inroads the speculative spirit was making among farmers and their friends in the small towns of the Midwest—the ticker and the blackboard had brought new evil into these communities. The legislator believed that the Chicago Board of Trade was merely a bucket shop that had a monopoly on legality. The concern over this invasion had been growing, and Senator Cummins had mentioned it in his 1913 speech. The stringing of private commodity wires had hastened what looked like an irreversible trend.

Herbert Hoover, former Food Administrator and Harding's Secretary of Commerce, was the most important witness before the Agriculture Committee. Members wanted to know what recommendations Hoover would make regarding exchange legislation in the light of his experience regulating grains during the war. Hoover's principal suggestion was a limitation on the amount and number of trades an individual could make in a given period. He noted that speculative manipulation was necessarily accompanied by very large trades; therefore speculators could be reached by imposing trade limits. He reminded the committee that he had always favored experience over inflexible law as a guide to reform, and recommended that the marketing problem be entrusted to an administrative board of experts. This distrust of statute, so typical of responsible business leaders since the time of the Hughes Committee report and before, irritated Congressman Tincher. He mentioned the resentment against the Reserve Board's deflation policy, and warned Hoover that the nation was in a mood for direct laws rather than power invested in any more boards. Hoover opposed the closing of the exchanges; he approved of hedging and thought scalpers were valuable as insurers, and he attributed the margin between producer and consumer in wheat, the narrowest margin in the world, to the efficient hedging process on American exchanges. He cited the growth of business morality over the years and remarked that the exchanges had virtually eliminated the corners that had wrought so much havoc in the past.[21]

Senator Arthur Capper of Kansas wrote a bill for the regulation of commodity exchanges, based on information gathered in the hearings. On the Senate floor he reviewed the history of the American farmers' struggle with the middlemen of the exchanges. He described the bill as an attempt to return to the great law of nature

[21] *Future Trading,* Committee on Agriculture. United States House of Representatives. 66 Cong., 3 sess. (Washington, 1921), 10-31, 50-73, 895-923.

"that appeals to the sense of justice in all men," and said his purpose was to eliminate the practices that upset the law of supply and demand. He admitted the speculators were right when they argued that they could not overcome the supply-demand principle in the long run, but he regarded the distortions and violent daily fluctuations as the unnecessary results of speculation. He claimed that J. P. Griffin, president of the Chicago Board of Trade, had failed to make good on a recent promise to correct abuses, and said that tips instituted by bears were particularly rife since 1920—as were false crop reports. Like others from the Midwest, Capper emphasized the human toll exacted by the grain exchanges. He blamed the pits for increasing embezzlement and suicide, and considered shocking the number of women who had been inveigled into trading. Countering the fact of the low middleman charge for wheat, Capper declared that he did not want his bread any cheaper if it came from widows and farmers who had gambled away their life savings. He wanted the private commodity wires confined to the big city terminals to keep temptation away from the smaller towns.

Senator Capper then answered the major objection to the bill—that it was government interference with business. He explained that the bill meant supervision, not regulation, that the Secretary of Agriculture was not given dictatorial power as some enemies of the bill were claiming. The exchanges would be left to use their own methods in combating manipulation and in conforming to the requirements of the act; the room for private initiative was very large and the hedging process remained unimpaired. Even Julius H. Barnes, president of the Chamber of Commerce, admitted that the improvement of the business conscience might be hastened by governmental encouragement. Capper said many exchange men agreed with Barnes that the law would increase public confidence and thereby stimulate business in the long run.[22]

The Capper-Tincher bill became law on August 24, 1921; it was known as the Futures Trading Act. Less than a year later, however, Section 4 of the Act, based upon Congressional taxing power, was declared unconstitutional. In *Hill* vs. *Wallace* Chief Justice William H. Taft made it plain that the Act had misused the tax power in that the tax was only incidental to the intent to regulate. In his written opinion, however, he hinted that a similar act based upon the commerce clause would find more favor with the Court. Following this lead, Farm Bloc members secured passage of a second measure, which was signed September 21, 1922, and was known as the Grain Futures Act.[23] Defenders of the exchanges claimed that this second Capper-Tincher law went too far, that the Secretary of Agriculture was given too much power, that the grain business was primarily intrastate and not within federal jurisdiction. They thought the Cotton Futures Act and the anti-trust laws were adequate to control the more flagrant cases of manipulation, squeezes, and corners. L. F. Gates, a Board of Trade member, told the house committee that outright abolition of the Board would be better than slow death under the Grain Futures Act, but Congressman Tincher accused him of bluffing. The opposition to the second Capper-Tincher measure was really half-hearted.[24]

The 1922 act was the product of a compromise between progressives and commercial interests. The more radical agrarians supported it reluctantly; the exchange people had been even more reluctant, and had secured

[22] *Congressional Record,* 67 Cong., 2 sess., v. 61, Pt. 5, 4762-4769.

[23] *Grain Futures Act,* Committee on Agriculture. United States House of Representatives (Washington, 1923), 1-10; *New York Times,* September 22, 1922, 2:5.

[24] *Grain Futures Act,* 25-67.

many small concessions. As finally enacted, the Act provided that:

1. A futures seller must be a producer or must make his contract through a member of a "contract market."
2. A "contract market" is one that the Secretary of Agriculture has certified as complying with government rules. These rules required the keeping of records on all trades for three years, making special reports on the request of the Secretary, and the elimination of false crop reports.
3. The exchanges must admit representatives of farm cooperatives and permit rebates to members of cooperatives. (Cooperatives had complained that commodity markets were refusing to admit them on the excuse that patronage dividends violated the no rebate rule of grain exchange members.)

The Act declared the business to be affected with the public interest, and included trading in wheat, corn, oats, rye, flax, and barley. A Grain Futures Administration was set up in the Department of Agriculture to administer the Act, and offices were opened in the exchange cities to handle the trading reports.[25]

First reactions to the law were cautious. The market had been dropping as the effective date approached. President John J. Stream of the Chicago Board of Trade observed that the Board was complying with all provisions and, if the law failed, it would be because of its own defects. Exchange officials lamented the departure of scared small-fry speculators; they urged the scalpers to return, claiming they had nothing to fear from the operation of the new act, but rumor had it that many old-timers were frightened off by the knowledge that all

[25] George Wright Hoffman, *Future Trading upon the Organized Commodity Markets in the United States* (Philadelphia, 1932), 371.

transactions had to be available for reports to the govern-ment. Market spokesmen had predicted this result; in-deed, when the Federal Trade Commission recom-mended daily reports from the Chicago Board of Trade, the Board threatened to close temporarily. It later ob-tained an injunction against the Capper Act, and the ex-ecutive committee of the Board urged modification of the law and continued to object to daily reports. A speaker, J. R. Mauff, told the Independent Millers' Association that the grain act should be repealed in the interest of both farmers and consumers; the National City Bank of New York backed the exchanges and condemned gov-ernment restrictions.

Reformers countered these protests. Senator Edwin F. Ladd of North Dakota denounced attempts to repeal the law, and introduced a Senate resolution accusing the Chicago Board of Trade of trying to bear the market ever since the second Grain Futures Act had been de-clared constitutional in April 1923.[26] The resolution, which was later agreed to, called for publishing the ac-tivities of the big professional speculators. The muttering of the commodity exchanges subsided with the passage of time, but reports on the trading of individuals con-tinued to be controversial.[27]

The concerted efforts of farm legislators to aid agricul-ture in the troubled years of postwar deflation produced results. The Packers and Stockyards Act of 1921, the Grain Futures Act, and the Co-operative Marketing Act of 1922 were designed to curb the alleged excesses of middlemen. The Intermediate Bank Credit Act of 1923 supplemented the Federal Farm Loan Act of 1916 by filling the remaining gap in the farm credit structure.

[26] Edward J. Dies, "Grain Marketing under Government Rule," *World's Work*, 46:425-429 (August 1923); *New York Times*, July 31, 1923, 34:3; October 31, 24:4; November 6, 32:2, September 22, 2:4, November 5, 30:1.

[27] *Congressional Record*, 68 Cong., 1 sess., v. 65, Pt. 1, 683. See Chapter 6 below.

President Harding acquiesced in Farm Bloc demands for farmer representation on the Federal Reserve Board by appointing Milo D. Campbell, a dairy cooperative leader from Michigan, but unfortunately Campbell died shortly after his appointment.[28] The achievements of the Farm Bloc between 1921 and 1923 were substantial, but they did not eliminate agricultural discontent.

III

Meanwhile the improving business morality that Herbert Hoover thought he saw in the commodity markets did not seem to extend to the stock markets. Stock trading accelerated with the war and continued to expand afterward. Citizens acquainted with Liberty Bonds during the war were later more easily converted to stock trading by slick hucksters, and bucket shops, more subtle than their prewar counterparts, mushroomed. A movement to obtain a national blue sky law grew as the magnitude of postwar stock swindles became known, and many newspapers had approved the 1920 deflation policy of the Federal Reserve Board as a healthy move to check postwar speculation. The popular magazines began, during the war, to expose the ruses employed by stock promoters. Only 500,000 people had held securities before the war, but, as a result of war bond sales, there were seventeen million security owners in 1918 and these new investors offered temptation to the stock swindler.[29] The *Outlook* ran frequent warnings, and *World's Work* printed a series called "Pirates of Promotion," which urged people to hold on to their Liberty Bonds and investigate prospective brokers.

As a prototype of the "Pirates of Promotion," George Graham Rice received detailed treatment. Rice, whose

[28] James H. Shideler, *The Farm Crisis, 1919-1923* (Berkeley, 1957), 172.
[29] "Club for the Speculative Frenzy," *Literary Digest,* 63:17 (November 29, 1919).

real name was Jacob S. Herzig, served his apprenticeship in the bucket shops and at the racetracks around
the turn of the century. About 1905 he went to the boom-
ing Tonopah-Goldfield area in Nevada and started a
news bureau and a mining newspaper which he and
other promoters used to sell worthless stock. Later he
started the Sullivan Trust Company in Nevada, when he
realized that people felt safer buying securities through a
bank. The trust company collapsed as the result of Rice's
manipulation, and took with it not only a Goldfield bank
but the good name of the Nevada governor who had un-
warily lent his name to the enterprise. After a year in
jail in New York on a mail fraud charge in 1910, Rice
emerged and published the *Mining Age,* another vehicle
for pushing the worthless stock of dummy companies.[30]

Rice was a particularly crafty operator because, unlike
most promoters, he had some of his stocks listed on the
Curb Exchange. The sucker could actually see how he
was doing and this whetted his appetite for profits. But
the only people who ever made money on Rice's securities were those who had bought early and sold out
while Rice was still manipulating the price upward in
order to unload. He and others with similar methods
naturally operated with patriotic camouflage during the
war—they would offer to take subscriptions for Liberty
Bonds free in order to compile sucker lists for future ref-
erence. Rice ran patriotic editorials on the front page of
his bogus newspaper, but inside he would suggest how
the reader could use his bonds as collateral for some
sure-fire stocks in Rice's companies. Sometimes he forecast profits in thousands of per cent.

These promoters usually knew one another, most of
them having trained together in the crooked brokerage
houses and racetracks early in the century. Their methods were very similar. After the war they did not resort

[30] Louis Guenther, "The Pirates of Promotion—George Graham
Rice," *World's Work,* 36:584-589 (October 1918).

to actual misrepresentations of fact; instead they created erroneous impressions, and interspersed plugs for their bogus stock with the names of respectable, nationally known stocks. The Post Office Department claimed it did not have enough inspectors to keep close tab on these gentry.[31] The swindlers shifted their emphasis with the times. When oil was the topic of interest, they peddled oil stocks; when that interest faded, they switched to mining; they also had invention schemes working. The promoter usually cited Bell Telephone or Ford Motor to persuade the sucker that others had made hundreds and thousands per cent profit by investing in new ventures. Beguiled by generalities, people were not careful enough in investigating specific propositions. The sharpers had many tricks for stimulating the client's enthusiasm. Sometimes they would send telegrams signed by the president of a dummy company telling the customer to buy in a hurry because a new vein, a gusher, or a government contract had changed the business outlook of the concern. After thus urging their clients to buy immediately, the promoters would "go short," followed by other sharpers around the Street, for they all foresaw the impending collapse of the stock in a few weeks or months.

According to *World's Work*, these men had virtually denuded the population of some sections of the country of their Liberty Bonds. Four hundred million dollars of the Bonds had been taken from Midwesterners within a few months after the war. The magazine urged legal protection for these new investors; it endorsed the British Corporation Act and approved the Denison blue sky law then being discussed. Because of the cleverness of this postwar breed of crook, *World's Work* recommended

[31] *Ibid.*, and Louis Guenther, "The Pirates of Promotion—Market Manipulation and its Part in the Promotion Game," *World's Work*, 37:393-398 (February 1919); Letter to the Editor, *World's Work*, 38:354-356 (February 1920).

that the law require nothing but the truth in stock promotion literature, instead of permitting much extrane-
ous verbiage calculated to mislead the reader. *World's
Work* ended its exposure series with long lists of promoters' names, aliases, and phony corporations, in order
to warn their readers against these jackals. Several years
later it could claim at least one "I told you so"—the brokerage firm of F. Kriebel, named on its list, collapsed
and was discovered to have been a bucket shop.[32] The
magazine's conclusions were also later confirmed by a
New York University Bureau of Research survey, indicating the lack of care of the average citizen in buying
stocks. The study showed that the buyers of promotion
stocks were largely businessmen, lawyers, and account-
ants who were seeking large profits. They invested an
average of $1,190, and 68 per cent made no investigation
before purchase.[33]

The Outlook ran some short, short stories with the
moral, "don't trust promoters," warning its readers that
the physical appearance of the culprits was deceptive,
that promises of 2 per cent interest per month were sus-
pect, and that the "hurry-up" approach was usually a
sign of fraud. In some obviously moralistic pieces,
George Witten warned young men and women against
selling promotion stock; it would lead to moral decay, to
a blasé and cynical attitude. He also told the sad story of
Bosworthy Brown, who persuaded a dying consumptive
to entrust his life savings to Brown's phony company. After his death, the victim's wife and children were desti-
tute because Brown's company failed. *The Outlook*
asked, "Why waste time with unknown speculations,
when investment possibilities are so good?"[34]

[32] Guenther, "Pirates of Promotion—Methods of the Industrial
Promoters," *World's Work*, 37:314 (January 1919), and "Pirates
of Promotion—The Wreckage," 37:509 (March 1919).

[33] Louis Guenther, "Who Buys Promotion Stocks and Why,"
World's Work, 50:221-222 (June 1925).

[34] "Why Bother with Speculations," *The Outlook*, 128:78 (May

After the war the *Saturday Evening Post* also devoted important space to stock market topics. Albert W. Atwood saw the 1920-1921 stock liquidation as the inevitable aftermath of an orgy, but suggested that parvenu speculators produced by the war were the chief victims. He thought that members of the new class were acquisitive, hence kept buying, and were not as adept at selling —at taking the bear side—as the old professionals and hence were more vulnerable to declines. The defeat of these *nouveaux riches* wizards, he observed, would be explained to many as a further demonstration of the power of "the interests," instead of as a chastisement of a new, inexperienced class. Atwood believed that there had been too much stock issued during periods of inflation to be accommodated in the subsequent deflationary periods. The exchanges permitted the listing of too many new companies, and the admission of too many new brokerage firms. He also criticized the government for not rationing credit more slowly and equitably during the war; stock exchange credit had been controlled since September 1918, although other items such as cotton had escaped.

The *Post* writer introduced another factor—taxes— arguing that the prevailing method of taxing stock profits intensified fluctuations. At that time stock profits were considered a part of income for the year in which the holder decided to sell, even though the profits might have accumulated over a three- or four-year period or longer. Atwood claimed that rich stockholders deferred taking their profits because of the large tax that would have to be paid; such persons contributed to the unnaturally high prices of securities. On the other hand, when panic finally did come, they sold the stocks on

11, 1921); George Witten, "Pretty Girls and Handsome Men," *The Outlook*, 138:173 (October 1, 1924); Witten, "Let Nothing Worry You," 138:552-557 (December 3, 1924); Witten, "Wolf in the Pack," 138:91-92 (September 17, 1924).

which they had accumulated losses over the years, and set this loss against their current income; consequently they were often able to avoid the tax completely or to pay a much smaller amount. Selling to establish losses for tax purposes was dubbed "tax-selling," and increasingly appeared in financial columns as an explanation for otherwise inexplicable sell-offs at the end of the year. Atwood thought that brokers were too indifferent to the public clamor. He urged the exchange to disseminate accurate information regarding its activities, especially the economic functions of short selling and legitimate pools. Why was it, for example, that reasonable people seldom objected to bull pools but heaped opprobrium on their bear counterparts?

After the 1920-1921 "shake out," there was some discussion of protecting the small investor, but Atwood was skeptical. He believed that the basic trouble was the "get-rich-quick" urge, and organizational measures would only slightly affect results. There was but one sure way to protect the investor, and that was to prohibit investment except in government bonds. The average man preferred to check the action at some bucket shop rather than earn a few per cent on a few hundred dollars in the bank, so as long as some men were spectacularly successful the promoters would thrive. The hope for a lucky strike would go on despite better business bureaus and state security commissions—even the big investors had "dogs and cats" in their portfolios. Financiers and exchange officials had ideas too about protecting the little man. Several suggested that the public should be urged to accumulate $500 to $1,000 before venturing into securities, and even then only on a cash basis. The public should seek out exchange members, because they had to meet more exacting requirements. Exchange president Seymour L. Cromwell admitted that it was difficult to get good securities distributed adequately through the population; costs were too high and people did not come to brokers' offices on their own initiative.[35]

Edwin S. Lefevre, also writing in the *Post*, explored the meaning of the word "manipulation," as used in relation to the stock market, and asked many people active in the Street for their opinions. Thomas P. Woodlock, an ex-editor of the *Wall Street Journal*, defined it as transactions aimed at inducing people to buy or sell from the manipulator. "Corners" or lying were not necessary; in fact, said Woodlock, what the newspapers used to call manipulation was simply plunging. "I never actually saw any in my years in the Street." Clarence W. Barron, of the Dow-Jones Company, defined it as moving quotations up and down by legal means. Barron noted that the crude schemes of the prewar era were obsolete; the ticker service furnished too many facts too quickly to make the circulation of false information really profitable. Theodore H. Prince, a picturesque figure in the cotton market, thought public opinion and stock exchange regulations had greatly circumscribed manipulators' opportunities. Sidney W. Curtis, a stock broker, believed that the Interstate Commerce Commission had subdued the great manipulators like Jim Fisk, Daniel Drew, Jay Gould, Colonel Vanderbilt, and Henry Keep, and that later financial titans employed professional manipulators like James R. Keene to run their stock operations for them.[36]

Lawrence Livingston, the subject of Lefevre's biography, *The Reminiscences of a Stock-Operator*, declared that the method of manipulation depended upon

[35] Albert W. Atwood, "Vanishing Millions—Aftermath of a Great Bull Market," *Saturday Evening Post*, 193:9 (February 26, 1921), and "Protecting the Small Investor," 194:6-7 (May 20, 1922). Atwood was the author of *The Exchanges and Speculation* (New York, 1918), a brief but competent description of the markets.

[36] Edwin S. Lefevre, "Stock Market Manipulation," *Saturday Evening Post*, 195:3-4 (February 10, 1923).

the particular conditions.[37] Most stories divulged manipulative methods that were obsolete and futile, and no one needed to study the methods of Jay Gould any more than a West Point cadet needed to study archery, said the former "Boy Plunger." The human factors, fear and hope, remained relatively constant. He approved Woodlock's observation that successful stock speculation was based upon the assumption that people would continue to make the mistakes they had made in the past. Livingston said it was pointless to discuss manipulation during booms; no subtlety was needed if the public were heavily in the market, and in booms the appeal was frankly to the gambling instinct. Edwin Lefevre's own opinion was that manipulation had become more subtle but was still present in the markets. Corners, wash sales, and false information had become too crude for a more sophisticated era; the tape now did its own advertising, and false impressions could be created via trading itself, unaccompanied by whispered tips and bribed reporters. As a forerunner of this modern technique he told the story of Rothschild hurrying to London after the battle of Waterloo. Reaching the city before news of the British victory, Rothschild would not tell who had won, but appeared dejected and retired to his home. The market interpreted Rothschild's behavior as an indication that the British had lost, and the price of consols went down. Rothschild bought secretly and was amply rewarded several days later, when the news of Wellington's triumph was established and consols went up. Lefevre concluded that there was just as much stock rigging as twenty-five years earlier; only the methods had changed. There would always be manipulation as long as there was a reward for doing it successfully.[38]

[37] Garden City, 1923. Excerpts appeared in the *Post* beforehand. As indicated before, Livingston was the pseudonym Lefevre gave Jesse L. Livermore, the well-known Wall Street bear.

[38] Lefevre, "Stock Market Manipulation."

Atwood confirmed Lefevre: tipsters and manipulators had not disappeared, they had just refined their techniques. Ten to twenty years before, tipsters had offered smeared, crudely printed sheets naming a stock and advising "buy for a five point rise." Now the dopesters were not so forthright in their recommendations—instead they assembled data to create bullish impressions. The growth of the statistical services helped, said Atwood; speculators could now focus on charts, trends, cycles affecting the whole economy. The public was interested only in action, not thought; action was easier. They waited to be told what to do and the promoters knew that the more positively the tip was stated, the quicker would be the response. The tipsters made their reputations in big bull markets where virtually all stocks rose, and sometimes they sent different advice to different clients, so that they always had some winners.[39]

Readers of the *Saturday Evening Post* and other magazines during this period, if they were at all perceptive, could gain valuable insight into the stock market game, how it had been played, and the new wrinkles being used to sell dubious stock to rising classes of the population. Although the *Post* was cautious about questions of government supervision or interference in the brokerage business, it presented fairly sound advice and indicated the more obvious pitfalls. Atwood's observation about too much stock being created during inflation to be sustained during the following deflation was particularly significant in view of the excess of securities issued later in the twenties.

The decade from Sarajevo to LaFollette's defeat saw the slow advance of the progressives at the expense of the agrarians and financial reformers. The agrarians

[39] Albert W. Atwood, "Wall Street Tipsters and their Methods," *Saturday Evening Post,* 194:14-15 (June 3, 1922).

stirred briefly in 1917; they hoped to close the trading markets during the war emergency and keep them closed afterward. They were vociferous again during the post-war deflation of 1920 and 1921 when the behavior of the Federal Reserve Board seemed to confirm their longstanding prejudices against regulatory boards.

The financial reformers could also count some victories in these years. They had been able to modify most of the stringent blue sky laws in the Western states and gain exemption from control for listed securities. They had staved off the Denison bill, which would have used federal power to coordinate and facilitate blue sky laws. They had the support of President Wilson during the war, which had helped minimize trading and price controls, notably in raw cotton. And in the new American Farm Bureau Federation, important in lobbying in Congress in the 1920s, they had an organization which was pro-agriculture but still had a strong respect for laissez-faire in the business world.

Nevertheless the progressive position improved during the war. For instance, Food Administrator Herbert Hoover chose to impose trading limits on individual commodity traders rather than close the markets altogether. This was a victory for regulation, and this principle was later incorporated into the Grain Futures Act. Also the Federal Trade Commission's *Report on the Grain Trade* provided seven volumes of the kind of data the progressives needed to frame a workable regulatory law, and incidentally to furnish them with the right kind of information for educating their colleagues and the public. The Grain Futures Act of 1922 was the first substantial victory in the exchange field for the progressives since they had differentiated themselves from the agrarians early in the century. Even here the triumph was not complete, since the coalition that secured the Cotton Futures Act in 1916 still claimed it was adequate for cotton marketing problems and cotton was not covered.

IV

Financial reformers, so often on the defensive after the 1907 Panic, liked to include among their recommendations the restriction of exchange speculation to classes occupationally and financially qualified. Academic experts increasingly suggested winnowing the customers, and wartime experience with the regulation of speculation seemed to suggest its feasibility. In these circles, enthusiasm for restriction was high when World War I ended.

But the notion of formal requirements for speculative activity was alien to America. The idea of controlling speculative practices in this fashion originated in the bureaucracies of Europe. In the 1890s German farmers had suffered in the world-wide depression and, like Populists in the United States, they were inclined to blame the futures method of commodity trading for much of their woe. Therefore, in 1896 the *Reichstag* passed a bill drastically curbing the exchanges. Prospective speculators were required to sign a register; manual workers and petty shopkeepers were prohibited from trading, and future trading in commodities and stocks was banned. This German registration law was repealed in 1908; during the years 1897-1908 fewer than four hundred persons had registered as speculators. Fluctuations were wider than before enactment of the law; and there were complaints of too narrow a market for securities. Small brokerage houses, faced with bankruptcy, succumbed to dealing with non-registered customers although they knew the contracts were not legally enforceable. The more daring speculators seemed to thrive on the economic and legal uncertainties of the situation but cautious investors transferred their accounts to France, England, and Holland. Farmers called loudly for enforcement of the law, but the registration plan was obviously a failure.[40]

Dr. Henry Emery, pioneer in the study of exchange practices, had publicized in American journals the ineffectiveness of the German statute. He regarded this German failure as positive proof of his neoclassical dictum that economic law was ultimately beyond legislative fiat.[41] American market experts were, therefore, at first loath to suggest adoption of the German method of trying to exclude incompetents by registration. Charles A. Conant, a prominent financial writer and currency expert, in 1908 stressed the desirability of eliminating from speculation "persons of small means who are not qualified by their resources or their knowledge . . . to take speculative risks," but declared it was not possible to do this in a country where laissez-faire was extolled and bureaucracy detested. While discrimination based on class might be feasible in Europe, in America it would contradict the classless ideal.[42] At about this time Governor Hughes' special stock market committee observed that:

A real distinction exists between speculation which is carried on by persons of means and experience, and based on intelligent forecast, and that which is carried on by persons without these qualifications. The former is closely connected with regular business. While not unaccompanied by waste and loss, the speculation ac-

[40] "Report of the Hughes Committee," *Public Papers of Charles Evans Hughes, Governor, 1909* (Albany, 1910), Appendix 1, 327-330; Parker, "Government Regulation of the Exchanges," *Annals of American Academy*, 38:454-457 (September 1911).

Section IV is from the article, "The Discussion of Speculative Competence in America, 1906-1934," reprinted here with permission from the *American Quarterly*, X (Spring 1958), 17-33.

[41] Henry Crosby Emery, "Results of the German Exchange Act of 1896," *Political Science Quarterly*, XIII:286-320 (June 1898); Emery, "Ten Years of Stock Exchange Regulation," *Yale Review*, XVII:5-23 (May 1908).

[42] Charles A. Conant, "Regulation of the Stock Exchange," *The Atlantic*, CII:307-314 (September 1908).

complishes an amount of good which offsets much of its cost. The latter does but a small amount of good and an almost incalculable amount of evil. In its nature it is in the same class with gambling upon the race track or at the roulette table, but it is practiced on a vastly larger scale. . . . A continuous stream of wealth, taken from the actual capital of innumerable persons of relatively small means, swells the incomes of brokers and operators; . . . a continual influx of new customers keeps this mechanism going. The most faithful policy will be found in measures which will lessen speculation by persons not qualified to engage in it. . . .[43]

But the committee concluded that the exchange could accomplish more in this matter than the legislatures. In 1911 Professor Carl Parker of Columbia University also came to this point of view but, like Conant, hesitated to propose any legal remedy. He wrote that:

to meet the evil of speculation what is required is the elimination . . . of . . . those who are unfitted by nature, financial circumstances, or training to engage in it. We select certain persons for the law, . . . medicine and the ministry by means of certain rigid requirements, because we think those arts of too great moment to permit untrained men to engage in them. But there is no law prohibiting certain persons from buying and selling property; to make such a law would strike at the roots of personal liberty. The right to buy and sell is a fundamental one, and even when a small sum is paid to seal the bargain, and when the portion of capital . . . to the amount dealt in, is small— even under these conditions, it is difficult to see how any law which does not seriously abridge the right of contract, could save people from themselves.

Instead of statutes or even rules, Parker foresaw recognition by brokers of their fiduciary relationship to the pub-

[43] *Hughes Public Papers,* 1909, 291-292.

lic, a decline of sharp practices and a gradually enlightened public—these would mitigate the evil of
speculation in the future.[44]

Defenders of the stock exchanges were less philo-
sophical on this point during the Congressional investigation of market practices in 1914. Under questioning
by Senator Robert L. Owen and his committee counsel,
Samuel Untermyer, exchange spokesmen forcefully
stressed public incompetence. While talk of "The Money
Trust," of stock pools, and incorporation of the exchanges was filling the air, Emery testified that the
greatest evil in the market was "the ease with which
the small piker is allowed to plunge beyond his means."
He retreated from his earlier hands-off position and ultimately suggested that brokers refuse all margin, i.e.,
credit orders. Reflecting a "financial reformer" attitude,
he argued that this matter should not be legislated but
left to the discretion of the brokerage fraternity.[45] Thus
in 1914 Emery saw speculative ignorance as the greatest
market evil but was unwilling to banish it outright because he thought the cost outweighed the benefits.

Four criteria for speculative competence emerged
during this period. The first, "financial responsibility,"
was mentioned by the Hughes Committee in 1908.
Did the prospective trader have resources sufficient to
trade safely without endangering his family, home or
business? And, more importantly from the point of view
of economic theory, did he have enough money to
avoid being shaken out of the market during a temporary dip in prices? The function of the speculator—
his supposed *raison d'être*—was, after all, to exert his
foresight in easing price transitions in the market, and
not to accentuate instability. The Hughes Committee
also noted the second criterion, fiduciary competence.

[44] Parker, "Government Regulation of the Exchanges," 454ff.

[45] *Stock Exchange Regulation*, Committee on Banking & Currency. United States Senate. 63 Cong., 2 sess. (Washington, 1914),
342-344.

Exchange officials acknowledged the merit of this; individuals whose occupations were too closely related to the market or its credit facilities were banned from trading. Exchange employees, certain bank tellers, and bank cashiers were prohibited from trading because they occupied positions of trust. The Hughes Committee commended the exchanges for this action; in 1922 the Chicago Board of Trade president called for a broadening of the ineligible category because of the great temptations created by many jobs in the security business. Although brokerage employees were generally forbidden to trade, partners could trade in their own accounts, for it did not seem possible to prevent such activity by those of entrepreneur status. There was no real opposition to excluding persons closely related to the business; it seemed only reasonable.

The third criterion for competence was business experience. The Federal Trade Commission stressed this factor in its *Grain Trade Report*. Did the would-be speculator have the requisite knowledge of business, the shrewdness associated with trade, to be a successful market operator? The F.T.C. suggested that mining, manufacturing and the domestic trades did not give one a suitable background for trading in the commercial markets. The fourth measure was that of temperament: a good operator must have courage and independence of mind. The ideal speculator, in both economic theory and the popular mind, was one who was not afraid of opposing the public clamor, one who was not stampeded by temporary reverses of fortune.[46]

It was natural that financial responsibility was a prominent factor in the discussion of market ability. The lax margin requirements of the early twentieth century permitted a client to put up less than 10 per cent of the total amount required, but later investigators recom-

[46] *Hughes Public Papers, 1909*, 308-310; Federal Trade Commission, *Report on the Grain Trade*, VII, 181, 193.

mended raising these margins to at least 20 per cent.[47] Disparity of income has ever been irksome in America, a major source of rural-urban friction from colonial times to the eras of "Sockless" Jerry Simpson, Arthur Townley, and "Kingfish" Huey Long. But if money was a source of envy, it was also an excuse; lack of it brought easy rationalization. John Doe figured he could be as good a man as "Mr. Big" if only he had the same amount of money.

The experience and temperament categories, however, were more delicate and controversial; the suggestion that there were aspects of competence other than money was not readily acceptable. Charges of deficiency of experience and temperament seemed to be directed explicitly at professional men, workers, and women. Should trading be restricted to the businessmen assumed to have the necessary skills, or would it be wiser to permit the whole public to participate even if it meant that 85 to 95 per cent would eventually lose?

In the commodities field also, by the end of the World War I decade, experts had become more outspoken in their advocacy of market ability requirements. James E. Boyle, a Cornell University agricultural economist, stated that certain occupations should be denied access to the commodity exchanges, and suggested a more restrictive policy with respect to ticker service in small towns.[48] In 1922 the Chicago Board of Trade president, in recommending restrictive measures, reiterated what he meant by unfitness: "Under the term incompetent are included all persons of trust, such as cashiers and bookkeepers; all persons lacking in the study and understanding of grain market conditions, all persons whose families or dependents may be injured by such speculation." Sentiment for restriction probably reached its

[47] *Stock Exchange Regulation* (1914), 800.
[48] James E. Boyle, *Speculation and the Chicago Board of Trade* (New York, 1920), 205.

height in 1920-1922, when the Federal Trade Commission was completing its *Report on the Grain Trade*. The Commission admitted that "Licensing of futures traders would involve a departure from usual American practice in the matter of letting individuals do about as they please in business matters, but their compulsory registration does not involve any real interference with private affairs." Consequently the Commission felt that some form of registration ought to be studied, in order to bring recalcitrant firms into line.[49]

In the latter years of the Progressive Era, geographic location became important and was added to the other factors bearing upon speculative competence: dilettante and rural participation was seriously questioned. In 1908 the Hughes Committee had foreshadowed this concern when it recommended that the luxurious uptown branches of the brokerage houses be closed. The committee believed that money, idleness, and liquor were not suitable accompaniments for speculation, that any man with acumen would prefer to go to the main offices where greater research facilities were available. The implication was that money and leisure were not the only prerequisites for admission to the ranks of the speculators.[50] As to the undesirability of speculation in small towns, more and more branch offices had been opened in such towns as the wire houses expanded. Rural Congressmen objected to the vitiating effect of introducing the acquisitive appetite into idyllic hamlets; they felt that such activity meant reduced efficiency at regular occupations and possibly dissatisfaction with home-town limitations.[51]

While the agrarians and progressives wanted speculation stopped in small towns because it was demoralizing them and concentrating the wealth in a few large

[49] F.T.C. *Report*, VII, 181.
[50] *Hughes Public Papers*, 1909, 304.
[51] Senator Cummins of Iowa, *Congressional Record*, 63 Cong., 1 sess., v. 50 (September 1, 1913), 4036-4037.

111

cities, the financial reformers wanted to strengthen the speculative structure by "shaking out" the unfit who were loitering about tickers in the country towns. The laws to end commodity speculation enacted by some state legislatures worked in favor of both groups: branch offices in these states would not solicit or accept small accounts or inexperienced investors, because the brokers knew the legal defenses of the customer were too great. Ignorance of market protocol was deemed prima-facie evidence of gambling intent, and gambling contracts being unenforceable, there was much opportunity for welshing. New offices were not opened in these areas and occasionally, when a client refused to make good on an obligation to a broker, the latter was inclined to let it go rather than stir up local sentiment against the brokerage business. Speculation in these restrictive states tended to fall into the hands of a few, and while the citizenry were probably not so badly mauled by the "big city boys" as they might have been, neither did they have the opportunity to try for a share of the profits that were being accumulated in the metropolitan centers.

The webs of wire had spun out from New York City and Chicago since 1895; the war years of 1914-1918 accelerated their expansion. The wire services, expensive to operate, naturally carried stock, coffee, grain, cotton, and other market items as well: enough data for those intrigued by forecasting and fluctuation. The high cost of wire service encouraged branch offices to solicit business assiduously, and managers wanted to set volume records for their offices despite the fact that they were paid salaries rather than commissions. The wire could handle small thousand-bushel deals that would have been unprofitable for old-fashioned cash grain merchants. The result was a good number of small, amateur accounts in non-restrictive states. The Chicago Board of Trade tried to prevent branch offices in towns of less than 75,000, but the move was narrowly defeated by the members. Cash grain merchants argued vehemently that correspondents in small towns exploited neophytes; their broker opponents claimed that the cash dealers wanted to prevent accurate crop information from reaching shippers in these parts. The Board, however, did set three branch offices as the limit permitted in a small town. Whether or not the Board was concerned primarily with amity among firms, the rule reveals its general position that solicitation in certain directions should not be pushed too far. The institution of radio broadcasts of farm prices in 1922 weakened the brokers' argument about crop information.

The view that citizens of small towns possessed less business acumen than their brothers in the city was based upon inference, and on the assumption that they contained proportionately fewer capitalists, speculators, and grain trade men—fewer of the classes supposed to be efficient in the market. The names of a few of the towns that early received wire service—Santa Barbara, Pasadena, Miami, Colorado Springs—are enough to suggest that mere smallness should not be equated with incompetence in speculation. The economic character of the town, not its size, would be a better determinant. In any event, the Federal Trade Commission, using a questionnaire, could not demonstrate that the business capacity of those trading via the wires from small towns was significantly inferior. As in the metropolis, those whose occupations were associated with risk and commerce—farmers, grocers, and salesmen—showed special interest in the vagaries of the ticker tape. They were aware of the risks they were taking, although somewhat vague about hedging as practiced in the commodity exchanges. Their reasons for initiating accounts were ordinary: (1) curiosity; (2) to make money; (3) intrigued by advertising; (4) a tip from a friend.[52]

[52] F.T.C. *Report*, V, 304-309, 127-142, VII, 198-205.

After 1923, talk of restriction in any form was drowned out by the clamor of the middle-class public for securities and commodities, but in the early thirties there were some who again demanded winnowing. George Wright Hoffman, academic authority on commodities, reaffirmed the conviction of economists that amateurs had no place in the markets.

> Those, for example, whose training is in a field foreign to cotton or grain . . . and who occasionally attempt to outguess the market do not in their net effort serve a useful purpose. To this group should be added those who lack adequate financial capacity. It is true that they . . . lend continuousness to the market, they may pay for part of the cost of maintaining an extensive news service, and may carry part of the hedges of trade interests. Some, too, from time to time anticipate market developments. But against these advantages are to be listed the losses of those who could not afford to trade, the adverse effect upon the market of those who fail to anticipate probable price changes and the ill effect of occasional widespread public participation. In many cases, too, those who do profit in their initial ventures pyramid their paper profits to lose ultimately. It is trading of this quality which encourages the plunger with a financial backing of millions to keep the market in a continual turmoil. Were it possible to do so, it would certainly be desirable from a social as well as an economic point of view to rid the market of the small and uninformed as well as the large market operator.[53]

Thus the expert would remove the sheep from the grasp of the wolves. By 1932 however, the need was less ur-

[53] Hoffman, *Future Trading*, 450-451. Dr. Hoffman was a University of Pennsylvania economics professor; from 1926 to 1942 he served as consultant to the Grain Futures Administration of the Department of Agriculture.

gent; many sheep had been devoured and the rest had become timid. Even the issue of wire service in small towns was solved by the Great Depression—branch offices in less prosperous areas were the first to close, and the financial tentacles of New York and Chicago retracted considerably.

While economists and reformers from 1907 on increasingly condemned market participation by an uninformed public, little had been done to determine objectively whether these charges of inability were in fact true—whether some groups *were* inferior in speculative skill. The increased speculation during World War I made the need for objective study seem more urgent. Activity in wheat and corn, for example, was tremendous, and in 1918 the Federal Trade Commission, a body organized in 1914 to encourage the improvement of business ethics, began a study of the grain trade. The Commission sought to verify the assertions and counter-assertions about traders and trading that had been made in debates ever since the Populist-sponsored Anti-Option bill of 1892.

The investigators, collecting on perforated cards data they believed representative of Chicago grain trading, analyzed occupations of customers of eight houses in the period 1916-1918. Their findings are summarized in the following table.

The "unknown" category presumably consisted largely of outsiders about whom the brokers had no information. Comparison with the male population only is justified because the commodity markets refused to accept female customers, and the preponderance of businessmen, especially those in the grain trade, is obvious. Also revealing, and pertinent to the question at hand, were the results with respect to dollars gained and lost by the various occupational groups—perhaps at last the suspected incompetence of the non-commercial classes could be documented! The table below shows the gains and

Occupation	Total Trading Transactions by Occupation (per cent)	Customers by Occupation (per cent)	U. S. Males 1920 Census (per cent)
Agriculture	4.56	16.57	29.85
Manufacturing & Mechanical	6.01	9.20	32.93
Professions	1.81	4.84	3.41
Mineral Extraction	.04	.53	3.29
Transportation	.73	1.50	8.62
Clerical	.19	1.91	5.14
Public Service	.13	1.03	2.27
Domestic & Personal Service	.33	1.46	3.68
Capitalists & Retired	8.61	4.04	——
Speculators	4.15	——	——
Unknown	10.82	23.94	——
Grain Trade	54.62	——	——
Other Food Trade	9.90	——	10.81
Other Trade & Commerce	8.92	——	——

losses of the sample, covering chiefly the years 1915 to 1917.[54] And these years presumably favored bull outsiders such as the farmer, because price rises predominated during the war boom.

Occupation	Gain	Loss	Net
Capitalist & Retired	$3,638,875	$ 220,328	$3,418,547
Other Food Trade	2,514,171	1,115,830	1,398,341
Agriculture	373,931	217,717	156,224
Other Trade & Commerce	714,359	640,123	74,236
Unknown Accounts	832,474	799,003	33,471
Transportation	44,484	30,074	14,410
Mineral Extraction	3,959	2,681	1,278
Public Service	2,311	5,289	−2,978
Clerical	3,426	11,572	−8,146
Domestic & Personal Service	6,793	26,519	−19,726
Speculators	134,026	172,684	−38,658
Professional	3,409	110,750	−107,341
Manufacture & Mechanical	810,383	1,410,091	−599,708
Grain Trade	3,920,763	4,832,310	−911,547

[54] F.T.C. *Report,* VII, 182, 196, 184. The total amount invested by each occupation was not reported.

The figures of the "Grain Trade" and "Other Food Trade" categories to a large extent represented hedges; presumably, therefore, the concerns had grain stored that had appreciated and thereby offset the losses on these futures contracts. There were few hedges among the remaining groups, however. Analysis also showed that those in "Agriculture" held their trades too short a time—less than fifteen days on the average—to be hedging; the farmers were simply speculating on the long side and, during this unusually bullish period, managed to come out ahead. Of all outsiders, they seemed to be the most consistently optimistic about future prices. The "Other Trade Commerce" group showed some proficiency; it contained few bankers, but many real estate and security salesmen whose speculative appetite led them into commodities. The Commission concluded that these men had the "speculative shrewdness" which is essential to a good speculator.

The disproportionate number of professional men trading in Chicago and their dismal performance calls for special comment. It is probable that the members of this group—doctors, dentists, lawyers, clergymen, and teachers—had the ebullient faith in individual enterprise characteristic of middle-class America at this time, and, lacking businesses of their own to invest in, disposed of their surplus funds in the market to simulate the thrills of real proprietorship. Their losses indicate that although they might have associated with those in the know, they were too slow to profit from such information. If professional men could not win when world conditions were pushing the market irresistibly up, how would they fare when professional bears of the grain trade competed with them in a falling market? The industrialists seem to have been similarly handicapped.

The *Report on the Grain Trade* was thorough in its survey of market ability. It declared that the classifications of Manufacturing and Mechanical, Professional,

Mineral Extraction, Transportation, Public Service, Clerical, and Domestic and Personal Service were all occupations too remote from the grain trade to possess requisite skill, and that since none of these needed hedging privileges, the market would benefit by their exclusion. In other words, 10 to 20 per cent of the traders were found to be inefficient and unnecessary to the maintenance of the market.[55] These findings applied only to the nation's major commodity market, but perhaps the data might have some bearing on stock-market trading characteristics. Unfortunately, empirical data on stock speculators for the twenties—their heyday—is not available, but some figures exist for the thirties. In 1933 economist Paul Wendt found the following distribution of occupations among customers of a typical New York brokerage house:

Occupation (Wendt, 1933)	
Other Trained Persons	14.9
Business Entrepreneurs	11.5
Executives	10.9
Widows, Housewives, Spinsters	10.2
Clerical	9.1
Salesmen	8.1
Skilled Laborers	5.9
Retired Persons	5.8
Unemployed & Unknown Accts	4.6
Estates, Corporations	4.3
Merchants	4.1
Students, Teachers, Clergy	3.7
Unskilled Laborers	3.7
Doctors, Dentists, Lawyers	3.3
PER CENT	100.0

Occupation (Elmo, Roper, 1940)	
Full Time Investors	18.3
Professional	21.6
Salaried Executives	33.8
Proprietor, non-farm	11.2
Salaried-Minor	8.9
Retired	4.9
Wage-Earner (factory)	.4
Wage-Earner (other)	.7
Proprietor (farm)	.1
Unemployed	.1
PER CENT	100.0

About 20 per cent of the clientele in the thirties were women; two-thirds of these pursued a career. According to Dr. Wendt's statistics, about 35 per cent (and accord-

[55] *Ibid.*, 182-196.

ing to Roper, 23 per cent) would fall into the non-commercial classes held incompetent by the commodity experts in the previous decade. Little was said, however, about the speculative deficiencies of specific occupations in the stock market, either in the twenties or thirties. Indeed, most of the time the experts were drowned out by "New Era" journalists and public figures who were more general and optimistic in their statements. Nothing was done to exclude those allegedly incompetent by occupation.[56]

There was one important segment of society, however, against whom the arguments and data for restriction were cited persistently and with some effect: women. For some years after the tide of general discussion about restriction had ebbed, discrimination against females continued on Wall Street. Market misogynists charged unsuitable temperament, lack of business experience, and sometimes of money; they had ancient and respectable opinion—as well as that of most financial experts—on their side. Not until 1927 were women permitted to participate on a relatively equal basis in the great game of stock speculation. Feminine pressure for equality had been partly assuaged in the political and social realms by 1920. The Nineteenth Amendment, the culmination of a long suffragette harangue, was finally approved; thus began the decade that was to celebrate in conspicuous fashion the emancipation of women. In the social sphere cigarettes, liquor, and unchaperoned evenings became the rule among many respectable people.

In the financial world, however, women had made slower and more surreptitious advances. Prior to the Civil War, when expansion was at its height, frontier rigors and excessive childbearing brought early death to many American women, but as the era of the West gave

<hr/>

[56] Paul Francis Wendt, *The Classification and Financial Experience of the Customers of a Typical New York Stock Exchange Firm from 1933 to 1938* (Marysville, Tenn., 1941), 50.

way to that of the industrial city and men strove franti-
cally for higher positions in urban life, women obtained
better medical attention and greater physical comfort.
The old trend reversed itself: wives began to outlive
their husbands, particularly the wealthier women who
had fewer children and fewer cares.

Thus in the early twentieth century the widow
emerged as almost the typical investor. The safety of
widows' investments came to be—by their own testimony—the *raison d'être* of many firms. Articles aimed at
women stressed the safety of bonds and the risks inherent in stocks. Until 1920, however, the typical woman
was inclined to leave her financial affairs to a close friend
of the family, usually a banker or a lawyer.[57] Even in
the Victorian era there had been a few women in
the security markets who were not relicts. The most
spectacular females to challenge male dominance in the
financial districts were the Claflin sisters, Victoria and
Tennessee. Born of eccentric parents in Ohio, they had
already established a reputation for exotic enthusiasms
before invading the Street—both were at one time followers of Stephen Pearl Andrews, the Utopian social
theorist. Their advocacy of Utopian socialism and free
love, and their general humanitarianism put the
Claflins in the chiliastic tradition of the Transcenden-
talists, but apparently the sisters saw no conflict between these interests and their efforts as stockbrokers.[58]
In 1870, after obtaining credit support from Henry
Clews by deception, and with the secret backing of
Commodore Vanderbilt, who had fallen under the spell
of their spiritualism, they opened Woodhull, Claflin
and Company. During their brief interlude in business
they published a weekly designed to expose fraud in the

[57] Justus G. Frederick, *Common Stocks and the Average Man*
(New York: 1929), 285-292.
[58] Alvin F. Harlow, *Dictionary of American Biography*, XX, 493-
494.

profession and demonstrate the improvement in ethics which their sex would bring to the Street.

Men of affairs did not view this minor invasion of the financial world with any great satisfaction. There were, of course, some men not directly connected with finance who were moved by the pseudo-gallantry of the era to defend the feminine crusaders, but aside from these the opinion was that women were unfit for speculation. In the minds of the males of Wall Street, it was only the paternalistic protection extended by brokers, or simple luck, that ever saved women traders from being swamped by losses. And when a woman was threatened with reverses, she became beseeching and immodest.[59] In 1906 a stockbroker, in an exposé of his calling, remarked that "we do not like women customers, and execute orders from them only when we cannot . . . refuse them, as they are usually bad speculators and troublesome as clients." Henry Clews summed up the pre-Harding view of these stock market dilettantes: women were better in other realms. They lacked the mental characteristics required for speculation. Women were too impulsive and impressionable; they took market reversals as personal affronts. Their perspective on a given situation was too narrow and personal to be economically productive in the market, and they were too impatient, expecting a fortune to accumulate in a few months. Like all amateurs, they underestimated the knowledge and skill required, assuming themselves deserving of big rewards for little ability.[60]

After World War I the hardy band of female financial pioneers was augmented by a new generation of young middle-class women who yearned for new freedom and quick, exciting gain. The accumulation of funds in fe-

[59] "Confessions of a Stock Broker," *The Independent*, LXI:1465-1469 (December 20, 1906); Paul S. Warden, "Kiss Your Money Good-by," *American Magazine*, XC:55 (October 1920).

[60] Henry Clews, *Fifty Years in Wall Street* (New York, 1908), 438-446.

male hands had accelerated; they began to own large portions of stock in the nation's leading corporations; in a few cases they owned over 50 per cent of the shares outstanding. They did not, of course, control the companies in question in anything but a technical sense, since they were dependent on the judgment of men familiar with the business. Many of these shareholders were housewives who used their dividends to supplement the family income.[61] And so, in the speculative atmosphere following 1923, the new position of women could not be ignored by rising young investment companies. The staid firms of Wall Street, sustained by a wealthy clientele, might keep the swish of skirts from their board rooms, but the growth of finance naturally drew into the business some men for whom the protocol of brokers meant little and profits meant much. The large reservoir of funds held by women was too tempting a market to ignore; they were not reluctant; they bubbled with the prosperity delirium. Many of them repeated their menfolk's catchwords of prosperity with none of the qualifications or uncertainties, as children repeat the opinions of their parents without the rationale.[62]

This irrepressible horde of female investors reached sizable proportions by 1927. A woman dickered unsuccessfully for a seat on the New York Stock Exchange in that year; and there were women acting as partners in various brokerage houses. Articles about this phenomenon began to appear in national magazines; a few were encouraging, more were amused and skeptical of feminine abilities in this line. The number of respectable investment houses that opened their doors to women increased, although they continued to argue that it was more trouble than it was worth, and some of them claimed that women were given to calling on the tele-

[61] *New York Times,* February 16, 1927, 29:3.
[62] Jeanette P. Nichols, *Twentieth Century United States; A History* (New York, 1943), 291.

phone too often to see how they were doing. Special rooms and women brokers appeared to accommodate this new source of revenue, and those of the fair sex who loitered about the tickers in time of loss were dubbed "mudhens."[63]

A woman broker, trying to look realistically at the situation, observed that professional women accustomed to commercial ways were, by and large, well-disciplined and efficient in their financial affairs. In her view it was the women of the older generation—those once-decorative products of the finishing school—who knew little of finance and supposed themselves unduly important, who were the proper targets for male wrath. Even these self-centered bores were not wholly responsible for their condition; men had deliberately kept them ignorant.[64]

But there was contradictory evidence. An insurance company survey showed that, six years after receiving their benefits, only 1.3 per cent of the widows had lost money via the proverbial speculation and promotion route; most of them had invested conservatively. Another woman broker thought market competence more a matter of temperament than sex; she said there were both men and women whose accounts she would not want for this reason. She added that women were more often inquisitive and therefore might be more trouble in the office, but this curiosity about the facts behind the company's shares was a healthy sign in an aspiring trader. A bank officer observed that, with training, the women were as good as the men.

By 1928 speculation had fanned out to include more than upper-middle-class widows, housewives, and career women. Quotations over the radio attracted a large fol-

[63] *New York Times,* January 14, 1927, 1:2; Eunice F. Bernard, "Ladies of the Ticker," *North American Review,* CCVII:405-410 (April, 1929); "Wall Street Bids for the Woman Speculator," *Literary Digest,* XCI:86 (November 17, 1928); *The Progressive,* XX:99 (July 1929).

[64] *Saturday Evening Post,* CCI (September 8, 1928).

lowing, and employees close to their bosses began to act on tips. Working girls were being recruited into the market ranks. Woman brokers called on the girls in the evenings after work, to apprise them of the income and profit potentialities of stock. One such broker, operating in northern New Jersey, found the girls "sensibly alive" to the advantages of good securities; she had 150 customers and was thereby able to support herself and her aging mother. Another woman, a stenographer, extolled the virtues of thrift; in a magazine article she told how $100 could become $3,000 without neglecting charities. Thus were women assimilated. By 1928 their market defenders had gained an audience and their critics had diminished—the most underprivileged element had a strong foothold in the financial world.[65] The 1929 Crash did not alter this; women have constituted more than 20 per cent of brokers' customers ever since.

The epitaph for discussion of formal requirements for speculation was written in 1934. In that year, while the New Deal Congress had several regulatory bills before it, the Stock Exchange Research Staff of the Twentieth Century Fund made its report and final recommendations for exchange reform. These experts rejected "more careful scrutiny of the financial and moral standing of their customers by brokers" as an impractical remedy for existing evils. They also rejected the notion of limiting trade facilities to avoid tempting the allegedly imcompetent—but only after thoughtful consideration.

One of the most powerful stimuli to stock market gambling on the part of the outside public is the easy and pleasant access to the market provided by the stock ticker and the comfortable board rooms of bro-

[65] Barnard, "Ladies of the Ticker," estimated that women comprised 20-35 per cent of the customers in the late twenties. *New York Times*, January 5, 1928; Helen L.S., "The Business Woman's Investments," *Magazine of Wall Street*, XXXVI:1199 (1925).

kerage houses, especially since recent inventions like the electric board and the translux tape. The feverish and exciting atmosphere created by these devices . . . kindles and magnifies the urge for gambling. In addition, the best advertising medium which the pool operator has . . . is the ticker. It whets the appetite of the speculator beyond resistance as it records the pool's success in terms of mounting volume of sales.

The report concluded that the public would probably be better off with less highly developed facilities, but that there was no way to bring this about by legislation. The remedy had to be education to the point where people based their judgment on the intrinsic worth of commodities and securities.[66]

The lengthy discussion of speculative competence left a major question unanswered: was it the lack of skill of portions of the public or the unscrupulousness of traders and brokers that was primarily responsible for market instability in these years? Writers and scholars have generally preferred to castigate the few rather than the many, presumably believing that amelioration could more easily occur by inciting the many against the few. A study of a typical brokerage business between 1935 and 1937, however, suggests caution in assigning too much blame to the few or assuming that 1929 was a thorough lesson to the many. The study showed that the firm's recommendations to buy and sell, if followed, would have yielded 142 per cent on capital per month; but an analysis of the firm's customers revealed that most suffered losses for this period. The great discrepancy between advice and results indicates that the public preferred to make its own judgments even when expert advice was available free.[67]

Seen in its broadest perspective, discussion of specula-

[66] Evans Clark, *et al., Security Market Control* (New York, 1934), 180.
[67] Wendt, *The Classification . . . of Customers,* 210.

tive competence was merely one daub on a larger canvas of early twentieth-century expertise, which stressed efficiency and claimed science for its authority. Not yet sensitive to a wider audience, the specialist was openly arrogant toward the layman. The sociologists Madison Grant and Lothrop Stoddard were defining the "racially unfit"; psychologists were suggesting an I.Q. minimum for suffrage; Taylorization was the rage, and the Harvard Exquisites were writing for each other, not for the untutored public. In this milieu the consideration of speculative competence appears only as an innocuous parallel, a by-product of a general reaction to over-rapid social change and the emergence of new social elements.

Taking the discussion of competence together with accompanying market behavior, it seems that the experts were on the whole correct in believing that amateurs meant market instability. But any device to exclude certain social or economic classes would have had to be a temporary expedient; it could not have endured in a democratic economy where new leadership is continually displacing the old. The real problem these experts and commentators faced, therefore, was one that has plagued most of human history: how to assimilate a very large group—and one given to extremes of gullibility and suspicion, because it lacks experience—without deranging the structure that has been carefully erected over a long time. With market restrictionists largely ignored, it was an open race to make good speculators of doctors, lawyers, ministers, mechanics, and women before they could destroy the market by their initial errors. That race was lost, but there were other important contributory factors. After the Crash the memory of that debacle was deeply enough seared into the participants to bring about a natural winnowing in the market, and assimilation has since gone forward at a more modest rate.

126

CHAPTER 4

THE TWENTIES: "SONS OF THE
WILD JACKASS"

*S*ENATOR Robert M. LaFollette was decisively defeated in his third-party try for the Presidency in 1924. Woodrow Wilson died that year, and "Fighting Bob" the next; so did Senator Edwin F. Ladd, the "expert" of North Dakota's Nonpartisan League. This sequence of events has provided most historians with a convenient terminus for their discussion of progressivism and insurgency; they have been silent on insurgency between 1925 and 1929, except perhaps to remind their readers that George Norris was still urging government operation of Muscle Shoals and William E. Borah was continuing his fight against armaments.[1] Maybe this neglect of the radicals—at this time concentrated largely in the Senate—is justified: although they spoke often, they gained few victories and were a small body of Old Believers surrounded by the Philistines of the "New Era."

[1] For example, Eric F. Goldman, *Rendezvous with Destiny* (New York, 1952), 314-315; Russel B. Nye, *Midwestern Progressive Politics* (East Lansing, 1951), 347, 350; John D. Hicks, *The Republican Ascendancy, 1921-1933* (New York, 1959), 102-105. An important exception to the above generalization, however, is Arthur S. Link, who emphasizes the continuity between the Wilson Era and the New Deal. See especially his "What Happened to the Progressive Movement in the 1920s?" *American Historical Review,* LXIV:833-851 (July, 1959); Richard Hofstadter claims that the 1920s "Congressional Progressives were on the whole a fake" and cites with approval a critic who charged them with "underlying party regularity," *The Age of Reform; from Bryan to F.D.R.* (New York, 1955), 285. Their Senate voting record, 1925-1933 refutes this claim, however; it shows a definite and consistent insurgency in socio-economic matters, a pattern scarcely altered from 1910.

Yet despite some outbursts of provincialism, these Sons of the Wild Jackass, as Senator George Moses of New Hampshire dubbed them, should receive credit for putting their fingers on the vulnerable spots in the American economy of the 1920s.

These insurgents have been slighted because they had no formal organization. They announced no program and there were no important conferences comparable to those of the Farm Bloc in 1921 and 1922. This was in part because they were too individualistic, too heterogeneous, to compromise their convictions in any formal document. There were Roosevelt and LaFollette Republicans, Wilson and Bryan Democrats, and Henrik Shipstead, the Farmer-Laborite. Economic democracy was the core of whatever unity they had.[2]

I

Improvement in farm prices and income in 1923 and 1924 had temporarily lessened dissatisfaction and comforted the Republicans in an election year, but farmer demands soon became insistent again, as the farmers' standard of living continued to lag significantly behind that of urban dwellers. The chief vehicle of farm political pressure in the later twenties was the McNary-Haugen bill. It proposed a two-price system: crop surpluses were to be sold abroad for what they would bring, and a tax—an equalization fee—on the portion of crops sold domestically would be used to compensate the producers who had been forced to sell their products abroad at world prices. The tariff, it was assumed, would

[2] Ray Tucker and Frederic Barkley, *Sons of the Wild Jackass* (Boston, 1932), i-iii. See also Cedric B. Cowing, "H. L. Mencken: the Case of the 'Curdled' Progressive," *Ethics*, LXIX: 255-267 (July 1959), for an explanation of the postwar progressive heterodoxy in terms of David Riesman's theory of social character.

The introduction and section II are from the article, "The Sons of the Wild Jackass and the Stock Market," reprinted here with permission from *The Business History Review*, XXXIII (Summer 1959), 138-155.

protect the domestic market. Reliance on the protective tariff was probably the only aspect of the plan that Eastern Republicans found palatable, and they attacked the equalization fee feature as paternalism and class legislation—in other words, as too favorable to the farmers. From 1925 to 1929 the McNary-Haugen plan was bruited about Congress. Twice it passed both houses only to be vetoed by the President; in spite of the overwhelming support of the South, the Midwest and the Far West, the corporation-dominated administration was able to block this form of farm assistance.

Rural discontent over the disparity between farm prices and manufactured goods and resentment of the marketing system continued, especially in the South. If the Cotton Futures Act of 1916, which reduced the number of grades deliverable under a futures contract, was operating to diminish speculation, its effect had been lost in wartime and postwar market activity. And despite official encouragement of the Co-operative Marketing Act of 1922, farm cooperatives were being thwarted in their efforts to obtain seats on the commodity exchanges. The boards of trade argued that the rebates made to members of cooperatives were contrary to the exchanges' rules against fee splitting and therefore made the cooperatives ineligible for exchange membership. This question was the subject of much litigation during the twenties.

In 1926 Senator Thaddeus Caraway resumed the fight against futures trading. The Arkansas Senator was a logical leader in the new assault. His years in the House and Senate had given him experience, and opposition to cotton speculators in general had been a major concern of Arkansas' national legislators ever since Reconstruction.[3] Caraway's bill to place a prohibitive tax on cotton fu-

---

[3] *Options and Futures,* Committee on Agriculture. United States Senate. 69 Cong., 1 sess. (Washington, 1926), 3-28; *Congressional Record,* 70 Cong., 1 sess., v. 69, Pt. 8, 8269-8279.

tures contracts was similar to many previous bills; he merely augmented the familiar arguments of the Progressive Era with some current statistics. But in 1926 Caraway could find little support for his tax except among dirt farmers and their cotton factors in the South. Secretary of Agriculture William M. Jardine, ex-Secretary Henry C. Wallace and J. W. T. Duvel of the Grain Futures Administration opposed it. The Senate finally defeated the measure, 47 to 24, in 1928. The faithful yeas were, as usual, from the anti-speculator tier with some allies from the up-country South.

Caraway renewed the attack the following year with a bill that would ban futures outright. The new measure was debated at the moment of the Reserve Board's "direct pressure" against stock market loans and so attracted some attention from a public newly aware of this speculative danger. The Arkansan boldly stated that the futures ban was the most important bill presented at the session. He knew, he said, that a lobby was working in the cloakroom and sponsoring forums against the bill at many Rotary Clubs. Nevertheless he was blunt: "Everyone who believes that the gambling interests ought to be protected, although agriculture shall perish, will vote against this legislation."

Various Western and Southern Senators spoke. Lynn Frazier of North Dakota claimed farmers had received twenty cents less per bushel on their wheat the past July because of market manipulation, and cited the Federal Trade Commission report on the concentration of trading in a few hands. William H. King of Utah told of his legislative attempt, four years previously, to deny bank credit to speculators. "Tom-Tom" Heflin of Alabama reminded his colleagues that Thomas A. Edison was predicting a panic. Heflin urged cotton spinners to buy and store their cotton rather than hedge on it; hedging was not safe in a dangerously fluctuating market. Smith Brookhart of Iowa noted that cooperative banking had reduced speculation in England. "Cotton Ed" Smith of South Carolina did not think Congress could control what an individual did with his money. When the discussion of futures and speculation subsided, the Senators voted down this second Caraway bill, 47 to 27. The three converted to Caraway's side since 1928 were Elmer Thomas of Oklahoma, Charles Waterman of Colorado, and Wesley L. Jones of Washington.[4]

The futures trading issue had never really captured the attention of the general public. To overthrow such a well-established system would have required an aroused citizenry of sizable proportions and, aside from a few spectacular corners at the turn of the century, such trading had not stirred much interest beyond the producers, the brokers and their bankers and journalists. Since the Populist challenge of 1892 the exchanges themselves had adopted many new regulations, which together with the 1922 law had reduced the more obvious abuses; in later years the big operators—unlike Hutchinson, Pardridge, and Leiter—were more circumspect and less notorious. The futures issue had originally been raised by disgruntled agrarians in the late nineteenth century; they had been joined in the Progressive Era by some progressives and financial reformers, but now opposition was reverting to the agrarians again, a group proportionally much smaller than before. A cycle had been completed without success: evidently a system involving hedging and scalping was to prevail in the United States.

The vote on the second Caraway bill suggested that many Senators were concerned about speculation in 1929, but intransigents on the futures question had been slowly declining since 1892. Chester H. Gray's testimony in 1928 illustrated this. Gray represented the American Farm Bureau Federation, a large organization

4 *Ibid.*, v. 70, Pt. 3, 3214, 3358ff.

that spoke for many of the more prosperous farmers. He recalled the Federation's support of the 1922 act and praised its enforcement; he noted that the Farm Bureaus had "progressed" from their 1920 anti-exchange stand—although there were some demands for amendments to the 1922 law, the farmers were now at least willing to let the exchanges exist—and he warned that an increase in abuses could cause farm sentiment to revert to its earlier negative position.[5] Lester J. Dickinson, a Republican from northwestern Iowa, had introduced a bill in Congress that indicated just how far this tolerance of commodity exchanges had gone in the Farm Belt itself. Section 4-L of his bill set trading limits of two million bushels, but there was a proviso whereby the limit could be reduced during an emergency. Bona fide hedging and government trading were exempt, and Section 4-J required that trades of 500,000 bushels or more be reported. Thus a Farm Bloc Congressman was tacitly accepting future trading and merely suggesting limits on the transactions of the very big traders. The idea of placing maximums on the trading of individuals—used by Herbert Hoover during World War I and suggested by him to a Senate committee in 1920—had finally made such inroads that a Farm Congressman sponsored the principle.[6]

II

The election of Calvin Coolidge over John W. Davis and LaFollette in 1924 occasioned a rapid rise in the stock market. This reflected the glee of business at the prospect of further prosperity and the continuation of

[5] *Grain Futures Act Amendment,* Committee on Agriculture. United States House of Representatives. 70 Cong., 1 sess. (Washington, 1928), 34-41.

[6] *Ibid.,* 1-4, 34-41.

the economic policies of President Coolidge and his Secretary of the Treasury, Andrew Mellon.[7]

The big blond radical from Minnesota, Henrik Shipstead, arose in the Senate to comment upon the renewed stock speculation; it was January 1925. The Farmer-Laborite, elected in 1922, was still a relative newcomer to that body; his address was carefully worded and fortified with statistics from financial journals. He declared that the prosperity of October-December 1924, was based on false premises; production and employment were both below the levels of 1923. He accused the Treasury Department, the Federal Reserve Board, and the administration itself of encouraging credit for stocks while no similar credit relief was being extended to legitimate business or agriculture. The focus of his anger was the reduction of the rediscount rate to 2-2½ per cent by the Reserve Board; the prevailing rate for the years 1919-1923 had been 5-5½ per cent. Shipstead quoted Dr. H. Parker Willis, a noted banking authority, as saying that the Federal Reserve, through its open market operations, was causing inflation. But "the greatest menace which I see in the present situation is the effect upon the 100 million minds which make this the world's greatest nation, when it at last dawns upon the common man . . . that our boasted national prosperity hangs, not upon the productive industry and wage earning toil, but upon the use of government financial functions in aiding the stock-market operations. A few weeks' stock speculation may cost the faith of the American people!" Shipstead called for remedial legislation to correct credit abuses and to aid agriculture.

The bubbling stock market was gradually making the Federal Reserve System and its allocation of credit a center of controversy. *LaFollette's Magazine* attacked the boom as artificial; it claimed that the Federal Reserve

[7] Russel B. Nye, *Midwestern Progressive Politics* (East Lansing, 1951), 348.

System was being made to carry the burden of speculation. This political periodical, published in Wisconsin,
charged that the New York Federal Reserve Bank had
kept its rate at 3 per cent, ½ per cent less than the other
eleven Reserve Banks, for the deliberate purpose of increasing speculative credit.[8] Thus the Midwest progressives, always sensitive to economic aspects of American
life, were among the first to publicize the danger to the
economy of excessive stock speculation. Robert M. La-
Follette, Jr., who had succeeded his father in the Senate,
introduced the following resolution, which was referred
to the Committee on Banking and Currency, on January
18, 1928:

> *Resolved,* that it is the sense of the Senate that the
> Federal Reserve Board should immediately take steps
> to restrict the further expansion of loans by member
> banks for speculative purposes and as rapidly as is
> compatible with the financial stability of the Nation,
> require the contraction of such loans to the lowest pos-
> sible amount and be it further,
> *Resolved,* that the Federal Reserve Board be di-
> rected to report to the Congress what legislation, if
> any, is required to prevent the future use of the funds
> and credit of the Federal Reserve System for specula-
> tive purposes.

Three weeks later a Senate subcommittee began hearings, and young Senator LaFollette appeared to elaborate upon his resolution. Self-assured and to the point, he
argued that the use of the credit of the Federal Reserve
System for speculative loans was a violation of the Federal Reserve Act. Section 13 of that Act, after defining
the categories of paper subject to rediscount, concluded

[8] *LaFollette's Magazine* (March 1925), 42-43. In 1930 Senator
Shipstead blamed the easy credit policy of the Federal Reserve
Board for the false prosperity of 1925-1929 and the crash. *The
Progressive* (December 20, 1930).

"but such definition should not include notes, drafts, or bills covering merely investments or issued or drawn for the purpose of carrying or trading in stocks, bonds, or other investment securities, except bonds and notes of . . . the United States." In support of his case "Young Bob" also quoted Carter Glass and Robert L. Owen, the legislators who had steered the Federal Reserve Act through Congress in 1913. The chief purpose of his resolution, said LaFollette, was to call the attention of the Senate to the great increase in loans on stocks and bonds by members of the Reserve System. In 1921, $778 million was involved in loans of this type; in 1925, $2.1 billion; on February 1, 1928, the total had reached $3.8 billion. LaFollette acknowledged that the problem presented was complex, but hoped that some legislative remedy could be found to return the Federal Reserve to its original goals.[9]

Brokers' loans constituted a new topic of discussion in the mid-1920s. Banks in New York City had for decades made loans to stockbrokers both on call and on time. The size of these loans in New York City had been computed for some years but in 1926 the Federal Reserve Board decided on a policy of publicity and began to publish the totals of brokers' loans in the *Federal Reserve Bulletin*. Although the totals published were for New York City only and included loans made to dealers to float new issues, they nevertheless gave the public a barometer to watch in regard to stock speculation, because most such activity was conducted through members of the New York Stock Exchange and credit was most often used for the purchase of securities by their clients.[10]

[9] *Brokers' Loans*, Committee on Banking & Currency, United States Senate, 70 Cong., 1 sess. (Washington, 1928). At the suggestion of Senator Carter Glass, the committee later amended the resolution by removing the words following "speculative purposes" in paragraph one; evidently Glass and some other moderates did not favor limiting loans "to the lowest possible amount."

[10] *Ibid.*, 2-3.

The publication of these totals, rising inexorably month by month to new highs, naturally created discontent and concern in the classes and sections of the nation that were not participating. With a heritage of Populism and already aroused by the injustices of the commodity markets and rural credit facilities, Senators from the western part of the Midwest were the logical and inevitable spokesmen for the opposition to excessive stock speculation. After 1926 the rise in these loans was there for all to see.

The first witness called by the subcommittee on the LaFollette resolution was Henry Parker Willis, editor of the *New York Journal of Commerce* and a former Secretary of the Federal Reserve Board. Willis declared that banking rather than legislative reforms were needed, that negotiation with the more important banks in New York City would accomplish more than legislative interference with such things as interest rates. He regarded direct control of member institutions as neither legal nor desirable. Although Willis admitted that the cancer of brokers' loans was a menace to the stability of the nation, he was sure that an injunction from Congress to the Reserve Board would be too vague to accomplish the desired end. He told the committee that mere passage of the LaFollette resolution might itself be sufficient warning to check this tendency. Willis' attitude was typical of that of a large group of bankers and respectable citizens who, while admitting danger, wished to rely on negotiation, indirection, and the emergence of character in public officials.

Senator Smith Wildman Brookhart, a committee member, was impatient with Willis' point of view. At the outset of the hearing the Iowa insurgent had requested that the subcommittee also consider his banking bill, designed to remedy the brokers' loan evil. "I am not a believer in the theory that we can control speculation by raising and lowering the rates in some board," said Brookhart.[11] The remedy, he felt, was to be found only through law since the law, not the Federal Reserve Board, was primarily at fault; Congress should therefore act.[12] Brookhart, a nominal Republican, had attached himself to the progressive wing of that party, headed in Iowa by Senator Albert Baird Cummins; he served in Iowa Progressive councils in the 1912 Bull Moose campaign. When age sapped the progressivism of Senator Cummins, Brookhart took up his cudgel against the railroads, and the agricultural discontent of the postwar period brought him political success. He won Senate seats in 1922, 1924, and 1926, although in the middle year he was counted out by a Senate campaign investigating committee that feared his radicalism. He was temporarily read out of the Republican party for supporting LaFollette in 1924.[13]

The Iowa Senator—born in Missouri—seemed to be a blend of Southern moralistic nativism and solid Iowa equalitarianism. He campaigned hard for veterans, mothers, and "drys"; attacking middlemen, he advocated cooperatives based upon the Rochdale plan, and demanded government ownership of the railroads.[14] He was convinced that the Federal Reserve Board had strayed from its original objectives. Speculation was five or six times as great as when the Reserve Act was

[11] Lewis H. Haney, Lyman S. Logan, and Henry S. Gavens, *Brokers' Loans: A Study in the Relation between Speculative Credits and the Stock Market, Business, and Banking* (New York, 1932), 3-43.

[12] *Brokers' Loans* 19, 23-24, 6-7. Cf. Richard N. Owens and Charles O. Hardy, *Interest Rates and Stock Speculation* (New York, 1926), preface. These two economists announced that they could find no evidence for the theory that stock prices were controlled by short-term and call loan rates.

[13] *Time Magazine* (January 19, 1925). The two-year term, 1923-1925, was to fill the vacancy caused when Senator William S. Kenyon accepted a judgeship.

[14] Reinhard H. Luthin, "Smith Wildman Brookhart of Iowa: Insurgent Agrarian Politician," *Agricultural History*, XXV: 187-197 (October 1951).

passed in 1913; but more importantly, local banks were refusing to lend to the people of Iowa. The banks preferred to obtain a safe 1¾ per cent by redepositing in New York City or lending on call there at 4-5 per cent. Yet before the inauguration of the Reserve System, said Brookhart, farm loans were considered the safest in the world. The flow of funds from local banks in the hinterlands to the big banks and Stock Exchange in New York City aroused the concern of other Senators also: Earle B. Mayfield, a Democrat from Texas, and William B. Pine, an Oklahoma Republican, voiced their disapproval.

Brookhart then presented his solution to the problem. He estimated that 75 per cent of Iowa's money was invested in New York City; he was not subdued by the claim that the funds were safe there. He wanted to stop speculation and bring Iowa money back to Iowa where it could benefit his constituents—to achieve this he had designed a drastic measure. At that time the Reserve System required that 25 per cent of a member bank's reserves be deposited with the regional Federal Reserve Bank; the Iowa radical proposed that the remaining 75 per cent also be thus deposited, so that the entire reserve could be controlled by the Reserve System. In this way Brookhart hoped to prevent excess funds from finding their way into the call markets of New York. He also suggested that member banks be *directly* prohibited from making speculative loans. Senator Carter Glass of Virginia, banking expert of the Senate, at this point reminded Brookhart that the American system of government was traditionally dualistic, that member banks would not accept drastic invasions of their privileges; they would merely withdraw from the Federal Reserve System and join the various state banking systems. But Brookhart had a solution for that too: state banks that failed to conform to the regulations of the Reserve System would be denied the use of the mails. He introduced a bill to this effect.[15]

The question of the soundness of the rural banks that the insurgents wanted to protect was then raised. The controversy came to a head when Oliver W. M. Sprague, professor of banking at Harvard, testified. Sprague denied that the money concentration in the East was depriving other areas of needed credit. Local bankers were lending in the New York money markets because they could not obtain sufficient loans in their own sections of the country. There were too many small, shaky banks; many of them had invested too heavily in local enterprises and discovered their mistake in the deflation of 1920, according to Sprague, and they were now diversifying their risks. He admitted that this development aided urban at the expense of rural elements, but the money concentration in New York actually represented an advance over earlier banking methods in that it provided a great impersonal reserve, free from local conditions and prejudices.[16]

Senator William B. Pine of Oklahoma disagreed vehemently with the economist. Pine, Methodist banker and oil man, was taking an insurgent position consonant with the temper of Oklahoma voters in 1928. He did not believe that the withdrawal of funds lessened the threat of bank failures. Sprague, however, seemed oblivious to regional prejudices; he told Pine that he was less fearful of speculation in securities than of speculation in land.

[15] *Brokers' Loans*, 6, 8, 19, 64, 75, 83. Joseph Stagg Lawrence, *Wall Street and Washington* (Princeton, 1929), quoted Brookhart as saying, "Unless something of this kind is done we are now headed for the greatest panic in the history of the world." Lawrence, a Princeton professor who served as economic consultant to the New York Stock Exchange, ridiculed Brookhart, declaring that the proposals of Midwest radicals could not be taken seriously (309-314).

[16] *Brokers' Loans*, 32-33. Experts had long claimed that there were too many small, inadequate banks. John M. Chapman and Ray B. Westerfield, *Branch Banking; its Historical and Theoretical Position in America and Abroad* (New York, 1942), 128-129.

Overspeculation in securities was an evil that could quickly be corrected and the loss confined to a few individuals, whereas inflated land values could cause a collapse in industry and consequent unemployment. No statement could have antagonized the insurgents more. The view that security speculation should be permitted but land speculation suppressed seemed to suggest a double standard for rural and urban areas; the implication was that farmers could not safely participate in national prosperity or take a hand in the traditional American game of speculation. Brookhart produced figures to show that the great deflation of 1920-1921 was erroneously attributed to land speculation by the farmers; in reality, said the Iowan, the events of 1920 were, as always, caused by bankers and speculators in the cities and not by industrious husbandmen. For example, in Iowa in 1920 the index of land value was 213 when the general price index was 241. The inflation in land had not kept pace with other price rises during World War I.[17]

But Sprague continued to turn the knife in the wound. He observed that since the demand for food was less elastic than the demand for industrial products, the farmer was doomed to vicissitudes independent of the general trend. Economic distress in the Midwest was caused by too many small banks and not by the flow of funds to New York. Call loans, the kind made to New York stockbrokers, were the safest possible commercial loans, said Sprague; they might be called any time after noon on the date of issue, and losses on them were negligible. (The current size of brokers' loan totals had no important bearing on the national economy!) Senator Brookhart thereupon shifted from economic to moral grounds. Speculation was immoral and illegal, he said, and depositors' money should not be used as the "kitty" in what was essentially a gambling game. The Senator

[17] *Brokers' Loans*, 33-35. 1913=100.

wanted to believe, however, that there was a direct relation between stock speculation in New York and the depression in Midwest agriculture. He insisted that a reduction in brokers' loans would ease the burden of the farmer, but Dr. Sprague continued to deny it.[18]

Several weeks after these acrimonious hearings, the Senate subcommittee reported favorably on the LaFollette resolution. Chairman Peter Norbeck of South Dakota, a well-driller and a Republican, said in an accompanying statement:

> . . . the history of booms is that the higher they go the more suddenly they break. It is no defense for the "Street" to say that the risks are widespread. That is only another way of saying that the losses will not fall so heavily on the centres, but will be borne by the whole country. This is not surprising. The speculative buyers are not the experienced class; they are the lambs. The higher the market goes, the more widespread the condition. We can find small consolation in the fact that the losses will be borne by those least able to bear it, scattered over every state in the Union.[19]

The committee report also quoted with approval the observations of Carter Glass in 1913:

> Under existing law we have permitted banks to pyramid credit upon credit and to call these credits reserves. It is a misnomer; they are not reserves. And

[18] *Ibid.*, 39, 45, 54, 62. Dr. Sprague did acknowledge that current stock prices were too high for prospective earnings.

[19] The Senate Banking & Currency Committee voted 7 to 5 in favor of the resolution. For: Brookhart (R-Ia.); Fletcher (D-Fla.); Frazier (R-N. D.); Glass (D-Va.); Mayfield (D-Tex.); Norbeck (R-S. D.); Steiwer (R-Ore.). Against: Barkley (D-Ky.); Edge (R-N. J.); Phipps (R-Colo.); Sackett (D-Ky.); Wagner (D-N. Y.). In view of their later support of New Deal reforms, it is interesting to note the nay votes of Alben Barkley and Robert Wagner. *Commercial & Financial Chronicle*, 126:II:2737 (April 30, 1928); *New York Times*, May 13, 1928.

when financial troubles come and the country banks call for their money with which to pay their creditors, they find it all invested in stock gambling operations. There is suspension of payment, and the whole system breaks down under the strain, causing widespread confusion and almost inconceivable damage.[20]

Glass's words of 1913 were reproduced to demonstrate that the supporters of the Reserve Act intended it to rectify the speculative credit situation.

But the LaFollette resolution, although reported favorably, remained on the Senate calendar throughout 1928. LaFollette later blamed "the friends of speculation" for preventing its adoption.[21] The *Wall Street Journal* believed that the agitation against Wall Street was really "sour grapes"; speculation could be dangerous of course, but stock market activity was the least hazardous kind—it acted as a safety valve. In contrast to farmers' loans, brokers' loans could be liquidated instantly; 1919 proved that: "Congress may rest easy if it is worried only by stock speculation." Even a year later *Barron's* declared that overspeculation tended to curb itself. The financial magazine chided "Young Bob," claiming that he wanted to reduce brokers' loans to the 1921 level, even though such a step would stop industrial expansion. The *New York Times,* on the other hand, was favorable; editorially it said of the resolution: "It only aims at preventing further aggravation of the present situation."[22]

While LaFollette's resolution languished on the calendar, the progressives made another foray against Wall Street speculation. William H. McMaster, a Republican from South Dakota, acting on behalf of his colleague,

[20] *Commercial & Financial Chronicle,* 126:II:3061-3062 (May 19, 1928).

[21] *Congressional Record,* 71 Cong., 1 sess., v. 71, Pt. 1, 2324.

[22] *Wall Street Journal,* May 15, 1928; *Barron's,* March 5, 1929, 12, April 30, 4; *New York Times,* May 13, 1928.

Peter Norbeck, submitted an amendment to the pending tax bill: it called for a tax on call loans of five cents per \$100 or fractional part thereof. Assuming the average life of a call loan to be 60 days, McMaster estimated that the levy would raise \$12 million and could be used to offset the contemplated refunds to be made elsewhere in the tax bill. The Yankton banker told the Senate:

> There has been a wild orgy of speculation . . . in the last two or three years. Hundreds of millions of profit have been made and to anyone who is familiar with the . . . history of the stock exchange, while many millions are in the hands of lambs, it will be . . . only a short time when there is going to be a frightful shakedown in the stock market . . . and these profits again are going to revert to the rich and be safely stored in their strong boxes.[23]

The McMaster amendment was immediately rejected by the Senate in a voice vote. But the Dakotan brought the matter up again two days later; he asked for a formal roll call vote. It was defeated, 44 to 18. Only the staunchest anti-speculators stood with McMaster for the call loan tax.[24] The failure of the insurgents to muster more than 18 votes for the tax is perhaps attributable to the burden which such a tax would place upon some small businesses accustomed to using call loans to finance their operations. James Couzens, Ford Company millionaire from Michigan, was the only Senator from an

[23] *Congressional Record,* 70 Cong., 1 sess., v. 69, Pt. 9, 9203. This was the customary type of loan made to brokers who re-lent to clients buying stock on margin.
[24] The anti-speculator eighteen were: Black (D-Ala.), Blaine (R-Wis.), Brookhart (R-Ia.), Couzens (R-Mich.), Cutting (R-N. M.), Dill (D-Wash.), Harris (D-Ga.), Howell (R-Neb.), Johnson (R-Calif.), LaFollette (R-Wis.), Mayfield (D-Tex.), Neely (D-W. Va.), Norris (R-Neb.), Nye (R-N. D.), Sheppard (D-Tex.), Shipstead (F-L, Minn.), Thomas (D-Okla.), and McMaster. Norbeck was absent but of course favored the tax. *Ibid.,* 9203-9204 (May 23, 1928).

industrial state to vote for the tax. In view of the rapid rise of brokers' loans in 1928, however, it would be hasty to say that this tax was too drastic.

In the same month of 1928, however, the anti-speculators won, with powerful allies, a minor skirmish in the struggle with Wall Street. An amendment had been offered to the tax bill to reduce the stock transfer tax from two cents per $100 to one cent. This 50 per cent reduction had already been approved by the House as part of the over-all plan to cut nuisance taxes. The Democratic regulars were interested in reducing federal taxes, especially during this lush period of Republicanism. Using the traditional arguments of Jeffersonianism, they charged that President Coolidge and Secretary Mellon were retaining unnecessarily high wartime tax rates in order to lavish government largesse on the industrial enterprises of the North; like the tariff, most Republican taxes were unfair to the South.

The spokesman for these Democrats, Furnifold Simmons of North Carolina, took the lead in advocating the reduction to one cent. The levy was a burden to business, especially to those companies involved in employee and customer stock ownership plans, as well as to cooperatives of all kinds. The revenue to the Treasury, said Simmons, was inconsequential anyway. In reply Reed Smoot of Utah, charged with steering the tax bill through the Senate, told his colleagues that this tax was unobtrusive and brought in $8.8 million to the government. He implied that the tax bill had been carefully considered by committee experts and that changes like the one proposed might well prevent reductions in other provisions, such as income and corporation levies. The corporations, he said, favored keeping the two cent rate, for it served as a deterrent to speculation in securities.

Simmons challenged Smoot on this. The tax did not hit speculators, said the Carolinian, because market operators traded in a floating supply of stocks held in the names of brokers, and not transferred upon each sale through the corporation registrar. The tax applied only to stock in cases where ownership was transferred on the company books. Smoot contested this interpretation, and when Thaddeus Caraway of Arkansas, long-time foe of cotton speculators, asked if the transfer tax hampered gambling, Smoot answered yes. Caraway said in that case he would support the two cent rate. Aware that the corporations also favored the tax, he predicted that the vote about to be taken would reveal how much more influential the corporations were than the farmers. Earlier that day Caraway's amendment to ban cotton futures trading by taxation had been beaten, 47 to 24, when the independent farmers had stood alone. Now, said Caraway, the business interests want to keep the two cent rate on transfers whereas the "gamblers" prefer the reduction. Could a coalition of farmers and businessmen, he asked, overcome the speculative interests in the United States Senate?

When the clerk called the roll, there were 48 yeas and 30 nays; the transfer tax was retained at the two cent rate. The corporation–Western farmer alliance had triumphed over those who would have reduced the tax on speculation. This was one of the two instances after 1925 in which anti-speculators won a vote.[25] They suc-

	To Retain (Yea)	To Reduce (Nay)	Not Voting
New England	7	3	2
Middle Atlantic	3	4	3
South	6	13	5
Central & Eastern Midwest	8	5	3
Anti-speculator tier	10	1	1
Far West	14	4	4
	48	30	18

[25] The other victory was the voice vote passage of the Heflin resolution in 1929; see p. 150. Like all votes on speculative matters since 1892, the vote to retain the transfer tax at two cents had a definite sectional pattern. Here is the vote by section:

145

ceeded on this occasion because some twenty Senators from the East and Midwest, chiefly representing corporate interests, chose to continue this transfer tax rate in preference to other more onerous taxes, and voted with the insurgents. Evidently the anti-speculators could win a vote in Congress only when their interests coincided sufficiently with those of corporate business to form a coalition against the speculative interests that were strong in the East and parts of the South. The real defenders of speculation in this vote proved to be the Simmons group of Southerners, the conservative planter advocates of states' rights and lower federal taxes.[26]

But as 1928 unfolded and speculative credit kept climbing, the policies of the Federal Reserve Board, investigated by the banking subcommittee early in the year, continued to be the point of controversy. During the 1920s, Democrats publicized the Federal Reserve Act as the major achievement of the Wilson Administration; their partisan defense of it had been intensified by the violent criticism of the Reserve Board during the 1920 farm deflation.[27] It was inevitable that the 1928 Democratic convention would refer in some way to the Reserve System and its relation to speculative credit. The party of Jefferson and Jackson, like the rest of the country that year, was focusing primarily upon domestic business rather than international affairs or social welfare. In fact, John J. Raskob, the Democratic manager, was accused of trying to make Al Smith more politically attractive than Herbert Hoover to businessmen.[28] Senator Carter Glass of Virginia, the frail Lynchburg editor who liked to be remembered as the "father" of the Reserve Act, was the natural choice to labor over the Democrats' Federal Reserve plank at the convention in

26 *Ibid.*, v. 69, Pt. 8, 8276-8277.
27 *Democratic Campaign Book* (1924), 20-24.
28 Frederick Lewis Allen, *Only Yesterday* (New York, 1931), 302-303.

Houston. A true Virginia Piedmont product, Glass combined a fierce Scotch-Irish Calvinist temperament with a gracious Episcopalian constitutionalism. The result was a socially conservative critic of speculation, one who was contemptuous of the Western "Jackasses" and cautious in supporting remedies that might infringe upon states' rights. But he was outspoken, and finally drew up a plank that called for changes, and justified the criticism he had been directing toward the Board and the Coolidge Administration.[29]

The Republican insurgents also had strong opinions on the Federal Reserve question. Senator LaFollette, their leader, submitted a plank to the Republican convention that demanded that the Reserve Board check the flow of credit into the stock market. This proposal was part of the Progressive Republican platform which he put before the main body of the GOP, but the convention rejected the progressive version, and no mention of the Reserve Board was made in the platform finally adopted.[30] The phraseology of the two Federal Reserve planks—the one by Glass for the Democrats, the other by LaFollette for the Republican progressives —points up the differences that divided cautious, financial reformers of the South and East from the more radical progressives and agrarians of the dirt-farmer South and rural Midwest:

Democratic

The Federal Reserve system, created and inaugurated under Democratic auspices, is the greatest legislative contribution to constructive business ever adopted. The administration of the system for the advantage of

[29] "Has the Federal Reserve System Promoted Speculation?" *Review of Reviews,* 78:256-260 (September 28, 1928).

[30] The GOP had rejected LaFollette Progressive platforms at every convention since 1908. Nye, *Midwestern Progressive Politics,* 337.

stock market speculators should cease. It must be administered for the benefit of farmers, wage-earners, merchants, manufacturers, and others engaged in constructive business.[31]

Progressive Republican

We denounce the conversion of the Federal Reserve System into an instrument by which the nation's credit is used for the advantage of stock speculators. We favor such amendment of the Federal Reserve Act as may be necessary to ensure that the credit facilities of the system shall be used for the benefit of American farmers, merchants, manufacturers, homebuilders, and other constructive purposes.[32]

While the planks are similar, it is apparent that the Republican progressives, having less of a vested interest in the Reserve System, were more concerned with making it an instrument for economic reform, while Democratic wording stressed the role of that party in its conception, and the Democrats did not mention anything as definite as an amendment. Indeed, the plank at the Houston convention may have been a concession to Senator Glass, an elder statesman, and probably did not have the support of the Democratic party as a whole. Glass wanted to dramatize his part in passing the 1913 Act whereas run-of-the-mill Democrats had no such interest. LaFollette, on the other hand, could count on the enthusiastic support of almost two dozen of his colleagues.

As 1929 opened, the Reserve Board was still timid, still dilatory in taking action against the speculation threatening the national economic structure. Financial circles were uncertain as to the course the Board would take. The Board had not been allowed to forget the charge that it was responsible for the 1920 deflation, and

[31] *Proceedings, Democratic National Convention* (Houston, 1928), 187.

[32] *New York Times,* January 24, 1928, 3.

feared the same criticism again—from brokers instead of farmers—if it attempted any drastic curtailment of credit. Finally the Board acted; it not only raised the rediscount rate, but it sent a strong letter to each of the twelve district banks. The letter announced a policy of "direct pressure" on individual member banks to reduce their stock market loans. While admitting that the Board was not the arbiter of security speculation or stock values, the letter carefully defined the Board's responsibility in keeping Federal Reserve credit away from speculative channels.[33] The gravity of the situation had overcome any Jeffersonian fears about the threat to decentralization posed by the "direct pressure" approach. The Federal Reserve warning was well received, except among some brokerage houses in Wall Street. The *Duluth Labor World* saw the Reserve Board letter as a confirmation of the analysis Senator LaFollette had made at the time of his resolution in 1928. Because of the large portion of money being lent to brokers by "others"—private individuals and corporations—in 1929, the Duluth paper believed that the stock market had finally gone beyond the control of Federal Reserve authorities. Its remedy was extreme: a complete ban on margin purchases.[34]

The belated action of the Board also had repercussions in the Senate. J. Thomas Heflin, the sentimental Klansman with the Prince Albert coat, introduced a resolution that required specific recommendations from the Federal Reserve Board to curb speculation. The Alabaman's resolution was similar to the one LaFollette had introduced the year before. Elmer Thomas of Okla-

[33] *Wall Street Journal,* February 7, 1929.
[34] According to the *Literary Digest,* the majority of American newspapers supported editorially the Board's action. For a list of papers endorsing the action see "Can the Federal Reserve Board Check Speculation?" *Literary Digest,* 100:78-82 (February 23, 1929). *Duluth Labor World,* February 23, 1929, v. 2:6; March 9, 4:1; March 16, 4:2.

homa arose to remark that Heflin's measure was too weak; he wanted immediate action by Congress. Carter Glass at this point reminded the Senate that the Reserve Board was not charged by law with regulating stock exchange activity; its only jurisdiction was over Federal Reserve credit. On February 11, the Senate passed by voice vote the Heflin resolution, slightly amended:

> *Whereas* in press dispatches recently, the Federal Reserve Board has complained that money is being drawn from the channels of business and used for speculative purposes, and that some of said speculation is illegitimate and harmful; therefore be it
>
> *Resolved,* that the Federal Reserve Board is hereby requested to give to the Senate any information and suggestions that it feels would be helpful in securing legislation necessary to correct the evil complained of and prevent illegitimate and harmful speculation.

During the debate on the resolution, Senator Heflin shouted that Wall Street had become "the most notorious gambling centre in the universe" and "a hot-bed and breeding place of the worst form of gambling that ever cursed the country. . . . Whereas the Louisiana lottery slew its hundreds, the New York State gambling exchanges slay their hundreds of thousands."[35]

Five days later Representative Hampton Pitts Fulmer of South Carolina, later to become chairman of the House Agriculture Committee, gave full voice to the position typically taken by the Southern agrarians. Congress, he said, should move slowly in permitting boards and bureaus to interfere with private business. Powerful groups were threatening small enterprise and disregarding the laws of God, of land, and of ethics, cried Fulmer, and he condemned the duplicity of brokers who were

[35] *Congressional Record,* 70 Cong., 2 sess., v. 70, Pt. 3, 3202-3207 (February 11, 1929); *Commercial & Financial Chronicle,* 128:I:993 (February 16, 1929).

sucking the citizenry into the market. He cited in populistic fashion the increase in millionaires from 7,000 in
1914 to 40,000 in 1928, and he made a prophecy:

> It is my prediction that unless Congress does some-
> thing to regulate these speculators and gamblers, or
> some genius who has the welfare of legitimate busi-
> ness and the country at heart can bring about a re-
> adjustment in the use of credit which will turn some
> portion of it to channels where it is most needed, we
> are headed for one of the most serious economic crises
> in the history of the great Republic.[36]

The progressives by and large approved the "direct
pressure" tactics of the Reserve Board in 1929; they
lamented the fact that the Board had not acted earlier,
before credit had reached such dangerous levels, and
they could not see why the Board could not stop stock
speculators, because it had been so effective in deflat-
ing farm land inflation in 1920.[37] The strong stand of the
Board did check the expansion of brokers' loans in the
spring of 1929. But public enthusiasm was then too powerful, and gradually the markets built up immunity to
the words of the Board. When the summer began, the
old craze returned despite the warnings of government
authorities.[38]

At this point Senator William E. Borah of Idaho made
a suggestion. A strong individualist who usually found
himself in the progressive camp, Borah had not taken an
active part in the Reserve Board controversy; he had
been preoccupied with international affairs. In the June
World's Work, however, the Senator offered a familiar

[36] *Ibid.,* 3699-3700. Fulmer's colleagues did not have a high
opinion of his abilities. His appointment as chairman was regarded
as a triumph of the seniority system. Wesley McCune, *The Farm
Bloc* (Garden City, 1943), 49-50.

[37] *Ibid.,* 3205-3207.

[38] Aaron M. Sakolski, "American Speculative Manias," *Current
History,* 30:860-868 (August 1929).

solution for curbing the speculators. He proposed that American exchanges adopt the English system of settling loans fortnightly. If loans could be made to brokers only on a two-week basis instead of on call, Borah believed that many sources lending money to Wall Street would dry up—bankers would not want to commit themselves to 14- or 15-day loans in place of immediately callable obligations. The daily settlement method in use in the United States was inferior, said the Idaho Senator, because it facilitated stampedes; the two-week plan would level out many of the call rate flurries characteristic of turbulent markets and, by reducing liquidity, would diminish credit available to speculators. Senator Borah warned the exchanges to act before state legislatures or Congress acted; if the Street really feared the crudities and impetuosity of legislators, the wise course was to clean house itself. "Shall the call-money market on the daily settlement plan go on until a great world-wide smash comes, or will constructive efforts be made at the source to alleviate and cure the situation before it is too late?" The Coolidge-Hoover bull market was, after all, no exception to traditional rules; there was bound to be a period of deflation following the current one of inflation.[39]

In the same month, during a debate on tax exemptions for government securities, several Senators took the opportunity to appraise the stock market position. James Couzens of Michigan, perennial critic of Mellon tax policies, took his fellow automobile tycoon, William Crapo Durant, to task for making light of Federal Reserve Board warnings; Couzens claimed that Durant

[39] William E. Borah, "Call Money and Stock Gambling," *World's Work*, 58:33-34 (June 1929). Lawrence in *Wall Street and Washington*, 295-296, bitterly assailing Borah's plan, said that Borah had no right to ask banks of the nation to lend only for two-week periods, that the plan would not deter speculators. In addition, he accused Borah of harboring a prejudice against Wall Street that rested upon "profound substrata of dour Calvinism."

was not disinterested but had a definite interest in speculation. Couzens was also critical of the Reserve Board. The Board was "dumb," or it would have moved earlier against stock gamblers. It should have spoken frankly and openly in the beginning; there had been too much secrecy and rumor. The Federal Reserve System was organized as a protection for industry:

> I contend that the object has been largely defeated by the failure of the system itself properly to recognize its responsibilities and duties. I contend that the present situation should never have been permitted to reach its present proportions. I contend that it has cost industry, manufacturing, retail and other business, as well as farming, hundreds of millions of dollars that cannot possibly be justified under any conception of the organization of the Federal Reserve System.[40]

The grisly reckoning that the progressives had been forecasting came in October, 1929. Within a month $30 billion in stock values had been wiped out; gradually the nation was to learn that this was the forerunner of the Great Depression.

Right up to the 1929 precipice Senate progressives from the Midwest warned the public of the dangerous situation. Whereas their allies from the Southwest, the agrarians, were afraid of bureaus, boards, and administrative law, and sometimes lost their way in demagogic moralizing, the Midwesterners exercised their bent for economic analysis and led the fight to apply governmental curbs to stock market credit. True, their legislative triumphs were few and minor: a favorable committee report on the LaFollette resolution in 1928; a voice vote victory for the similar Heflin resolution a year

[40] *Congressional Record,* 71 Cong., 1 sess., v. 71, Pt. 3, 2325. Senator Couzens' general progressivism at this time is discussed in Harry Barnard, *Independent Man; the Life of James Couzens* (New York, 1958).

later; and a coalition triumph in retaining a small transfer tax. But their remedies of tighter credit control and taxation of speculative gain have since been adopted as sound. These legislators publicized as best they could the economic inequities in the nation, specifically the farm recession, exchange abuses, the draining off of funds to New York City, and the ominous rise in brokers' loans. Reiterating these facts in the national arena was their contribution.[41] The record shows that the "Sons of the Wild Jackass"—LaFollette, Couzens, Shipstead, Borah, et al.—were better oracles in the 1920s than the hucksters of false prosperity—Coolidge, Mellon, Raskob, and Durant.

[41] Cf. Theodore Saloutos, Farmer Movements in the South, 1865-1933 (Berkeley, 1960), 282ff.

CHAPTER 5

THE TWENTIES: BULLS, BEARS,

AND COMMENTATORS

I

*I*N THE twenties a number of factors combined to fan the flames of speculation. World War I had helped to secularize society, and Biblical literalism was in retreat before science; the advance of technology and of business had emphasized efficiency, facts, and statistics. After 1922 industrial production rose rapidly and prosperity increased, except in some major farm areas. Sociologists Robert and Helen Lynd found in their *Middletown* investigation a growing tendency among young, lower-class men to forego a problematic future for immediate "big money."[1]

As such influences drew more people into the stock and commodity markets and into real estate—notably, in Florida—it was natural that journalists and financial experts should reexamine American dicta regarding speculation. A typical article on this subject appeared in the *Atlantic Monthly* in 1925; it was a revaluation of the investment-speculation relationship. The frugal bondholder was portrayed as a chump, a doctrinaire who thought that to renounce the likelihood of capital gain was virtue in itself—as one who was smug enough to believe that he was avoiding the taint of speculation by buying only bonds. Bonds, it was shown, were far from immune from price and dollar fluctuations. In fact, because of shifts in the purchasing power of the dollar, a bond might fall in real value although the company's credit

[1] Robert S. and Helen M. Lynd, *Middletown: A Study in American Culture* (New York, 1929), 81.

standing remained firm. The purchase of bonds was really a speculation unless one was trying to hedge against future commitments; in effect the bondholder was betting that the bond would remain at approximately the same value and that the purchasing power of the dollar would rise. The logic of the bond purchaser seemed to be that because he was getting only 3 to 5 per cent, he was incurring no risk; actually bondholders were engaged in "risk for no gain." Having swept away the web of myth surrounding bonds, the writer addressed himself to the problem of reconciling investment with its disreputable sister, speculation. Investment, he said, was risk without hope of capital gain; speculation, on the other hand, was merely investment *with* the hope of capital gain.[2]

Clearly this brand of financial heresy would give even the sturdiest coupon-clipper pause, and it was perhaps not the best food for the neophyte investor. Albert W. Atwood, of the *Saturday Evening Post,* believed that the increased popularity of common stocks must in slight degree be ascribed to a book published in 1924, *Common Stocks as Long Term Investments,* by Edgar Lawrence Smith, author of the *Atlantic Monthly* article mentioned above. Smith demonstrated in twelve tests that bonds would have been more profitable than stocks in only one case. He felt that the only way to keep from going down was to be sure you were going up. Atwood, however, in describing Smith's views, was perhaps mindful of the pocketbooks of the "little men" who read the *Post,* for he did not subscribe wholeheartedly to the anti-bond revolt. Because of human frailty, because of the tendency to get in and out of the market at the wrong time, he advised his readers to diversify their portfolios, to buy some bonds and some stocks. Investment trusts were then new and untried; for this reason people should continue to buy some bonds. After all,

[2] Edgar Lawrence Smith, "Speculation and Investment," *Atlantic Monthly,* 136:542-547 (October 1925).

the chances of losing the whole sum were much less.[3]

The Magazine of Wall Street also took cognizance of the trend away from the conservative bond. "The rapid rise in the cost of living that was caused by the War has led investors to discover that both principal and income may shrink painfully in purchasing power, though the dollar value of both remained fixed. Huge real losses have thereby been sustained through investments which, according to all the old standards, were universally accepted as the last word in safety. . . . The tendency among modern investors is to buy not for income as of old, but for both income and profit."[4] It is difficult to say how influential any of these anti-bond outbursts were, but this type of reasoning, perhaps less formalized, was undoubtedly a prime factor in the dormancy of the bond market while stocks were in frenzied flux.

Meanwhile the orthodox justification for the speculative process was appearing in thousands of brochures, newspapers, and conservative financial organs. This point of view was summarized by Edward H. H. Simmons, president of the New York Stock Exchange, in answering a question from *The Magazine of Wall Street*: "Does speculation play any part in the determination of real security values?" Simmons replied in the affirmative. "Speculation," he said, "plays a major part in determining the real value of a given security. By means of a widespread publicity which the Stock Exchange gives to the quotations of stocks listed on its board, and the equally broad publicity which it insists shall be given corporations whose securities are listed as to their earnings and financial position, the public is afforded an opportunity to determine for itself whether or not current prices really reflect their fair values. . . . Speculation

[3] Albert W. Atwood, "Secret of Riches; Common Stocks," *Saturday Evening Post*, 200:31 (June 2, 1928).
[4] *The Magazine of Wall Street*, 41:30 (November 1927).

157

merely intervenes to adjust present prices to more or less future but seemingly probable values. Naturally such prophetic changes are only as accurate as the consensus of the most experienced and expert human opinion can make them." Speculation must have been essential, since without it the great manufacturing industries, the mining enterprises, and the huge railroad systems of the country could never have come into being. According to this theory, the speculators of the previous generation were men of vision and foresight; they had the courage of pioneers.

Simmons took special pains to distinguish speculation from gambling because the latter term had frequently been applied to the Stock Exchange by "irresponsible" critics. The resemblance was superficial, he asserted: "Speculation consists in the purchase and sale of property with the aim of making a profit between the buying and selling prices, under the inevitable risks attendent upon such an operation. Gambling, however, consists merely in the wagering of a sum of money on some future fortuitous event, having no necessary relation to the purchase or sale of property. The risks of speculation are thus the inherent risks of property ownership; those of gambling are unnecessary and artificial risks created solely for the purposes of deciding wagers of money."[5] In discussing this question, Simmons did not distinguish between the speculation of the early nineteenth century, which represented direct investment in hazardous enterprises adding to the nation's resources, and the speculation of the twentieth century, which centered on the transfer of shares and gained much of its momentum through manipulation and the lag of information between insiders and outsiders in the markets. Even after Simmons' careful exposition, there remained those who suspected that some security fluctuations

[5] *Ibid.*, 41:186ff. (January 1928).

were "unnecessary and artificial" and created solely for the purpose of making money.

John T. Flynn, the exuberant economic journalist, writing in *Harper's* at about the time of the Crash, took a much harsher view in exploring the ethics of speculation from the Roman Catholic point of view. Flynn attacked the traditional defenses of the exchange economists, accusing them of creating definitions to separate speculation from gambling merely to ease the public conscience. One such proposition was that a gambler created risk in order to bet on it, whereas a speculator simply assumed a risk incidental to some economic activity. Flynn said this distinction was false because it was not necessary to create a risk in order to gamble. If, for example, a man purchased a high-grade security for cash but with the intention of selling on a quick rise rather than relying on the growth of the enterprise, he was a gambler. It was the motive that was important, not the nature of the security nor the mode of purchase. Flynn accused the exchanges of promoting a campaign to throw a halo around gambling. The journalist went on to say that there was no inherent immorality in gambling, that Roman Catholic moralists had set out four conditions necessary to making gambling ethically defensible: (1) The gambler must be able to win without causing injury to others; (2) There must be no fraud present; (3) Free will must be operating; (4) There must be some sort of equality among participants. Flynn noted that number four was the element usually lacking in the stock markets; he did not believe that there was enough equality of knowledge to make the market ethically justifiable. He called for the gathering of statistics on various phases of exchange operation, because currently the experts were simply citing each other for corroboration. And he cynically suggested that a government commission rather than a Congressional committee should gather data, because the latter would lead to a political show.[6]

Late in the speculative craze, the moral dangers of speculation were strongly expressed. The *Christian Century* ridiculed the rationale of the "New Era."

It is the old spirit of daring, we are told, that returns today to impel Americans to speculate. But the pioneers planned and worked. Today people are shutting their eyes and letting 'er go. If this is the way to a position of recognized standing in the community, why work? Why save? What kind of society will it be that is composed of get-rich-quick, something-for-nothing citizens? Up to date, the American churches have said practically nothing on the issues raised by gambling in its postwar forms. . . . Ministers shy away from the issue. (Some of them are too deeply involved in the current craze to be in a position to speak out.) The gap between the New Testament and the mind of the man who sits in the pew wondering what Amalgamated Wireless is going to do tomorrow is too wide to be bridged by most sermons. For the sake of its own message, and for the sake of the future moral stability of society, it is time that the church was facing this issue, making up its mind what it wants to say about it, and saying it.[7]

Charles Merz in *Harper's* asked what effect the quest for sudden profits was having on the average investor's relish for the humdrum task of earning his daily bread.

There has been a breaking down . . . of certain ethical values and many household mottoes which were only recently in their prime. There was a time when, outside of certain circles in a few large cities, specu-

[6] John T. Flynn, "Speculation and Gambling," *Harper's*, 160:201-208 (January 1930).

[7] "Playing the Stock Market," *Christian Century*, 46:255 (February 21, 1929).

lation in the New York Stock Exchange was widely regarded as mere "gambling." There was also a time when a host of such maxims as "a penny saved is a penny earned" emphasized the importance of steady application and close-fisted economy, rather than the persistent playing of successive hunches, as the most promising means of self-advancement. The spectacular profits reaped by nitwits at some points in this astonishing bull market have come among these maxims with the disruptive force of science among the fables of the Bible.[8]

Lewis H. Haney, the economist turned journalist writing in the *North American Review*, advocated a return to conventional financial principles. Calling speculation investment was simply rationalization, and buying with the hope of increasing principal was pure speculation, he wrote. The tendency to consider a dividend as safe as bond interest was really a sort of escape for those who wanted to speculate. With the future as uncertain as it was in the summer of 1929, the old virtue of saving should not be discounted, Haney wrote prophetically. But apparently few people agreed.[9]

II

The progressive writers also deplored the ethical level of brokers at that time; they were accused of unscrupulous commission seeking. Writing in the *Nation*, Robert Ryan, a conscience-stricken ex-broker, observed that some brokers had taken advantage of the helplessness of the small customer, and presented factual examples. He cited a case in which his broker-partner was given an order by a customer to sell some Arabian bank stock "at the market." Such an exotic issue circulated

[8] Charles Merz, "The Bull Market," *Harper's*, 158:640-646 (April 1929).

[9] Lewis H. Haney, *et al.*, *Brokers Loans*.

only over the counter. The partner did not bother to inquire as to the current price of the stock; instead he sold the stock to another partner of the firm at $415. Had he been assiduous in pursuit of the customer's interest, he could have obtained $448, the over-the-counter price at that time. Of course, when the broker informed the customer of the sale at $415, there was little chance that the customer would know that he should have received $448; even if he had had an inkling of the current price, the broker had a multiplicity of excuses for the disparity, the chief of which would be the "at the market" order. This type of order was a sort of *carte blanche,* a perfunctory act of faith that assumed the broker would obtain the highest price possible at the moment.

Other examples involved favoritism shown by the broker to the big operator. This was done in a number of ways, Ryan claimed, and often amounted to outright dishonesty. For example, Big Customer A has learned secretly that a company whose stock he holds will pass a dividend. He tells Broker X to sell his shares at a favorable price. Broker X, always attentive to such clients, dutifully spreads the rumor in the ticker room that Y stock is ticketed for a rise, and the small traders around the ticker rush to get aboard Y stock for the anticipated rise. Meanwhile Broker X stealthily unloads Customer A's block of Y shares in the artifically high market brought on by the rumor. Ultimately, of course, when the news of the passed dividend becomes general, the price plummets, leaving the small operators "holding the bag." The small speculator, Ryan contended, "remains completely unaware of these practices. In a rising market such methods may be employed without losing the customer's business, for a speculator will overlook small irregularities as long as he continues to make money; and in a declining market when the broker gets away with an equal amount of dishonesty, the customer blames the results on market drops." Ryan then sketched the expedient philosophy of these brokers: "If a customer loses all his money, or so dislikes the actions of Mr. X's firm that he withdraws his business, Mr. X is completely unconcerned. As he remarked to me, 'Suckers are born every minute; the glamor of easy money gets them all. One goes, two come in. Win or lose, we get our commissions.' It is an easy-going philosophy which has been so completely proved true by many Wall Street brokers that they have no reason to revise it." Ryan suggested the prohibition of trading by brokers since a dual role tempted them away from allegiance to the customer's interests.[10]

In remarks intended for general circulation, the habitués of the Street were inclined to be more optimistic about prospects of profit for the little man. When John Gunther interviewed Arthur W. Cutten, the former wheat plunger from Chicago, that secretive insider was still claiming (as late as 1929) that the exchange was a fair game. "Everybody has a chance. That is everybody who isn't a fool. But a man can't expect to make money on a stock if he buys without any faintest notion of what the stock is—as many fools do. . . . The two things a man needs most to play on the market are nerve and vision." Merryle S. Rukeyser told the many readers of *Collier's* about an astute Iowa farmer who bought when he read in his country newspaper about depressed business conditions in the city. Putting away the stocks that he had purchased, he forgot about them; he subscribed to no financial organs or tip sheets. When he read in his paper of rising business conditions, the farmer sold all his holdings. "Thus he is one of the few consistently successful speculators," Rukeyser observed.[11] The moral would

[10] Robert Ryan, "Brokers and Suckers," *Nation*, 127:154-156 (August 15, 1928). See also David Salmon, *Confessions of a Customers' Man* (New York, 1932).

[11] *Time*, 14:43 (July 22, 1929); Merryle S. Rukeyser, "How to Make Money in Wall Street," *Collier's*, 78:32 (November 13, 1926).

seem to be that success in the stock market depended not so much on inside information or vast funds as on the good old American attributes of common sense, patience, and conservatism—paying for securities in cash, not trading on margin.

Some brokers argued that many of their new customers had the means and the "abdominal investiture" to hang on to a good thing in the face of fluctuation; anyway they thought the gods were on the side of the small investor, judging from market performance. Public-spirited writers labored manfully to dispel the non-trader's possible myths and prejudices. Cromwell, in 1926, deplored the fact that the exchange figured in the popular mind chiefly as the marketplace for the big investor, and stated that the exchange was not a financial octopus, but a financial center whose function the public "has never understood." Cromwell implied that there were large segments of the population who had the erroneous impression that in buying stock one had to match wits or knowledge with the exchange itself, as one played against the house at a casino. If this inference were correct, it would explain the emphasis placed by financial firms on the actual mechanics of stock market operation. Cromwell added, "Particularly does the exchange strive to facilitate the purchase of small amounts of shares, to protect the small investor and to place him on exactly the same plane as the large investor. Every effort to direct his investing power into safe and legitimate channels demands the utmost support."[12]

Thus the majority of brokers and business leaders sought to effect what looked like an impossible compromise—to admit novice traders into the market but to educate them to be investors and not speculators. Brokers always had to weigh the personal factor of huge

[12] "Bulls, Bears, and Lambs," *North American Review*, 227:28-34 (January 1929); Seymour L. Cromwell, "The Small Investor," *Outlook*, 142:250-252 (February 17, 1926).

commissions, predicated on high volume, against the social factor of inevitable panics that might threaten the
entire security business. Needless to say, in the early
years the brokers were more disposed to work for a
heavy turnover, knowing that new lambs would replace
the shorn ones. There were of course some dissenters,
who perceived the unhealthy air around the ticker tape
in 1927 and 1928. Clarence Walker Barron scolded little
market traders who tried to follow the big operators; he
thought it should be obvious that the big boys always
acted before informing the public. He advised the small
speculator to follow the known facts. This was a wiser
course than trying to follow strangers, declared the
elderly financier; it was a survival of the fittest.[13]

As speculation became more pronounced in late 1928,
many elements of differing economic and political per-
suasion felt it necessary to remind the public of its short-
comings in the market—to drive home the idea that ex-
ceptional knowledge and ability were required just to
keep one's head above water in the Street. Everyone
knows that this united front against bullish speculation
failed. But as the day of reckoning approached, writers
spoke with unaccustomed candor. One Wall Street broker estimated that 80 per cent of the people in the bull
market were lambs who made commitments without
understanding values; another 10 per cent consistently
made money; the remaining 10 per cent, although incon-
sistent, usually finished ahead. Even the magic name of
Harvard was invoked; in a study conducted by that institution, results showed that 97 per cent of the margin
players lost money, 2 per cent broke even, and 1 per
cent came away with a profit. Rukeyser accurately
summed up the prevailing situation: "Statistical demon-
strations of disappointments sustained by amateur traders are powerless to check the nationwide impulse to

[13] *Barron's*, 8:7 (June 25, 1928).

participate in prosperity without working." He added frankly, "Some marginal traders succeed for a time, but ultimately most of the lay plungers fail. They constitute the suckers who create opportunities for more analytical financiers. . . ."[14] H. I. Phillips, in a whimsical article in the *American Magazine,* found it absurd to think that "whenever the Durants and the Cuttens plan to shoot a stock up 150 points, their first step is to notify all the master barbers of America." Fortunes could not be made by amateurs.[15]

We have already seen that the idea of formally regulating speculative competence never got very far beyond the discussion stage, that it lost ground after 1923 when there was money to be made from recruiting new "investors."[16] As 1929 opened, however, important financiers, believing that the public had brought too much instability into the market, began to discriminate against small operators. As columnist Arthur Brisbane wrote, "The big people want to discourage gambling by little people."[17] The method most often chosen to achieve this was the raising of minimums, in margins and accounts. In some houses, trading on margins of less than twenty-five shares was forbidden; a minimum of $1,000 equity was required for an account, and a minimum commission of $5 was fixed. In other houses the minimum was $2,000 and margins were upped to an average of 35-50 per cent in 1929; only Curb stocks of the highest quality were carried on margin at all. There was no doubt that the "little men" had been in the market in numbers in 1928; this was apparent from the enormous increase in odd-lot trading (trading in lots of less than a hundred

[14] Merryle S. Rukeyser, "Wall Street's Speculative Optimism," *The Nation,* 127:514-516 (November 14, 1928).

[15] H. I. Phillips, "My Stock Market Operations," *American Magazine,* 107:54-55 (March 1929).

[16] See Chapter 3 above.

[17] Arthur Brisbane, "Today," *Omaha Bee-News,* June 6, 1929, 14:3.

shares). One odd-lot house, DeCoppet and Doremus, was alone responsible for 10 per cent of the day's trading. Wall Street sources reported that the higher minimums did reduce trading by small fry, as 1929 wore on.[18]

The discouragement of the small investor was expected to contribute to the curtailment of speculative credit. The *Commercial and Financial Chronicle* offered three reasons for this: (1) because small traders had been borrowing as much as they could, and were an important factor in swelling brokers' loans, the new restrictions ought to force them to reduce their credit and thereby reduce brokers' loans; (2) many small fish, prevented from trading by higher margin requirements, would probably buy securities outright and thus reduce brokers' loans also; and (3) the elimination of many of the small fry was expected to give the market a stronger technical position, that is, a market less susceptible to sharp swings in sentiment.

Some prominent businessmen finally sensed, in 1929, danger from an overenthusiastic public. Typical of this conservative business-oriented criticism was that of John Foster Dulles, Wall Street corporation lawyer and later Secretary of State. Dulles was not bound by academic traditionalism; he was a participant in the business world at one of its most sophisticated centers, yet he was cautious in his approach even when many were urging more drastic action. In April of 1929 while the market was recovering from the reaction to the Federal Reserve warning, Dulles said, "The problem . . . does not involve deciding whether or not stock prices are too high or whether brokers' loans are inherently excessive, or whether the Federal Reserve Banks have the legal power, which I do not understand they assert, to discriminate against any class as a recipient of credit. The

[18] *Commercial & Financial Chronicle,* 128:1669 (March 16, 1929); 1163 (February 23, 1929); 2010 (from *New York Times,* March 28, 1929).

problem is primarily one of psychology. A speculative mania has threatened to sweep the land. I have heard no one contend that it is healthy. . . . There is . . . the danger that our credit base cannot, under present conditions, meet potential speculative demands as well as the economic needs of the nation as a whole. . . . The past ten years exemplify a monetary policy which has adequately met our national needs and brought us unprecedented prosperity. If those who have administered that policy warn that its continuance is imperiled, it behooves all prudent men to heed."[19]

Dulles, in other words, rejected the idea of trying to dampen stock speculation by making money more plentiful, hence cheaper and less of a lure to individuals and companies that were lending on call in New York. He also doubted the legal power of the Federal Reserve Board, and did not seem to want to face directly the mounting brokers' loans. Industrialist Charles M. Schwab was bolder. Before sailing for Europe, the steel magnate told dockside reporters that he feared a stock market crash. He emphasized that because of the hordes of small traders in the market on margin, any crash would not only wipe them out but would reverberate through the economy, seriously affecting all segments of business.[20]

Paul M. Warburg, banker and an original member of the Federal Reserve Board, came out strongly against speculation and investment trusts, describing the latter as "incorporated stock pools."[21] The banker claimed the

[19] *Ibid.,* 1163-1164; 3118-3120 (May 11, 1929).

[20] *Time,* 13:56 (March 18, 1929).

[21] For a brilliant analysis of the 1929 Crash, see John Kenneth Galbraith, *The Great Crash, 1929* (New York, 1955), and for the role of investment trusts in fanning the flames of speculation, see especially Chapter IV entitled "In Goldman, Sachs We Trust." See also George Soule, *Prosperity Decade,* 298-300. Investment trusts mushroomed belatedly in the United States in 1927-1929 to meet the alleged scarcity of stocks on the market. The trusts were supposed to enable "the little fellow" to diversify his portfolio

Federal Reserve Board had lost control of the money situation by failure to take decisive action before inflation reached such proportions, and said that no central banking system should permit expansion unless it could also stop it. Warburg, however, was inclined to blame structural defects in the system rather than the Board itself. A hundred and twenty men on twelve district bank boards were too widely separated in opinion and too bewildered by political influences to adhere vigorously to a common policy. But Warburg's statement did not annoy the speculators, who were inclined to take it as an admission that they controlled the situation. In his monumental study of the Federal Reserve System published in 1930, Warburg analyzed the situation in more detail. The conservatives, he wrote, opposed the disciples of the "New Era"; they agreed with the Reserve Board's views—bravely expressed in the beginning, but later strangely muted—that the loan pyramid on the stock exchange constituted an element of grave danger. But they were disheartened or alarmed at the Board's apparent unwillingness or inability to bring the ominous runaway movement to a halt.[22]

III

Despite these warnings, the majority of magazines re-

---

somewhat in the manner that the "big fellow" was supposed to do. Thus "the little fellow" bought the securities of non-operating companies that traded in many and varied stocks. He expected that the company would pass along to him the dividends and capital gains that accrued from this diversified holding, less of course the expenses of management and financial counsel. Usually the managerial charges were high and the shares of these investment companies were overpriced because of the 1920s' tendency to overrate managerial and financial expertise. But these companies did make it possible for the small investor to have an interest, albeit indirect, in more companies than would otherwise be possible, considering his modest means.

[22] Paul Moritz Warburg, *The Federal Reserve System; Its Origin and Growth, Reflections and Recollections* (New York, 1930), I, 508.

flected optimism about the financial future, even in 1929. Although some articles alluded to the ineptness of the amateur or to the unusually high price-earnings ratios, they probably left the reader with no hint of impending panic. The mild wrist-slapping aimed at speculative abuses was canceled out by talk of prosperity, efficiency, and "the constructive forces" behind the stock market fever.[23]

But veteran *Saturday Evening Post* writers Edwin S. Lefevre and Albert W. Atwood were not infected with the "New Era" virus. Drawing on their years of experience in the Street, they gave the thoughtful among their readers definite reason for uneasiness. In January of 1929 Atwood carefully examined the pathology of the market. Recent buying, he said, was not based on reasoning but simply on the fact that prices had risen; a rise led the public to expect more and more returns. The public was blind to think that a 25-30 point rise in a stock in one year could be justified by a 1-5 per cent increase in earnings. Whereas the current level of prices might be justified by five years of continuous growth, most of the purchasers expected to hold their stock for only a few months. Excessive anticipation of growth and earnings, said Atwood, always led to depression and unemployment, and he recalled 1901 and 1905-1906; in those years also the public had been infected with a "New Era" psychology, only to be jarred back to reality later.[24]

Edwin Lefevre struck the same note. He wandered through the Street to sample the temper of the crowd, and found that customers were ignoring their brokers' advice to sell out, that they were more interested in what the big boys were doing than in reports of com-

[23] These observations are based primarily on twenty-seven signed articles that appeared in ten magazines during 1929. Articles from the *Saturday Evening Post* are treated separately.

[24] Albert W. Atwood, "The Great Bull Market," *Saturday Evening Post*, 201:6-7 (January 12, 1929).

pany earnings. The psychology, he thought, was the same as in past booms, despite greater volume and many technical improvements in the exchange apparatus. Lefevre interviewed an aging banker who deplored the substitution of banker- for owner-control, and scored speculators who persisted in buying into these companies anyway. He reported the advice of two foreign businessmen, a Swiss and a German, who claimed American prosperity was wasteful and inflated; they were withdrawing their money and returning to Europe. The banker believed that the American people were disregarding 5,000 years of history by following the leadership of privates rather than that of generals in the market, and he said that all the warning signals anyone could ask for were present.[25]

Thus these writers, who were active in Wall Street circles for many years, underlined the repetitive cycles that seemed to be inherent in market behavior and psychology, and deduced that the market balloon would soon burst. They did not say when, but they assumed that the bigger the balloon the more disastrous would be its collapse; and they did not exhort their readers directly, but constantly called attention to the danger signals. Aside from the *Post,* the *New Republic* and *Forbes Magazine* were among the very few that consistently warned against economic conditions. The *New Republic,* an "egghead" publication with a small circulation, hammered away at the thesis that an income distribution curve increasingly askew was concentrating money in the upper brackets and dampening consumer purchasing power, thus leading to overproduction. Other writers for this magazine warned of economic doom, and prophesied that the big fellows would leave the little ones holding the bag. Advertising was egging the public

[25] Edwin S. Lefevre, "With the Blue Chips this Time," *Saturday Evening Post,* 201:3-4 (February 2, 1929), and "Bulls on America," 201:25 (February 16, 1929).

on beyond its depth; brokers' loans indicated the precarious state of our economy; disaster could come at any time.[26]

Early in 1928 B. C. Forbes, the epigrammatic editor of *Forbes Magazine*, also began to issue dire warnings, siding with the Federal Reserve Board against the speculators. Throughout the year he called attention in his editorials to the widening gap between earnings and stock prices, and other *Forbes'* writers echoed his sentiments. In April Robert W. Schabacker suggested switching from stocks to bonds and cash; a bull market, he said, ignored all warnings, but not forever.[27] Forbes himself was inclined to stress credit conditions. There was no "New Era" in credit, he wrote, and the current bull leaders like William C. Durant and John J. Raskob were market novices, men who had experienced meteoric rises in industry, but were ignorant of stock market history. In the fall *Forbes Magazine* bore down hard on the influx of "bootleg" money. Merryle S. Rukeyser had claimed in an article entitled "Are Bootleg Loans a Menace?" that small bankers and traders, ignorant of central banking functions and responsibilities, were fomenting unwarranted feeling against the Federal Reserve Board. Forbes carried this theme further in his editorials, suggesting that borrowers as well as lenders had social responsibilities. At the end of 1928 he noted that Wall Street was more conservative than its patrons, that the big pool operators were not from the Street. If a crash came, he said, blame should rest elsewhere.[28]

[26] "Great American Lottery," *New Republic,* 54:206-208 (April 4, 1928); "Paying for Wall Street's Joy Ride," 55:293-294 (August 8, 1928); "Four Wheel Brakes on Speculation," 58:4-5 (February 20, 1929).

[27] *Forbes Magazine,* 21:21 (March 1, 1928); 21:28 (April 1, 1928); 21:11 (April 15, 1928); 22:29 (August 1, 1928); 21:13 (May 1, 1928).

[28] *Ibid.,* 22:15 (September 12, 1928); 22:28 (December 15, 1928). Bootleg money, or bootleg loans, were loans made to stock-

As 1929 opened, Forbes forecast a collapse during the year, a collapse so serious that it would have an adverse effect on all business. Deploring the gambling spirit rampant in the markets, he again endorsed the Reserve Board's restrictive measures. Stocks, he said, were too high, and money was too high.[29] In June, when President Simmons of the New York Stock Exchange made a bullish pronouncement, Forbes was angered. He called it an act of "irresponsibility," for he had been maintaining that only non-Streeters were foolish enough to lure the quotations higher. As the year went on, he continued to forecast disaster, and on October 15th he charged that high speculative money rates were thwarting new construction. Merryle S. Rukeyser followed the *Forbes* line, reminding readers that the Federal Reserve Board should not be made the goat for a collapse; the Reserve System, the result of political compromise, was built not for leadership but for checks and balances. The Board, by pursuing a tight money policy and using "moral suasion," had done everything it could do. After the Crash, Forbes reprinted many of his editorials to emphasize his prescience. Over $1 billion of bootleg loans were called during the week of October 30th; thus he could claim that his forecast about the instability of outside loans had proved accurate. While he had not predicted the day of the debacle, almost all of his writings were relevant to what actually took place in the fall of 1929.[30]

Organized labor did not follow market developments

---

brokers by private corporations or individuals, rather than banking institutions. It was generally conceded that the lenders in such transactions were less "responsible" and less well-informed financially.

[29] *Ibid.*, 23:11 (January 15, 1929).

[30] Merryle S. Rukeyser, "Which are Abler, the Federal Reserve Board or Big Bankers?" *Forbes,* 23:20 (June 1, 1929); 24:11 (December 15, 1929).

so closely as did the magazines discussed above; like the general public it became aroused only during periods of excessive activity, and representatives of labor never testified at any of the many Congressional hearings regarding stock and commodity market practices. The *American Federationist*, organ of the American Federation of Labor, had surprisingly little material on the 1929 Crash and its prelude. In an article entitled "Overproduction and Business Depression," Elmer Wood disparaged the notion that there was a dangerous gap developing between profits and consumers' incomes which would lead to overproduction, and ascribed this fear of excessive output to both conservative businessmen and radical socialists. A gap could not occur, he theorized, because there would be a new adjustment whereby more capital per worker would be used; business depressions were caused by maladjustment of factors, not by a generally excessive output. Thus the *Federationist* seemed to endorse the narrow interpretation of neoclassical economics.

But the labor paper wholeheartedly supported the Federal Reserve Board's 1929 warning. It claimed that the construction industry was showing the effects of money diverted to the stock market, that farmers were having trouble getting fertilizer credit, and reminded its readers that labor was particularly interested in seeing that speculative credit did not undermine business stability. After the Crash, the *Federationist* commented on the large increase in incomes over $5,000 reported by the Treasury Department, and attributed it to speculative profits made on the exchanges. It noted that the total amount of wages in manufacturing and railroading was less in 1929 than in 1928. After quoting New York Stock Exchange President Simmons to the effect that the Crash was brought on by excess of capital (and consequent over-financing), the *Federationist* suggested that this condition be alleviated through the payment of higher wages.[31]

Labor, the publication of the railway brotherhoods and affiliated unions, had somewhat more to say about economic conditions and speculation. It reported Senator Smith W. Brookhart's prediction that an economic explosion was in the offing if present methods were continued, and also noted that the progressives were interested in curbing speculation; it suggested that their chief motive was to deprive a handful of men of the power to mark stocks up and down. The paper seemed to approve the anti-speculation warning of the Reserve Board, but several weeks later it published an editorial criticizing the Board as "Our Financial Autocracy," and by April, *Labor* admitted there had been no abiding result from the F.R.B. warnings. The paper also quoted with approval the *Wall Street Journal's* criticism of the secrecy of the Reserve Board in determining its policies. Thus organized labor was torn by the same ambivalence that divided members of Congress; it wanted the speculators stopped but feared the power of a banker-dominated administrative body like the Federal Reserve Board.

During the summer of 1929 *Labor* warned of the growing disparity of income between wage-earners and speculators and, unlike the *Federationist,* maintained that this would mean overproduction and depression since prosperity depended ultimately on mass purchasing power. The exchanges were no more than crooked gambling houses. In August the union organ hoped that the smash of Insull stocks would destroy the popularity of the customer stock-ownership plans which many utility companies had instigated. As for the Crash itself, *Labor* rea-

---

[31] Elmer Wood, "Overproduction and Business Depression," *American Federationist,* 36:I:65-71 (January 1929); "Excessive Stock Speculation a Menace," 36:I:534ff. (May 1929); *ibid.,* 37:I: 339-340 (March 1930).

soned that the small investors were wiped out, but that margins averaging 35 per cent cushioned the return to economic realities. *Labor* particularly resented the action of the New York bankers who stepped in to mitigate the liquidation which had come in the wake of the Reserve Board warning. Somehow the Federal Reserve System had failed to transfer control from Wall Street to Washington, as its framers had hoped it would.[32]

The more radical *Industrial Worker*, in which Marxists Lewis Corey and Scott Nearing occasionally had articles reprinted, was published by the Industrial Workers of the World, and advanced the income disparity thesis more persistently and vehemently. Like the other labor papers, however, it seldom dealt specifically with the speculative markets. The line—on the whole an accurate one at the time—was that in 1928 the nation had stopped advancing industrially, although advertising-minded newspapers were concealing this fact by playing up prosperity. True prosperity did not depend on inflation; the discrepancy between mass purchasing power and big incomes caused speculation. Because the I.W.W. (more commonly known as the Wobblies) was composed largely of Western miners, lumberjacks, long-shoremen, and migratory workers, their paper devoted much space to the problem of unemployment, especially technological unemployment. Since they were working for ultimate abolition of the wage system, they naturally opposed the employee stock-ownership plans because they undermined the workers' class-consciousness. The Wobblies interpreted these plans as sops designed to spur the workers into speeding up production.

Organized labor lost ground in America after LaFollette's defeat in 1924, so its warning voice was much less powerful than even the pronouncements of Midwest progressives. The extreme radical view, expressed by

[32] *Labor*, February 16, 1929, 3:2; April 13, 3:1; March 2, 4:1-2.

the *Industrial Worker,* apparently did not extend beyond a tiny fraction of the working class, and the labor
papers as a whole did not deal with market topics with
enough familiarity to convince non-union readers.[33] The
struggle for public opinion was between the anti-Wall
Street South and Midwest on one hand, and the urban
East and its enclaves in the Midwest, the Rockies, and
on the Pacific Coast on the other. Organized labor did
not have an important voice in it, and few suggestions
for reform came from that quarter.

The soundest market advice came neither from Wall
Street brokers nor from agrarian or labor malcontents;
it came from those persons, familiar with the markets
and the thinking of traders, who nonetheless retained
some detachment. Inevitably writers in organs like the
Wall Street Journal or *Barron's* were drawn, in times of
crisis and controversy, to a defense of Wall Street against
outsiders; this was a natural group loyalty. Their advice
therefore was apt to be partisan at the wrong times.
Similarly, dedicated agrarians or laborites were unreliable because they were chronically alarmist, and their
fund of practical information about the Street was
usually inadequate. The best advice—and this could be
an endorsement of government by experts—came from
men who knew the Street but were not of it, men whose
functions as reporters or analysts were more important
than their ties with the Street.

IV

Just how wide was the participation in speculative
trading in stocks in the months before the 1929 Crash?
The literature of the time conveys the impression that
"everybody" was following the ticker with an eager eye.
"This has been a children's crusade, not an adventure for
a few hard-boiled knights; and no historian of the years

[33] *Industrial Worker,* June 8, 1929, 3:1. The *Industrial Worker*
staff estimated its circulation at 5000 to 6000. March 26, 1927, 2:1.

1924 to 1929 can afford to ignore the evidence that the butcher, the baker, and the candlestick maker have been in this market on an unprecedented scale."

The democratic glow evoked by the market debut of the little man warmed many writers to the point of scribbling optimistic generalizations. They hailed the small investor as the backbone of America; they told him that he was the stabilizing influence the market needed, and that, if he were to invest prudently, the old treacherous volatility of the security markets would disappear. Furthermore, the influx of small savings was a democratizing and homogenizing force. "When the country follows the same tips, finds comfort in the same reassuring signs that normalcy is here to stay . . . we know . . . that this is a united people." The commentators, in the following typical quotations, also noted that the market lure was typically American. "The market has fitted perfectly into the interests of a highly mathematical nation which can really give its heart to no sport which cannot be tallied in batting averages . . . strokes per hole, or stolen bases. Every night the American public knows precisely where it stands in this contest. . . . Down to the last eighth the ticker posts the winners and losers."[34] "Millions of the population, who formerly were indifferent to stock market fluctuations, now eagerly scan the quotations. . . ." "It is the universal testimony of stockbrokers that their orders now come from everywhere and all sorts of people." "Statistics do not portray the psychology of an imaginative nation. And it is in the emotions of a rich people, exploring the mysteries for the first time, that we must look to find the secret behind the romantic bull movement in stocks that has shattered all world's records. . . ."[35] The *St. Louis*

[34] Merz, "The Bull Market." For the reaction of the Duluth Labor World see ch. 4 above.

[35] Aaron M. Sakolski, "American Speculative Manias"; *Current History*, 30:860-868 (August 1929), "Playing the Stock Market,"

Globe-Democrat noted that the people had become market-minded, that interest in the market was greater than any other news on page one. The tendency of the newspapers to give the market close prominent display on the front page was eloquent testimony of widespread interest, since editors were sensitive to the demands of readers. And the *Globe-Democrat* hypothesized a cautious average reader; he gave his most attentive perusal to the less active issues, to the ones "little regarded by speculators and organizers of pools."[36]

Seymour L. Cromwell, ex-president of the New York Stock Exchange, writing in 1926 when the speculative blister on the body economic had only begun to swell, proclaimed the universality of prosperity. In the pages of the *Outlook* he presented various statistics illustrating the broad and democratic base of capitalistic enterprise. Cromwell admitted that prior to World War I only a few hundred thousand people were investors, but the Liberty Bonds, he argued in conventional fashion, had accustomed great numbers to the advantages of securities. In 1917 only 9.5 per cent of income in the $1,000–$5,000 income group came from stock dividends; the same group received 22.7 per cent of such income in 1921, according to Cromwell's figures. After that date the per cent accruing to those who earned under $5,000 was increasing, while the proportion going to those in the $20,000 and up category was decreasing. In 1926 over 50 per cent of the New York Central Railroad's stockholders were employees; on the Pennsylvania the figure was 25 per cent, and the number of shareholders in the fabled American Telephone and Telegraph had increased 600 per cent since 1913. Cromwell thought that these facts, combined with employee stock plans,

Christian Century; "Forces Behind the Fever," *Outlook*, 150:1391-1392 (December 26, 1928).
[36] *St. Louis Globe-Democrat*, August 10, 1929, 14:2.

removed any worry about infiltration of radical doctrines into the working classes. Still he did not allow himself to be completely carried away by this idyll of brotherly profit for he added soberly, "It would be going too far to draw a Utopian picture of all American industry entirely owned by the workers."

Most writers viewed the employee stock-ownership plans as exceedingly beneficial. For one thing this "wise policy" would prevent the United States from developing a "caste system like England's." Only through equities could labor share in the profits: his few shares of stock would bind each workman to the capitalistic system and would bolster the American competitive structure. "In other words it is more important for a machinist in an automobile plant in Michigan to get a few shares of stock which, through appreciation, may pension him when he becomes old, than it is for him to fight for seventy instead of sixty cents an hour in wages."[37] Thus Atwood, for example, sensed the workers' drive for security but not the method by which it was finally to be achieved.[38]

While press agents of democracy and prosperity hailed the arrival of the small operator as a unifying influence, there were many close to the Street who questioned his sagacity. Robert Ryan, in the *Nation,* looked back over months of tidal activity in the market and voiced his skepticism: "These amateurs were not schooled in markets that had seen stringent, panicky drops in prices. They came in on a rising tide. They speculated on tips, on hunches, on 'follow-the-leader' principles. . . . They would sell or buy on the slightest notice, usually obeying implicitly the advice of their broker." Chester T. Cromwell, another financial writer, went further; he charged that the influx of novices, far

[37] Seymour L. Cromwell, "The Small Investor," *Outlook,* 142: 250-252 (February 17, 1926).
[38] Atwood, "The Great Bull Market."

from exerting a unifying influence, was giving the exchange a bad name among certain classes, and in some regions was even giving rise to cries for government control. Most objectionable features of the exchange had arisen with the growth of the gambling public. "The small investors seldom enter the market in numbers until stocks are on the upgrade, frequently not until the tail end of the rise, when the reaction is about to set in. The shorn lamb then blames the brokers for his own error of judgment." Small fry could not learn to act independently; there was a heavy turnover of customers, and "the average amateur lasts only as long as the bull market."[39]

There were, of course, a few dissenters from the dictum that everyone from bootblack to banker was augmenting his income in the stock market. One of them, Lewis Corey, writing in the *New Republic*, adopted a viewpoint that was to gain more adherents in the dismal years after 1929. He said the belief that millions from all walks of life were making speculative profits was "surprisingly pervasive, another proof of the myth-making power of the press-agents of prosperity." The number of shares traded, so frequently a cause for exultation on the Street, was not, according to Corey, a reliable index of stock dispersion. "Speculation, unlike the lottery, is not mass gambling, the price being still beyond the reach of most of the American people." To substantiate his claim that speculative profits were going to the few, Corey presented the following table:

DISTRIBUTION OF PROFITS AMONG INCOME GROUPS

Income Group	Amount	Per Cent
Below $3000	$1,033,393,449	7.1
$3000-10,000	3,837,552,168	26.3
Over $10,000	9,702,466,414	66.6

[39] Robert Ryan, "Brokers and Suckers"; Chester T. Cromwell, "What the Stock Exchange Really Does," *Outlook*, 148:659-661 (April 25, 1928).

The amounts listed are "profits from sale of real estate, stocks, bonds, and net capital gains." Thus 94 per cent of the employed got only 7.1 per cent of the profits, and speculators were "overwhelmingly of the upper middle-class and the very rich." Corey accused the wealthy of using their influence to impede reformist efforts to curb speculation. Nor was prosperity itself uniformly dispersed. "The frenzied speculation prevailing since 1925 coincides with a relative decline of prosperity measured in terms of the production and mass consumption of goods." Production and distribution, relative to the increased population and increased exports, had been standing still since 1923. Corey's thesis was that frantic speculation was further concentrating the wealth, that speculative profits accrued to the rich few, giving an aura of prosperity beneath which the economy was stagnating.[40]

How reconcile the statistics of Corey with the voluminous testimony in such magazines as the *Saturday Evening Post,* the *Atlantic Monthly,* and the *Literary Digest,* all referring to the widespread participation of the public? Was the little man speculating in the market or not? There seem to be three possible answers to this question. The first answer is no—that only the upper middle class and the rich were in the market: this was the Corey hypothesis. But is it reasonable that a man with a $25,000–$50,000 annual income would buy large blocks of risky utility or railroad stocks on 50 per cent margin? Would a man of such means want to take such a chance? True, a few insiders seeking control or mani-

[40] Source: Bureau of Internal Revenue as given by Corey. Lewis Corey, "Who Gains by Speculation?" *New Republic,* 58:247 (April 17, 1929). See Theodore Draper, *The Roots of American Communism* (New York, 1957), 61-62, and 295-299 for Corey's Marxism and relation to the early Communist party in the United States. In his later years Corey became a vigorous anti-Communist and even retreated from his Marxist economics. His real name was Louis C. Fraina.

pulation of a company might wish to do so, but for investment purposes the rich man usually seeks safe, low-yield, tax-exempt bonds or at least promising "blue chips" for the major portion of his funds. Actually 1916 was the peak of the domination of corporation stock by the rich; by 1921 this group owned a much smaller proportion of all corporate stocks than they had five years before, because rich men had switched to tax-exempt securities. From 1921 to 1927 their proportion was fairly constant.

A second possibility was that stock trading was confined to the middle and lower classes. This hypothesis cannot be entertained seriously. All large industrialists were inclined to hold some stock, especially in their own firms, and market operations by these insiders were closely followed. On the other hand, there were 806,068 employee stockholders in 1928, largely the result of campaigns conducted in the mid-twenties when the market for stock among the rich was drying up. It should not be inferred, however, that all of these employee stockholders were speculators. The number of the latter was undoubtedly small, for all employees together owned less than one per cent of the stock outstanding in the United States. It seems probable, however, in view of the little man's well-known penchant for directing his investment toward familiar, tangible products, that astute workers in such fields as the automotive industry did buy some stock in their employers' companies. Prior to 1929, when automobile shares began to lag behind the market, sizable profits could have been registered in most of the major automobile stocks.[41]

[41] Gardiner C. Means, "Diffusion of Stock Ownership in the United States," *Quarterly Journal of Economics*, 44:568-575 (August 1930). For every $100 invested on January 2, 1923, the following return could have been obtained on July 1, 1928, including market value plus dividends: Chrysler, $1,997; General Motors, $1,034; Packard, $1,002; Nash, $939; Hudson, $469; Studebaker, $200. *Time*, 12:28 (July 2, 1928).

The third possibility is a special synthesis of the first two and is, therefore, the most probable: that the great body of market traders was composed of wealthy insiders, upper middle-class dilettantes, and the lower-class elements of "little" men and women who came into contact with the preceding groups. This last category would include chauffeurs, barbers, office clerks, maids, secretaries, waitresses, taxi drivers, bellhops—yes, and bootblacks—in short, those who, by the nature of their work, encountered the persons who had interest in and knowledge of security markets. This group, of course, was small and was concentrated in the more important financial centers—New York, Philadelphia, Chicago, Boston, San Francisco, and Cleveland. Even these financial foci harbored large numbers of factory workers and petty tradesmen who never met those who might stimulate their speculative itch. A possible exception were the employees who held and occasionally speculated in the stocks of their employers; employee ownership plans were confined, however, to the larger concerns and these discouraged their workers from selling the stock. Thus the much-publicized little men probably were in reality members of a special class who performed services for those who were active in the market.[42] If this third hypothesis is, indeed, the correct one, the selection of the bootblack as the symbol of the little man in the market was unfortunate; it led to seemingly contradictory testimony by those who deemed it essential to claim that he was either in or out of the financial swim. Confusion is dispelled if one considers the bootblack as a member of the special class described above; the many anecdotes of columnists and people on the Street gain new authenticity, for it seems only logical that they should have

[42] A list of occupations of those trading in the Chicago Board of Trade in 1934 supports this general hypothesis about market dilettantes. *Congressional Record*, 74 Cong., 2 sess., v. 80, Pt. 8, 8289-8292. See also Barnard, "Ladies of the Ticker."

received the impression that "everybody" was following the market when it was true of the lower economic group with which they came into contact. If the share-cropper had been chosen to exemplify the small investor in the market, the controversy would have been obviously absurd.

Assuming that the small operator was in the market, just how successful was he? Did he profit in a moderate way from the great circus, or was the exchange really siphoning off the savings of lesser folk into the pockets of a few insiders? Contemporary answers to this question were colored for various reasons. The political left, of course, was committed beforehand, as it was on virtually all questions; it viewed the stock exchange as an ingenious mechanism through which a cabal with superior knowledge and animal cunning was enriching itself at the expense of the people. Thorstein Veblen's dichotomy of financier and industrialist lent itself well to the sequence of events in these years. The political right, on the other hand, had aristocratic reservations and a paternal attitude; it did not want to go far in democratizing the market because it feared the excesses of the populace. This was evidenced by refusal to accept female accounts, by discriminatory charges, and by a high minimum on the amount invested—also by public pronouncements against "bootleg" loans—all actions aimed at discouraging the dabbler in stock margins.[43] These cautious gentlemen felt that the delicate market mechanism was safer when confined to the "strong hands" of old timers who understood economic concepts, could withstand reverses, and would not rock the speculative boat. Thus quite early in the story the familiar alliance of right and left was found working to halt the tide of speculation. Nor was this merely an American phenomenon; in France the same antipodal cooperation occurred. Spokesmen for the

[43] *Commercial & Financial Chronicle,* 128:I:1669 (March 16, 1929) from the *New York Times* of March 10.

two positions, operating from different value systems, attempted to convince the public that it could not win —the right wing implied that ignorance was the handicap, the left wing that it was the nature of the structure which made conspiratorial activity inevitable. Until late in 1928, however, these were small voices.

V

The notion that the Federal Reserve System had made panics impossible was held by a large number of Americans in the 1920s, on the theory that previous panics had resulted from credit stringency, and the malevolence of large bankers and speculators. The Federal Reserve System, it was believed, was so constructed as to prevent artificial or selfish manipulation of credit. Elastic currency and credit enabled the System to roll with the punch—to accommodate itself to the vagaries of public psychology. The current and modern method of hand-to-mouth purchasing—buying only as needed with a minimum of inventory—was believed to be another factor militating against panic, for there ought to be less anxiety with less capital tied up in inventory. In the words of Theodore M. Knappen of *The Magazine of Wall Street*, "having survived such a period of stress and strain as that of 1920-21, we are justified in having great confidence that our financial system will be equal to any trial the future may have in store." This magazine ran a poll to check such assumptions about the Federal Reserve System, and leaders of business opinion answered the question, "Is it possible to have future panics comparable to those of 1893 and 1907?"[44] While it is hazardous to draw any conclusions from so tiny a sample, it is interesting to note the greater skepticism among editors and publishers. Could it be that journalists, off the re-

[44] Theodore M. Knappen, "The Answer of the American Business World to a Vital Question," *Magazine of Wall Street*, 41:100-102 (November 19, 1927). These are the replies to the questionnaires.

cord, were inclined to be more objective and better informed than businessmen?

Secretary of the Treasury Andrew W. Mellon, the Pittsburgh aluminum millionaire, had been called the "second Alexander Hamilton," and in some respects this was apt. Mellon was guided by the immediate fiscal demands of the situation, and never explored the social ramifications of the plans he advocated. Like his chief, President Coolidge, he ran his department as he would run his own business: as frugally as possible. It was rumored in the spring of 1929 that Mellon opposed the raising of the rediscount rate because the bull market was evidence of Republican prosperity, but also because raising the rate would make more difficult the flotation of Treasury loans. This narrowness of vision on the part of the Treasury secretary caused speculators to believe that they had "a friend in high places," and Mellon, by tax reductions to the wealthy, fostered optimism in that quarter; he and President Coolidge made encouraging statements whenever it seemed that the frenzied speculation might abate. They showed no fear of a crash or recession. Earlier, from his summer home in Quebec, Chief Justice William Howard Taft had announced that while he sympathized with losers in the market, "it was nice to have so much idle money around."[45]

Ex-Senator Robert Latham Owen also abetted the "stand pat" cause. Owen, with Carter Glass, had steered the original Federal Reserve Act through Congress in 1913, and had sponsored the stock exchange regulation

	Impossible	Possible, but not probable	Possible, but not improbable
Bankers	17	10	5
Business & Industry	11	8	1
Contractors & Builders	4	4	1
Editors & Publishers	9	4	5
Merchants	13	5	3

[45] *Time Magazine,* 13:56 (March 18, 1929); 12:14 (July 9, 1928).

bill in 1914, but now he was harsh in his criticism of the Reserve Board's efforts to thwart stock speculation. In an article entitled "How Far Can the Federal Reserve Go?" the ex-Senator from Oklahoma listed what he considered the legitimate duties of the Board; they did not include the right to check speculation. "No bank has any question of getting all the money it requires, so that a bank panic or money panic, as such, has been made impossible by the Federal Reserve Act." Owen was evidently still thinking in terms of 1913, when the main fear had been of a "money trust" that might cause a credit stringency at crucial times; now, however, the problem was an oversupply of credit to the wrong people for the wrong purposes. Did the framers of the Reserve Act really intend to protect the System against overspeculation as well as currency shortage? Glass said yes; Owen said no.

The idea that brokers' loans were absorbing credit needed by business was a misconception, according to Owen. He argued that the Reserve rate of 5 per cent, raised deliberately to check the speculators, was making it unprofitable for member banks to make regular commercial loans at 6 per cent. In other words, in getting at the speculators, the Reserve Board was blocking the channels of credit and threatening to bring about a business slump by depriving private industry of cheap loans. Owen went on, "Brokers' loans are an unavoidable part of the agency of the Stock Exchange through which the commercial and industrial companies get money for the nation's business by selling their stocks and bonds. They are an indispensable agency for supplying credit." They were so safe that they could be made eligible for rediscount by the Reserve Banks.[46] When the Reserve Board attempted to exert "moral suasion" to curtail speculative

[46] Robert L. Owen, "How Far Can the Federal Reserve Go?" *The Magazine of Wall Street*, 44:20 (May 4, 1929). For a conservative account of the Federal Reserve Board's effort to check stock speculation in the spring of 1929, primarily by "moral sua-

loans by member banks, Owen was irate. The Board, he said, could not make public policy. "Speculative buying and selling has existed since the foundation of this government and *is* in accord with public policy."[47] Owen, like Mellon and Coolidge, concentrating on legal phrases and banking procedure, could not see the forest for the trees. There were many others who took a laissez-faire attitude toward the stock market. Theodore H. Gammack concluded, after examining all positions, that interference with delicate central banking operations by Congressmen would be a "disaster." *Barron's Magazine* scoffed at the notion that bootleg loans constituted a threat to market stability—bankers could easily replace the funds even if all the call loans were called at once. The Reserve Board should use its powers to improve the public's investment skills; such paternalism would be acceptable.[48]

Louis T. McFadden, of Pennsylvania, Chairman of the House Banking Committee, opposed the "moral suasion" efforts of the Reserve Board. If the market must boil over, let it; threats seemed to be unavailing, said McFadden, and if business indexes should turn down, money rates should be liberalized to encourage investment, even if this meant encouraging stock speculation. Business comes first; too much attention has been paid to the stock market.[49] Congressman James O'Conner of Louisiana phrased the standpat position in more florid terms. He declared that "the world could not afford . . .

---

sion," see Seymour E. Harris, *Twenty Years of Federal Reserve Policy* (Cambridge, Mass., 1933), I, 201-214, and II, 539-551.

[47] *Commercial & Financial Chronicle*, 128:II:3443 (May 25, 1929).

[48] Theodore H. Gammack, "Look Out for Congress," *Outlook*, 151:346 (February 27, 1929); *Barron's*, April 22, 1929, 9:26; Seth Axley, "Are Brokers' Loans a Menace?" *ibid.*, May 20, 1929, 9:3.

[49] *Congressional Record*, 70 Cong., 2 sess., v. 71, Pt. 3, 3018 (February 7, 1929). After the 1929 Crash, McFadden blamed the House of Morgan.

to stem that wonderful tide which has made for a development of natural resources and opulent growth of a stupendous civilization paling into insignificance the glory that was of Greece, the grandeur that was of Rome. . . . As a result of education which is constantly making progress among all the people, soon or late strength of character will come that will protect . . . people from playing the part of fools that rush in where angels fear to tread."[50] The most important pro-speculator argument was advanced, appropriately enough, by the Senator from New York, Royal S. Copeland. He argued that the high capital gains tax caused many investors to postpone selling their securities, and thus led to a shortage of money for business purposes. Copeland's solution was a reduction in the capital gains tax. The New Yorker admitted the concentration of money in speculation, but claimed he had not heard of any other plan for disbursing it.[51]

When standpatters in the banking and business world in the East were seriously challenged concerning the trend of events, they could always fall back upon the incompetence of Western bankers. If the banking system was in trouble, they asserted it was due to the great excess of small, inexperienced banking institutions in the Great Plains region. Easterners had been working consistently during the decade for the enlargement of the national banking system by the establishment of branches, but they had been thwarted by legislators from the Midwest and the hill-country South; the Mc-Fadden branch banking measure had languished for two years in Congress before a greatly modified version was finally passed in 1927.[52] Eastern bankers asserted

[50] *Ibid.*, v. 70, Pt. 3, 3348-3350.
[51] *Ibid.*, v. 71, Pt. 3, 2321.
[52] Chapman and Westerfield, *Branch Banking*, 105-109. The McFadden Act provided for limited expansion of national bank branches outside of city limits and these concessions were achieved largely by trading votes for the McNary-Haugen bill.

that if there were any shortage of credit in the Midwest, it was because of improper banking methods; they refused to accept any relation between Midwest agricultural credit shortage and the climbing stock market.

Whether Eastern or Midwest bankers contributed more to the Crash is a question that cannot be answered conclusively. But loans to Wall Street by New York banks for their own accounts reached their peak on January 2nd, 1929; they declined to a low for the year on May 29th, and recovered only moderately during the fall. Thus Eastern bankers were not encouraging speculative credit but were gradually withdrawing their support from the over-optimistic Street. They began to do this in January, and the February warning of the Reserve Board merely confirmed them in their decision to effect an orderly reduction of loans to brokers. Out-of-town banks seemed to follow their New York brethren at a respectful distance. Loans from this source reached their height on February 6th, declining immediately thereafter and leveling off later in the summer. The small banks of the nation reflected the caution felt in New York.

It was the third source of brokers' loans that was most significant in 1929, the category called "loans from others" or "bootleg," consisting of loans made directly to New York brokers by non-bank lenders, i.e., corporations and individuals. The large supply of liquid funds in bank accounts and corporate treasuries proved to be a great temptation. It seemed foolish to let such money remain idle when the demands of a rising stock market kept the call loan rate between 7 and 12 per cent.[53] And so, although this source of loans had never been important in the past, it loomed large as 1929 wore on: except for a brief period after the Federal Reserve warning, bootleg loans reached new levels each week.

[53] *Wall Street Journal*, September 6, 1929, 12:4. The call loan rate was 2½ to 3½ per cent higher than the commercial rate between January and September 1929. Haney, *et al.*, *Brokers' Loans*, 161.

Although banks were withdrawing from the call money market, the "loans from others" more than offset this reduction, and the total of brokers' loans rose to what many thought were dangerous heights.[54]

New York bankers were much distressed. They noted that the funds came from all over the nation, from persons who did not know each other and felt no collective responsibility for the credit situation. Banks, for a variety of reasons, had always been interested in stability, but private lenders felt no such obligation, and the bankers wished aloud that means existed to reduce this lending by amateurs. They predicted that if a sharp reverse hit the market, these private lenders would be frightened and would call their loans, precipitating a money panic. In time of emergency, the public always called on the banks to throw in their reserves. There were many precedents: in 1890, 1895, 1901, and 1907 bankers, notably J. P. Morgan, had been summoned to relieve credit stringency caused by a hasty withdrawal of credit. The financiers did not see it as their duty to keep reserves ready for such an eventuality, and were reluctant to alter their banking policies to cushion the fall of private lenders. Yet what else could they do? In any crisis crowds would form in their offices demanding that they throw in funds to alleviate a credit shortage, so their best solution was to discourage loans by private lenders—there was no legal way to do more.

Some of the large corporations felt a responsibility to the national economy similar to that of the banks. These concerns announced that although they had liquid funds on hand, they would not permit them to be lent to brokers in New York, even though the call rate was 7-10 per cent.[55] Bootleg loans were also the subject of many

[54] *Wall Street Journal*, September 20, 1929, 10:4. As 1928 began "loans from others" amounted to 24 per cent of the brokers' loans total; this grew to 40 per cent in January 1929 and 57½ per cent by October (calculated from Haney, 220-221).

[55] *Wall Street Journal*, February 14, 1929, 1:2, February 4, 15:3.

editorials. Brokers' loans, divided into three categories, were published weekly in the financial journals, and the growing and conspicuous disparity between loans from banks and private loans was interpreted as a shift from strong lenders to weak lenders.[56] The result of this phenomenon of loans from "others" came in October with the Crash. As the bankers had prophesied, private lenders rushed to call their money, created a money panic and sent call loan rates to prohibitive levels. Inevitably the bankers were forced to step in with their reserves and try to restore some semblance of stability to the credit mechanism.[57]

By the spring of 1929 the situation had already gone beyond the powers of the nation's bankers. Any action would have to come from the federal government and would have to be drastic; the expansive forces were irrational and could no longer be curbed by the manipulation of interest rates or even by strong warnings.

The American Bankers Association had urged that bootleg loans be curbed, *Barron's,* October 8, 1928, 4.

[56] *Commercial & Financial Chronicle,* 128:I:665 (February 2, 1929); *Wall Street Journal,* January 21, 1929, 13:2. *Forbes* particularly stressed the shakiness of credit from private lenders.

[57] *Wall Street Journal,* October 25, 1929, 1:5.

CHAPTER 6

AFTER THE 1929 CRASH:

INVESTIGATION, COMPROMISE,

REFORM

*T*HE bubble that began in 1923 burst in 1929. Eighteen billion dollars in security values were wiped out between September and November. But few could foresee that this stock exchange catastrophe would be the beginning of a roller-coaster decline of economic activity. As 1930 opened, the Hoover Administration offered many assurances that business was fundamentally sound, that the effects of the great financial debacle would be as limited as business and government leaders could make them. Newspapers and magazines urged the maintenance of wages and exhorted businessmen to get back to work, to apply themselves to the honest tasks that they had slighted in 1928 and 1929 when their minds were filled with golf, market quotations, and thoughts of quick profit.[1] The spring of 1930 saw a gradual revival of brokers' loans; wounded traders were slinking back to the exchanges hoping, no doubt, to recoup some of their losses. The number of shareholders in American corporations continued to increase, and future trading was started in lamb and in black-strap molasses.[2]

The Crash of course brought forth many "I told you so's," as those who had been predicting calamity since 1928 enjoyed the dubious satisfaction of seeing their

[1] *Magazine of Wall Street*, 45:433 (January 11, 1930); *Business Week*, November 2, 1929, 52.
[2] *Commercial & Financial Chronicle*, 130:II:3236 (May 10, 1930); 131:I:377, 1506; *Time*, 16:39 (July 14, 1930).

forecasts realized. The agrarian and progressive groups in Congress were in a particularly favorable position in this respect; these men, in the face of overwhelming business and popular opinion, had consistently maintained their stand that the prevailing speculation was unsound and would lead to disaster. The abler progressives, moreover, had advanced many logical reasons for their beliefs. Now, in 1930, the Sons of the Wild Jackass could favorably compare the accuracy of their own statements with those of the men who had derided them as unsophisticated rustics. But the reformers did not exult in their triumph; they saw that the Crash would further weaken the nation's economy.

The movement to restrain speculators after the Crash took a number of paths, although they overlapped in chronology and subject matter. The first was investigation and attempted restriction of short sellers and futures traders, who were accused of precipitating the Crash and hamstringing recovery, especially in the commodity markets. The second was a move, not as popular as the first, to prevent the government-financed Federal Farm Board from gambling away the taxpayers' money and enriching favored cooperatives and commission men. The third path, still more obscure, was the revamping of the Federal Reserve System to close loopholes that had permitted the expansion of speculative credit. The fourth avenue of reform was through taxation and regulation: an attempt to regulate and discourage the more obviously shoddy practices of brokers and speculators.

I

It became evident, during 1930, that the fiasco of October was more than a severe financial panic. Despite the optimistic statements of business leaders and government officials, developments indicated that fundamental business conditions were *not* sound, that the stock panic was probably the climax of an economic infection which had been festering all through the post-war decade. The agricultural distress of the 1920s, brushed aside at the time by disciples of the New Era, was now emphasized, and seen as evidence of the conditions that led to collapse. Hindsight began its diligent work; observers recalled the rural bank failures, the reparations, the high tariff, and the regional unemployment of 1928 and 1929. The process of rationalization began in 1930 and continued, at least in political campaigns, for over twenty years.

Many explanations emerged; these became more complex as time passed, when facts of the period were gathered and correlated. Lack of purchasing power among farmers, high tariffs that blocked foreign trade, and debt payments, were prominent suggestions.[3] The most obvious cause of the collapse, however, to most people seemed to be the tremendous stock speculation, and the easy credit which had led citizens to overextend themselves—but this statement would not have been put so calmly at the time. In 1930 people wanted to know, not *what* was wrong with the economic structure, but *who* had been so cruel as to frustrate the popular dream of wealth without work, *who* had been responsible for pricking the bubble of prosperity? The interest in seeking scapegoats suggests that the public was not at first concerned with why the bubble had grown so large, but rather with who had dared to destroy it.

The political atmosphere of 1930-1931 was heavy with charges of conspiracy, fraud, and incompetence. The short seller was a natural culprit. Despite the learned articles and thoughtful testimony of various economists over thirty years, the public held to the idea that there was something faintly sinister, something almost un-American, about persons habitually "investing" to take advantage of market declines. The average person was

[3] Broadus Mitchell, *Depression Decade, From the New Era through the New Deal, 1929-1941* (New York, 1947), 181-183.

seldom a bear and usually did not understand the process by which one could sell now, cover later, and gain the difference between sale and subsequent purchase. Ordinarily only large operators took the short side of the market; when there were sudden and inexplicable declines in the exchanges, financial writers as well as farmers attributed it to bear pools. Talk of a "Money Trust" and a plutocratic elite, heard only in Socialist and agrarian progressive circles in the twenties, now became more generally fashionable. Who were these men who had precipitated a panic and a depression, who had sold America short for personal profit?

The public prints were full of bear charges and denials. Jesse L. Livermore, notorious stock market bear, in November 1929 denied that his operations had anything to do with the panic; in December Livermore hired a personal bodyguard.[4] James W. Gerard, former Ambassador to Germany, issued a list of sixty-four men who controlled America and who presumably were responsible for the current chaos; Senator Pine of Oklahoma agreed with the indictment.[5] John A. Simpson, new president of the Farmers' Union, interpreted business cycles as a plot of international bankers,[6] while Jacob S. Coxey, Sr., told a Senate subcommittee how the "big boys" inflated credit and then "pulled the string" for their own benefit.[7] Representative Louis T. McFadden claimed that the Federal Reserve Board was a tool of speculators affiliated with the House of Morgan; he was joined by Congressman Wright Patman of Texas, who charged Morgan with buying up bankrupt properties. Ex-Senator

[4] *Time*, 14:II:43 (December 30, 1929).

[5] *Commercial & Financial Chronicle*, 131:I:1315 (August 30, 1930); 1360.

[6] *To Abolish the Federal Farm Board and Secure to the Farmer the Cost of Production*, Committee on Agriculture, United States Senate. 72 Cong., 1 sess. (Washington, 1932), 6-7.

[7] *Prohibiting Trading on Margins on the New York Stock Exchange*, Committee on Judiciary. United States Senate. 71 Cong., 3 sess. (Washington, 1931), 37-40.

James Reed of Missouri blamed the growing unemployment directly on market manipulators, and even Senator
Copeland of New York found it expedient to excoriate
the "super-bankers" about whom he had been more
solicitous in the past.[8]

Politicians shrieked in protest when the Soviet Government was discovered selling short in the Chicago
Board of Trade. Moscow replied that it was simply
hedging purchases made in the United States and that
this trading was a very small fraction of the total short
sales here. Several Congressmen moved to outlaw such
transactions by foreign governments, as general xenophobia increased. Hamilton Fish, Jr., of New York led a
group of legislators around the country looking for Communists, and the Soviet short selling furnished an opportunity to blame foreigners for the economic situation.
It jibed well with the dubious thesis of President Hoover:
that the depression originated abroad, that the United
States was the victim of international vicissitude. Nativism, lurking below the surface in the Anglo–Saxon-domi-
nated South and rural Midwest, regained some of the
ground it had lost since the decline of the Ku Klux Klan
and the 1928 Presidential campaign. The farmers and
small businessmen of the hinterland of America had
always been susceptible to the notion that Eastern financiers were grasping, cosmopolitan, and not particularly
loyal to the interests of the United States. The close ties
to Britain and France of the investment bankers, especially the House of Morgan, and the presence of a number
of German Jews in the New York financial oligarchy, sustained this traditional prejudice. The disinclination of the
Allies to pay their war debts and the conference between
British and American bankers that led to a lower discount
rate in August, 1927, seemed but separate pieces in the

[8] *Commercial & Financial Chronicle*, 130:II:4546 (June 28,
1930), 134:I:771 (January 26, 1932); *The Progressive* (February
18, 1933), 1:8.

same puzzle. Congressman McFadden charged that the bankers were trying to make the United States pay the whole cost of the war, and suggested the danger of the infiltration of foreign ideas and experts—men who believed in Continental-style administrative rather than legislative law.[9] Senator Duncan U. Fletcher of Florida had earlier expressed his fear of a *droit administratif*, with laws administered by bureaus and committees without regard for statutes.[10]

It was in this atmosphere that the search for bears began. Probably because of agricultural influence in the Senate, investigations into the commodity markets got under way more quickly. The election of Simpson as president of the Farmers' Union in the fall of 1930 indicated that farmer opinion was again shifting to a more radical position; Simpson defeated Clarence E. Huff, a Hoover man. The threat made by Chester Gray in 1928 had become a reality: open opposition to the exchanges was again mounting with the failure of the Farm Board, and the familiar bills against futures trading were dusted off and reintroduced.[11] Meanwhile each rally of the commodity markets ended in a greater relapse, and their weakness was attributed to bears who were reaping rewards from the advanced state of uncertainty. The Federal Farm Board was struggling to stabilize wheat and cotton in the face of foreign overproduction and an ever-mounting surplus at home. A conference during the fall of 1930 between President Hoover and Richard Whitney, president of the New York Stock Exchange, was widely interpreted as indicating that the administration was determined to prevent bearish market activity. In January of 1931 George F. Baker, a noted financier, warned the public that further short selling was

[9] *Commercial & Financial Chronicle*, 131:II:2157 (October 2, 1930), 131:I:219 (July 12, 1930), 132:I:427 (January 17, 1931).
[10] *Brokers' Loans*, 27 (1928).
[11] *Congressional Record*, 71 Cong., 2 sess., v. 72, Pt. 12, 107, 177.

unwise and unpatriotic—but it continued.[12] Finally on July 10, 1931, President Hoover issued this tart statement:

> It has come to my attention that certain persons are selling short in the commodity market, particularly in wheat. These transactions have been continuous over the past month. I do not refer to the ordinary hedging transactions, which are a sound part of our market system. I do not refer to the legitimate grain trade. I refer to a limited number of speculators. I am not expressing my view upon the economics of short selling in normal times, but in these times this activity has a public interest. It has one purpose and that is to depress prices. It tends to destroy the return of public confidence. The intention is to take a profit from the loss of other people, even though the effect may be directly depriving many farmers of their rightful income. If these gentlemen have that sense of patriotism which outruns immediate profit, and desire to see the country recover, they will close up these transactions and desist from their manipulations. The confidence imposed upon me by law as a public official does not permit me to expose their names to the public, otherwise I would do so.[13]

Yet President Peter Carey of the Chicago Board of Trade asserted that the Board would close if any more regulation were imposed. J.W.T. Duvel, Chief of the Grain Futures Administration, came forward to refute the traditional argument that speculators generally stimulated the market, that they were more often long than short on the commodities traded. He described an experiment conducted between July 1, 1931, and May 31, 1932, to check this assumption. Duvel's findings were

[12] *Commercial & Financial Chronicle*, 131:II:2478 (October 18, 1930); 132:I:775 (January 31, 1931).
[13] *Commodity Short Selling*, Committee on Agriculture. United States House of Representatives. 72 Cong., 1 sess. (Washington, 1932), 27.

that the big traders were long only thirty days of this period—thirty days out of a total of 223; and on several days one man did over 15 per cent of all the trading. These results supported the modern theory that the big traders rode with the trend rather than trying to anticipate it.

The House Agriculture Committee held hearings in 1932 on several bills relating to commodity trading, with the usual parade of exchange and farm representatives. The idea of limiting individual trades had gained much ground since the Dickinson bill of 1928, and Chief Duvel continued to recommend both daily and total limits for traders.[14] John Vesecky, president of the Kansas Co-operative Wheat Marketing Association suggested a 500,000 bushel limit for any individual; he also wanted to authorize the Secretary of Agriculture to disclose the names of large traders. Simpson of the Farmers' Union would not, of course, accept the limitation principle. He reaffirmed the position—temporarily abandoned by the Union toward the end of the twenties —that all short selling should be stopped. "The stabilization of American business, industry, and agriculture is being retarded by short-selling operations on the commodity and other exchanges. . . ." The usual exchange arguments were augmented by tales of financial distress and inactivity. Russell Clark of the New Orleans Cotton Exchange told Congressmen that the cotton trade desired no more legislation, that 25 per cent of the firms had gone out of business, and that many cotton dealers were doing their own clerical work to cut expenses. The current low prices, he said, virtually precluded bear raiding or short selling. Sydney Anderson, a vice-president of General Mills and spokesman for the milling industry, declared that banning short sales would not

[14] *Commercial & Financial Chronicle*, 134:I:1680 (March 5, 1932); 135:II:3933 (December 10, 1932), 131:II:4138 (December 27, 1930).

benefit the farmers; it would simply make the market narrower and more uncertain. He subscribed to the Hoover dictum that trading in a large amount did not of itself signify guilt.[15]

The House committee finished its hearings in February and endorsed Congressman Marvin Jones's bill for regulating commodities. It also made some general recommendations: (1) that cotton be included with grain under the jurisdiction of the Grain Futures Administration; (2) that short selling be limited or prohibited; (3) that bucketing be prohibited; (4) that trading in privileges be made illegal. Early enactment was urged to curb the activities of large speculators.[16]

Not until March 4, 1932, when Congress passed the Hastings resolution, did an exhaustive investigation into stock market practices begin. Speculation had persisted in 1931 and 1932 but the market followed business indexes downward, punctuated by only a few rallies. Under these circumstances stock traders were reticent in their testimony about activities on the short side of the market. Aware that the committee was looking for devils who put the market down, the witnesses played up their operations on the long side. None of them would admit any significant short sales prior to September, 1929; they claimed that they did not take substantial short positions until well into 1930. In effect they admitted what some of their critics had charged, that they waited until a trend developed and then plunged in to take advantage of it. Therefore they did not, as formalistic economists liked to argue, stabilize the market by pitting their experience against the sentiments of the mob, but rather rode along with the mob, accentuating declines; they did not provide leadership but simply stood by, ready to take advantage of weaknesses

[15] *Commodity Short Selling*, 87-88, 45-46, 97-124.
[16] "Short Selling," *Congressional Digest*, 11:290-292 (December 1932).

they knew would occur.[17] Whether they called the tops or the bottoms was really immaterial—swings were bound to be wide with a large uninformed public in the market, and these men could make large gains by deliberately taking a position and maintaining it until it reversed itself. The lag in knowledge between the well-informed big traders and the little fellows who were gambling was enough in a big market so that some profit was assured. As Arthur W. Cutten put it, "the secret of success is holding on." Although these 1929 speculators persisted in being reticent and obscure, their statements and testimony gave something of their views. Cutten, the most famous grain plunger of the time, disliked reporting his trades and having a bureaucratic government shaking its finger over the size of his transactions. The knowledge that two or three ill-paid government clerks knew the size and timing of his trades made him so nervous that he had quit commodities and gone to New York to trade in stocks. The failure of the Federal Farm Board stabilization program demonstrated to Cutten the incapacity of the government in such matters. How did the government expect trading to lift prices when it scared away all the speculative money that usually made for an active and rising market?[18]

Other traders' opinions were more difficult to obtain. When Matthew Chauncey Brush, a big private operator, was asked about the investment ability of the average stock purchaser, he answered that he wished he could speak entirely off the record. For the record he termed

[17] *"Stock Exchange Practices,"* Committee on Banking & Currency. United States Senate. 72 Cong. (Washington, 1932), I, 224, 408.

The traditional economic defense during this period was by an economic consultant for the New York Stock Exchange, James Edward Meeker, *Short Selling* (New York, 1932).

[18] Arthur W. Cutten, "The Story of a Speculator," *Saturday Evening Post,* 205:12-13 (December 3, 1932).

their ability "pathetic." He told Senator Robert Bulkley of Ohio that short selling in no way impaired patriotism; he also seized the opportunity to address the Senate Banking subcommittee on the subject of the capital-gains tax. Like many Wall Street men, he felt this tax had contributed to the stock panic by reducing the supply of floating stock available. Once persons had a considerable paper profit on a stock, they were reluctant to sell because of the high capital-gains tax; instead they held on, or borrowed on the stock if they needed funds. The effect of this, according to Brush, was to reduce the supply of stock available and cause security prices to rise to unwarranted levels. Traders and bankers were inclined to dismiss short selling, manipulation, or defects in the banking system as causes of the collapse; instead they blamed an overly eager public. The market had gone up in 1928 and 1929 because of public demand, and it was only natural for old-time traders to form syndicates to take advantage of the rise.

These men explained pools as efforts to support a new stock until it had established itself as respectable in the public mind. Lag was always important in discussing markets and a new security needed promotion. Occasionally the accompanying ballyhoo might have been excessive and unwarranted by the facts, but a stock eventually found its proper value. Most pools therefore were not secret conspiracies, but ordinary syndicates given privileges by the concern offering the new issue. Those at all familiar with market practice would know this, and would buy or not, according to the intrinsic merit of the security. A stock specialist had no special advantage even though he had access to the listed orders, for usually the trading was so heavy that he did not have time to analyze the situation.[19] But however reasonable these explanations sounded, the Senators did discover pools whose members made vast sums in short

[19] *Stock Exchange Practices,* I, 289-321, 512.

periods without apparently incurring commensurate risk. Within ten days, for example, a pool in Kolster Radio made $337,000 per person when the stock bounded from 74 to 98 and then slumped to 70. In the freakish spring of 1929, however, practically anyone buying and selling heavily could have made almost as much on his own. In the House, Representative Fiorello LaGuardia introduced cancelled checks to show that many financial writers were given retainers to mention certain stocks in their newspaper columns.[20] When the committee completed its initial investigation of short selling, Richard Whitney and Peter B. Carey, presidents respectively of the New York Stock Exchange and the Chicago Board of Trade, called the attention of the public to the fact that the charges of deliberate bear conspiracies had not been substantiated: despite the advance claims of the committee counsel, no evidence of bear raids had been uncovered.[21]

Financial writers, in the belief that Congress was playing to the stands, generally took a tolerant attitude toward the search. One writer suggested that full data on the "shorts" be published to calm public fears. He cited, as an example, the figures for September 21, 1931, which showed only 9,369 short accounts averaging 400 shares per client and with no individual predominating. Another broker remarked, when criticism of short sellers was at its height, that most of the current short sellers were small amateurs whose attention had been called to the possibilities of bear activity by the highly publicized senate hearings.[22] But public antipathy toward short sellers increased rather than diminished as the depression deepened. Bears continued to be blamed for preventing economic recovery and for undermining

[20] *Ibid.*, 558-563, 439-464.

[21] *Commercial & Financial Chronicle*, 134:I:1680 (March 5, 1932).

[22] *The Nation*, 134:246 (March 2, 1932); *Magazine of Wall Street*, 49:18-19 (October 31, 1931); 50:86 (May 14, 1932).

efforts of the Federal Farm Board. Representative Adolph J. Sabath, a Democrat from Chicago, writing in the Pro column of the *Congressional Digest*, made his position plain to its high-school readers. He stated that he had opposed short selling for twenty years; he believed that the practice stimulated rumors and fears. The Congressman declared that the operations of bears were criminal in 1928-1932. Insiders began "selling against the box" in the early fall of 1929 in certain key stocks. The "big boys" had prolonged the depression, for these men always controlled the "tone" of the market. The ratio of short sales to total sales, which was always cited by market defenders to prove the small influence of short selling, was irrelevant to Sabath. Short sales, he believed, were highly concentrated in market leaders and worked sympathetically on the prices of the whole market.[23] Thomas Nixon Carver, the economist, thought that exchange reform would have to come from the outside. He observed that the exchanges had no incentive to distinguish between investor and gambler because both categories yielded commissions to the brokers. At the same time Carver exhibited the typical neoclassical distrust of legal restraints on economic phenomena; he felt that although a law would be powerless, it would, like laws against prostitution and gambling, signify public disapproval.[24]

There were even some business defections from the exchange point of view, generally from persons not intimately associated with the markets. The united front

[23] Adolph J. Sabath, *Congressional Digest*, 11:294 (December 1932). The term "selling against the box" means selling a stock short although already possessing the stock. When the operator decides to cover, he can either go into the market and buy the stock to make good on his contract or go to his safety deposit box and deliver the stock he already held. This was a favorite device of company officers who wanted to profit from a decline in the company stock without causing public uneasiness by selling it.

[24] Thomas Nixon Carver, "Selling Short," *The Atlantic*, 145:247-250 (February 1930).

against Western radicalism showed some fissures. Irving T. Bush, president of the Bush Terminal Company—a firm that handled 20 per cent of the freight into New York City—observed after the Crash that Americans were an emotional people and greed was difficult to control. He believed that some restriction ought to be put on promoters who were selling securities to the public, and said that the prime responsibility lay with our leaders; they should make only honest profits from the honest use of brains, otherwise public confidence would be undermined and a Sovietized economy would result. The choice as Bush saw it in December 1929, was between honesty and socialism—the leaders of finance would have to crush the promoter before he ate the core of our prosperity.[25] In the spring of 1932 Harold G. Aron, a New York City banker, assailed Richard Whitney for defending short selling. Aron charged that the market was dominated by twenty short sellers who were trying to recoup losses suffered in 1929. "For thirty years there has been a common-place saying in stock speculative circles that anyone can talk 'em down, but it takes money to buy 'em up. Since October, 1929 . . . there was not sufficient buying power to resist an organized effort to drive stock prices down. . . ." Short selling, said Aron, was an unfair tactic in hard times. The testimony of certain bankers a few weeks later in regard to their own dealings accelerated desertion from the exchange-investment banker camp.

Faced with investigations and the threat of drastic legislation against them, the markets moved to correct some of the abuses through the passage of new rules. The exchanges, of course, had been adding to their rules for many years but it always seemed to outsiders that these rules were too little and too late, enacted more for the purpose of staving off real regulation than to rectify evils. The New York Stock Exchange, effective April 1,

[25] Irving T. Bush, *The Magazine of Wall Street,* 45:357-358 (December 28, 1929).

1932, tightened its rules regarding the hypothecation of securities. The prevailing custom had been that brokers could borrow a customer's margined stock for another client who was short-selling that stock. The customer was not consulted, since he had agreed when purchasing the stock to allow such borrowing. This agreement was a stipulation in fine print on every agreement made between broker and client, but it was not familiar to the average customer. The effect of the clause was to give the broker a supply of stock, not actually his own, to loan to various short sellers, and it enabled brokers quickly to find stock to sell for short sellers. The exchange finally proposed to change this dubious practice by requiring written permission from the customer *each time* a broker desired to borrow his stock. Exchange authorities believed this requirement would lessen the supply of stock available for borrowing, since many customers would not sign such an agreement or the broker would hesitate to ask for permission too often; they predicted that the rule would cut in half the number of short sales being made and opposed the further suggestion that the names of short sellers be made public.

At the same time the exchange, by promulgating another new rule, seemed to have tacitly conceded the detrimental effects of short selling. Its historic position on short sales had been that there was no essential difference economically or ethically between a long and a short sale; both the Hughes Committee of 1908 and the Owen Committee of 1914 had endorsed this viewpoint. In 1932, however, the exchange set new limits for credit on short sales, making the required margin three times as much as for long transactions. It also began to require the reporting of short positions. Clearly the markets were yielding to public pressure.[26] The arguments

[26] *Commercial & Financial Chronicle*, 134:I:1304 (February 20, 1932); 1484 (February 27, 1932); also adopted by the Chicago

against short selling of stock on American exchanges had first become an issue during the Progressive Era. After the relatively mild protests of this period (1909-1917) the question did not become important again until 1930; most of the agrarian complaints against futures did not extend to the similar practice in the security markets, and it took the 1929 Crash to bring any change.

Is it possible, with the perspective of a generation, to establish the validity of these charges and counter-charges against the practice of short selling? What can we now say about the effects of short selling during the twenties and thirties? Were bears really organized to drive the stock market down? A thorough study of short selling and its effects, made by economists and statisticians from 1931-1932 data, failed to substantiate the claims of the bear critics of the time. The experts found that short sellers had a variety of motives: some were selling as speculators, some were hedgers; others were "selling against the box" or for tax purposes. They could find no relation between the amount of short interest in a stock and whether it went up or down; some went down, others up. An examination of the records of ten prominent market traders showed divergent tendencies; their short selling seemed to have different effects on different stocks. There was no evidence that short selling would necessarily depress a stock. The investigators completely corroborated the opinion of old traders that short selling was not a factor in the larger market movements. They were willing to concede, however, that there had been some socially undesirable short selling in the *early days* of the market. The experts also confirmed the idea, referred to several times previously, that short sellers did not attempt to call the turn in a stock but gradually took up a short position *after* a stock turned downward. There-

Stock Exchange, 1681 (March 5, 1932); 134:II:3740 (May 21, 1932).

fore short sellers, per se, could not be responsible for a market break but only for the accentuation of it.[27]

Thus in the stock market at least, evidence is now strong that the cries against the bears were largely irrelevant to problems of stock market fluctuation in the twenties and thirties. Those who were seeking to personify the forces against them, and those who exploited this public weakness, tried to make the bears the culprits in 1929. Although expert studies were generally against them, these critics finally won a major concession, for in 1938 the Securities and Exchange Commission instituted the ⅛th rule, which very greatly reduced short sales and made bear raiding virtually impossible. This was a concession to the anti-speculator view and was not based upon an objective study of the effects of short sales. Short selling is still possible if it is done in compliance with SEC regulations, and may be profitable occasionally in short-run downswings or special situations; in an economy which tends toward inflation, however, its usefulness has been much reduced.

But the principle of selling now and buying later to cover the commitment, which was involved in both stock market short sales and future trading in commodities and had been the central point of attack for market critics, had not been yielded. By the thirties, the ethical validity of this type of transaction was taken for granted in all except a few cash-crop farming regions.

II

The problems of the American farmer in a predominantly urban economy seem to be perennial; they have yet to be solved. Farmer participation in general prosperity has been too brief and has yielded too little, and even in the twenties discontent smoldered in many

[27] Fred R. MacCauley, *Short Selling on the New York Stock Exchange* (New York, 1951), Chapter 2.

staple crop regions. The complaints were familiar: lack of credit and lack of parity.

Congress passed the Agricultural Marketing Act in a special session in 1929, fulfilling Herbert Hoover's campaign promise and establishing an eight-member Federal Farm Board. Their duties were to: (1) minimize speculation in commodities; (2) encourage producer cooperatives; (3) prevent wasteful distribution; and (4) prevent or control surpluses. The Board was empowered to create corporate subsidiaries to implement these objectives. In May 1929 President Hoover appointed Alexander Legge, president of International Harvester, as Farm Board chairman.[28] Midwest Senators challenged the appointment because Legge headed the farm equipment trust—a traditional *bête noire* of the Farm Belt— but the Senate confirmed Legge, 67-12. Anti-speculators made similar charges of business bias against two other Hoover nominations, but Sam R. McKelvie of Nebraska and Carl Williams of the Oklahoma Grange, representing wheat and cotton respectively, were nevertheless confirmed by votes of 50-27 and 57-20. The opposition to Legge, McKelvie, and Williams had been minor when the President first announced the appointments in May, but the Board's lethargy in the four critical months that followed aroused resentment in the wheat and cotton areas.[29]

As 1929 ended and the country was disorganized by plummeting security and commodity prices, the Farm Board began its "stabilizing"—defined as mitigating wide seasonal fluctuations. Stabilization was, of course, most necessary in the big fungible crops, wheat and cotton. It was important to the Republican party and to President Hoover's prospects of reelection that the Farm

[28] *Business Week*, April 8, 1931, 26.
[29] *Congressional Record*, 71 Cong., 1 sess., v. 71, Pt. 4, 4610-4611 (October 16, 1929); *Chicago Tribune*, September 7, 1929, clipping from McCormick Collection, Wisconsin State Historical Society.

Board ameliorate conditions, because McNary-Haugen-ism had never really subsided.[30]

The Board had been granted $500 million to implement stabilization. Federal experts soon discovered that to stabilize commodity prices—to keep them up for the farmers' benefit—they would have to trade in the futures exchanges as well as in the cash or "spot" markets, and in February 1930, the two subsidiaries created by the Board entered the exchanges and began extensive buying and selling in the 1929 crop.[31] Although for obvious reasons the exact amounts of the government transactions were kept secret, rumors of the vastness of the operations quickly created opposition among traders and brokers. Private traders felt they were being elbowed out by Uncle Sam and accused the Farm Board of trying to corner the visible supply of wheat.

Opponents also claimed that the Board subsidiaries, intended to encourage farm cooperatives, were competing directly with private dealers. Businessmen recalled bitterly President Hoover's statement at the farm relief session of Congress: "No governmental agency should engage in the buying and selling and price fixing of products, for such courses can only lead to bureaucracy and domination."[32] Criticism mounted with each new bushel or bale that the Farm Board bought to maintain prices. Speculator Arthur Cutten crowed "I told you so," and demanded that the Board stop pouring taxpayers' money down a rathole in futile price-pegging efforts. As the government was forced to buy more to keep the price up, as the great surplus already stored became known, it became apparent that prices would slump seriously whenever the government curtailed its opera-

[30] Theodore Saloutos and John D. Hicks, *Agricultural Discontent in the Middle West, 1900-1939* (Madison, 1951), 406-407.

[31] *Business Week*, April 8, 1931, 26.

[32] *Commercial & Financial Chronicle*, 133:I:2016; William O. Scroggs, "Uncle Sam, Grain Trader," *Outlook*, 154:499 (March 28, 1930).

tions; and of course the Board did not plan to go on indefinitely. Here, said the speculators, was colossal proof of what they had been saying: no speculator, however large, could win against the conditions of the worldwide market. Despite invincible popular faith in the power of speculation, prices could not stray very long from those set by supply and demand; world conditions, not speculators, dominated price trends.

One of the results of Board speculative activity was the diminution of private trading, and a few brokers transferred their seats from Chicago to Winnipeg in 1930. Chairman Legge, testifying before a Senate committee in 1931, even cited the decline of private trading as an accomplishment of the Board. But, as *Business Week* noted, all the decline in private activity was not the result of Board policy; some traders simply saw greater profit possibilities elsewhere. Nevertheless, Farm Board critics noted that when private risk-takers were frightened out of the market by government competition, the burden of the Board increased: instead of stimulating trading and thereby stimulating prices, the Board was merely replacing private dealers who had withdrawn in disgust. The Board itself became aware of this "pegging paradox" and its annual reports were gloomy over the prospects of disposing of the surpluses.[33]

Because of the large world wheat crop, and particularly the increased Russian exports, the government found itself in the predicament of having to purchase very large quantities to maintain the price level it had promised the growers early in the season. The Board discovered that an artificial price could not be sustained indefinitely unless production could be controlled.[34] And

[33] Arthur W. Cutten, "The Story of a Speculator," *Saturday Evening Post*, 205:12-13 (December 3, 1932); "Uncle Sam, Plunger," *The Nation*, 130:351 (March 26, 1930); *Business Week*, April 8, 1931, 26.

[34] Charles P. Howland, "The Failure of the Federal Farm Board," *Yale Review*, ns 21:503-519 (March 1932).

so, amid mixed opinion, Chairman Legge and Secretary of Agriculture Arthur Hyde went on tour to convince the farmers that they should plant less. "Grow Less, Get More" was their slogan. But the farmers proved to be individualistic folk; agreements to plant less were defeated by farmers who planted more, hoping their neighbors would plant less, and that they would thereby improve their relative position. The agricultural colleges, moreover, had been preaching the doctrine of productivity, of two blades of grass where one had grown before. Patriotic appeals during World War I had also left their mark: production was virtue, restriction was sin. By the summer of 1930 government officials had to admit that efforts at domestic crop curtailment were ineffective.[35]

When the government entered the commodity futures markets, the anti-speculator element in Congress, which had steadfastly fought futures trading, options, and various other exchange practices, found itself in a dilemma. Reluctantly these Congressmen had acquiesced in Hoover's Farm Board plan, only to be offended later by his choices for its members. Now the Farm Board, responding to pressure from agriculture, was trying to raise farm prices by using the very methods that these men had consistently condemned. What were they to do? They came from states that needed federal assistance, but these were also the states where anti-commercial moralizing was still common, regions which expected their representatives to take definite stands for or against. Did the anti-speculators dare oppose the Hoover farm program on the ground that speculative activity, even by the government, was immoral and unsound? Hugo L. Black, Democratic Senator from an old Populist stronghold in Alabama, brought this issue to a head in Congress in February, 1931. He proposed the fol-

[35] Saloutos and Hicks, *Agricultural Discontent*, 422; *Business Week*, July 19, 1930, 5.

lowing amendment to the Farm Board section of the appropriations bill: "No part of the amount hereby appropriated shall be expended, and no loan shall be made out of such amount, for the purpose of dealing in futures or indulging in marginal transactions or any transaction whereby contracts are made for the purchase of agricultural commodities or food products thereof where no delivery . . . is intended."[36]

Senator Black thought it wrong to spend the taxpayers' money in speculation. Even if Chairman Legge were a competent businessman, the country was not ready to turn over vast sums of money for commodity speculation. If the Farm Board could not benefit the farmer except by gambling, it was time for the end of the Board. "Tom-Tom" Heflin, Alabama's senior Senator, agreed; he called for Congress to ban futures trading. Walter F. George of Georgia predicted the Board would lose all of its $500 million. What did the Farm Board know of the intricacies of trading? "Cotton Ed" Smith of South Carolina said the Board was not even supposed to hedge; it was supposed to take the stuff off the market entirely and let supply and demand operate. Kenneth McKellar of Tennessee could see no reason for the continuation of the Board. His cotton investigations had convinced him that the government-sponsored cooperatives, as well as the stabilization corporations, were speculating in cotton futures. If the market goes up, certain cooperatives win; if it goes down, the government takes the loss. McKellar reminded the Senators that the Board had received a mandate to minimize speculation, and Edwin S. Broussard of Louisiana, always sympathetic to New Orleans commerce, declared frankly that he wanted to restrict the Farm Board in the interest of the cotton merchants who were complaining about government competition.

[36] *Congressional Record,* 71 Cong., 3 sess., v. 76, Pt. 4, 4147, 4152, 4312, 4313-4314.

But appeals to anti-monopoly morality were not enough. Senator Wesley L. Jones of Washington, a Republican progressive, thought it unwise to limit the Board's activities when it was trying to aid the farmer. George Norris, the great Nebraska progressive, argued that the Black amendment would not change the marketing system but would only hamper the Board in its competition with private dealers; the Board, like other legitimate dealers, needed hedging privileges under the prevailing marketing system. The Farm Board was part of Hoover's farm relief and Congress should not hamstring it, said Norris, but he admitted that he had never had faith in the Board as a solution to low farm prices. Carter Glass, agreed with him. When the Senate clerk called the roll, the Black amendment was defeated, 55-26. The Republicans, with the major exceptions of Couzens of Michigan and Blaine and LaFollette of Wisconsin, chose to stay with the Hoover Administration. As Peter Norbeck of South Dakota concluded, the Farm Board plan was unsound but the farmers and the people were in favor of continuing the experiment.[37]

Not all the protests about government speculation came from the commodity business or from anti-speculators in Congress. There were some rank-and-file farmers who distrusted the Farm Board way of doing things and the men Hoover had chosen to rescue them from peasant status. Critics of the Board were also found among marginal farmers, those who had long felt that both the agricultural press and the Farm Bureaus were working

[37] *Ibid.*, 4312, 4313-4314. Legge resigned in March 1931. The anti-speculators were: Ashurst (D-Ariz.), Blaine (R-Wis.), Blease (D-S. C.), Bratton (D-N. M.), Brock (D-Tenn.), Broussard (D-La.), Caraway (D-Ark.), Connally (D-Tex.), Couzens (R-Mich.), Dill (D-Wash.), George (D-Ga.), Hayden (D-Ariz.), Heflin (D-Ala.), King (D-Utah), LaFollette (R-Wis.), McGill (D-Kan.), McKellar (D-Tenn.), Morrison (D-N. C.), Patterson (R-Mo.), Robinson (R-Ind.), Smith (D-S. C.), Stephens (D-Miss.), Thomas (D-Okla.), and Walsh (D-Mass.). Brookhart was absent but favored the amendment. For Norbeck's remarks, *ibid.*, Pt. 6, 5859.

against them and for the big growers. Anti-Board sentiment was particularly strong among Farmers' Union members in Iowa, Nebraska, and Oklahoma. The Pennsylvania and Vermont Farmers' Protective Associations opposed the Board; so did Milo Reno's Farm Holiday Association in Iowa. These groups saw the Farm Board subsidiaries as monopolies, operated by agricultural promoters who were eternally "farming the farmer" while pretending to espouse his cause. John A. Simpson, president of the Farmers' Union, told a Senate committee that prices on the Chicago Board of Trade were fixed by a handful of men, a cabal connected with international bankers who controlled the money in circulation. These men created booms and recessions by altering the quantity of money; they knew in advance what conditions would be and acted accordingly. Job Wells Brinton, an organizer for North Dakota's Nonpartisan League, saw the Farm Board as an invisible power building a privileged corporation—financed with government money —to control the marketing business. All these men, in constant fear of a conspiracy between big farmers and big business, believed that promoters and speculators were intercepting the funds that Congress had appropriated to aid the real farmers.[38]

But farmers as a whole—or at least their organizations,—felt compelled to support the Farm Board until its failure was very evident; it claimed to be helping them, and it had succeeded in maintaining prices, albeit for limited periods only. Moreover the cotton and grain merchants, foes of the growers, wanted to see the Board abolished; this fact recommended the Board to the farm-

---

[38] *To Abolish the Federal Farm Board*, 6-7, 33. Simpson had opposed Hoover and price fixing in World War I. His election as president of the Farmers' Union was a repudiation of Hoover's Farm Board. Gilbert C. Fite, "John A. Simpson; the Southwest's Militant Farm Leader," *Mississippi Valley Historical Review*, XXXV:563-584 (March 1949); Job Wells Brinton, *Wheat and Politics* (Minneapolis, 1931), 182-207.

ers. Many farmers agreed with President Hoover that Board trading did temporarily mitigate the tremendous deflation of prices that introduced the Great Depression.

By the summer of 1932 the Farm Board was floundering in its surpluses and willing to admit the failure of its policies, especially in view of its inability to restrict crops. At this time the Board was still trying to get rid of surpluses acquired in 1929, 1930, and 1931.[39] Farm relief was an important issue in the election of 1932 and Democratic presidential candidate Franklin D. Roosevelt had to have something to say when he crossed the prairies in search of farm votes. Was not Republican extravagance and speculation a natural theme? Said FDR in Topeka: "the Farm Board has squandered $100s of millions of the taxpayers' money; its surpluses have been a millstone around the neck of the cooperative movement. Farm Board speculative operations must and shall come to an end. . . . When the futility of maintaining prices of wheat and cotton through so-called stabilization became apparent, the President's Farm Board . . . invented the cruel joke of advising farmers to allow 20 per cent of their wheat lands to lie idle, to plow up every third row of cotton, and to shoot every tenth dairy cow. Surely they know that this advice should not—indeed, could not be taken."[40] These were ironic phrases in view of what Roosevelt's Agricultural Adjustment Administration did to those "little pigs" several years later. But Roosevelt's career as well as his actions during the first hundred days of his Presidency were to reveal that he was a pragmatist who had inherited less of the mental furniture of the past than had his contemporaries in politics. Anti-speculation was not a fundamental tenet with him (he had been a Wall Street lawyer), as it was

[39] Legge Clippings, McCormick Collection; *Business Week*, July 23, 1932, 11.

[40] *The Public Papers and Addresses of Franklin Roosevelt*, I, 709 (September 14, 1932).

with vestigial Bryan Democrats. By and large, FDR's attack on the Farm Board's methods may be dismissed as good politics.

Criticism of the Farm Board, particularly its invasion of the futures markets, came mostly from the political extremes; standpatters in the grain and cotton trades and the residuum of Populists and Nonpartisan Leaguers seem to have been the most persistent. In Congress Republicans generally supported it as part of Hoover's farm program, and Democrats were critical of it for this reason. But Black's anti-speculation amendment presented Midwest reformers with a dilemma: Whether to vote with the handful of Democrat agrarians for an end to speculation by the government or to vote with their Republican colleagues for the continuation of the Board's speculative activities. Their Republicanism and pro-regulation tendencies pulled them toward the Board; their anti-speculation sentiments pulled them toward its agrarian opponents. Only Blaine, La-Follette, and Couzens were overcome by the latter and defected to Black's amendment. Whether sound or not, the Farm Board was another regulatory device that seemed to undermine the agrarian, and strengthen the progressive position among the reformers.

III

Reform of the national banking system moved more slowly than the related efforts in agriculture and stock exchange regulation. It was several years after the Crash before the full weakness of the banking structure was widely recognized. Senator Carter Glass had intensified his campaign to revamp the Federal Reserve System, but his colleagues were slow in rallying to his cause. So was public opinion; in 1930, measures to prevent panics seemed too much like closing the barn door after the horse was stolen.

The Federal Reserve Act of 1913 had been a compromise between New Nationalists and the advocates of the New Freedom, including most of the Bryan followers. The act provided for a modified central banking system and a Federal Reserve Board to coordinate it. After the 1907 panic, bankers had demanded a central banking system to reinforce the state systems, for it was assumed that regional monetary stringency was the prime cause for the intermittent panics that had been occurring since 1819. Old Guard Republicans naturally leaned toward the Hamiltonian solution: a strong central bank and, after a careful study, Nelson W. Aldrich of Rhode Island, the GOP boss of the Senate, advanced the Aldrich-Vreeland bill to set up such a system. New Freedom adherents, on the other hand, favored an America of smaller concerns and greater individual competition; they distrusted the Aldrich bill as well as its author, believing that a central bank would tighten the grip of a financial oligarchy. Partly to combat this fear, the Reserve System was divided into twelve districts generally corresponding to geographical regions, with each District Bank supposedly autonomous, adjusting its policy and rediscount rates to the needs of the area served. The Federal Reserve Board was to be an independent agency, coordinating the system, aloof from both executive and legislative branches. Thus did the United States embark upon its third experiment with a national banking system. Between 1913 and 1929 there were many amendments to the act; generally these were to facilitate discounting by members, for some bankers thought the original provisions too cumbersome for quick action. This was especially true during World War I.[41]

After the war New Nationalist–New Freedom differences over Reserve System operations continued. Economic consolidation, strong at the turn of the century, had accelerated during the war and continued into the postwar decade. Big business hailed the mergers as prog-

[41] George Henry Soule, *Prosperity Decade,* 49-53.

ress, but those who clung to the New Freedom of Wilson and Brandeis were dismayed by the threat to local institutions represented by this concentration. Branch banking had become increasingly controversial after California sanctioned it in 1909. Success in California led bankers in other states to advocate it, but opposition developed among small state banks which feared the competition of national branches. Initially the anti-branch forces were numerically predominant in legislatures and, aided by the Pujo Committee findings, were able to impede the growth of national bank branches, but the banking crises of the twenties strengthened the pro-branch element politically. Conservative Eastern bankers went on record against speculative excess and tried to relate it to the claim that there were too many small banks in the farm states. As evidence they cited the many failures among small banks before 1929; they believed banking efficiency would be increased by larger, more diversified units.[42]

Anti-branch spokesmen were vehement in reply. They saw in branch bank expansion a surrender to all the forces they had been fighting since the days of Jackson and Biddle. Chain banking seemed particularly insidious to those who believed with the elder LaFollette that democracy was threated by a plutocracy indifferent to the wishes of the people. Banking chains could invade small towns, squeeze out local banks, and suck away funds without feeling obliged to cater to local

[42] John M. Chapman and Ray B. Westerfield, *Branch Banking; its Historical and Theoretical Position in America and Abroad* (New York, 1942), 84-115. Thomas W. Lamont, "Branch Banking," *Review of Reviews*, 87:22 (January 1933); Owen D. Young, industrial spokesman and author of the "Young Plan" for war debts, favored a completely centralized banking system that would eliminate state banking. *Commercial & Financial Chronicle*, 132:I:896 (February 7, 1931); branch banking with modifications had the support of Senators Glass, Bulkley, George, King, Costigan, Couzens, and Walsh of Montana, *Congressional Record*, 72 Cong., 2 sess., v. 76, Pt. 2, 2209.

needs. State banking systems would be menaced by a financial octopus reaching out from New York. Speculators and brokers would fatten even more than they had in the twenties if such expansion were permitted, for in 1930 only nine states allowed national branches, and these were bound by many restrictions.[43] Yet branch banking was not a party issue. Republican James G. Strong, a Kansas Congressman, declared that the spread of branches meant the decline of the middle class. Democrat Franklin D. Roosevelt, Governor of New York, believed that the "personal touch" was lacking in branch banking.[44] In the Senate Republicans Blaine, Brookhart, Frazier, Howell, LaFollette and Nye fought alongside Democrats Black, Bulow, Connally, Long, Sheppard and Thomas of Oklahoma to check the growth of national bank branches.

Deeply-held divergences on the old centralization question made the task of any banking reformer difficult. Proposals to reduce small country banks would divide the reformers; so would plans to strengthen the system by increasing the powers of the Federal Reserve Board. Even the progressives of 1913 had divided on the degree of centralization; this issue had set Norris against LaFollette, Poindexter against Bristow, Crawford against Cummins, and Owen against Borah.[45] Could banking reformers find a formula and present a united front thirty years later? Senator Glass tried to solve this problem in an omnibus banking bill, a political potpourri with provisions to please many divergent factions. Some banks, using wholly-owned security affiliates, had exploited the public in the twenties and oversold many dubious stocks. Therefore Glass proposed to separate the affiliates from their parent banks, a step acceptable

[43] Chapman and Westerfield, *op. cit.*, 129.

[44] *Commercial & Financial Chronicle*, 131:I:202 (July 12, 1930); *The Progressive*, 1:7 (June 28, 1930).

[45] *Congressional Record*, 72 Cong., 2 sess., v. 76, Pt. 2, 2207; *ibid.*, 63 Cong., 2 sess., v. 51, Pt. 2, 1230 (December 19, 1913).

to New Freedom disciples. Henry B. Steagall, chairman of the House Banking Committee, inserted an old Bryan reform, guarantee of bank deposits. This would appeal to small-bank advocates because it was the small institutions that were failing in large numbers. The big banks, on the other hand, claimed that deposit guarantees had been unsuccessful wherever tried.[46]

George L. Harrison of the New York Federal Reserve Bank explained to a Senate subcommittee in 1931 why the Federal Reserve did not check speculation before the Crash. He told Senators that in practice it was almost impossible to ascertain in advance what a member bank was going to use credit for. The member usually offered excellent paper, such as United States Bonds, or it borrowed under the fifteen-day rule on a general note *after* it had fallen short of reserves. Since it borrowed after advancing credit to its various borrowers, it was difficult to relate money borrowed from the Reserve Bank to specific loans made by the member. Could a Reserve Bank refuse credit if eligible paper were presented?[47] The fifteen-day borrowing privilege had been put into the Federal Reserve Act to hasten banking procedures during World War I. In the twenties what had been intended as an emergency measure had become common practice; the Federal Reserve had made rediscounting respectable, and thus largely circumvented the spirit of the act.

In Section 3 Senator Glass proposed to correct this evil: the Federal Reserve Board itself was empowered to investigate the nature of loans made by members in-

---

[46] Howard H. Preston, "The Banking Act of 1933," *American Economic Review*, 23:588 (December 1933); even after its passage banking expert H. P. Willis regarded the bank deposit guarantee as an incongruous rider.

[47] *Operations of the National and Federal Reserve Banking Systems*, Committee on Banking & Currency. United States Senate. 71 Cong., 3 sess. (Washington, 1931), 30-56. *Commercial & Financial Chronicle*, 130:I:329 (January 18, 1930); 134:II:3163 (April 30, 1932).

stead of leaving the matter to the District Banks. The Board was given the power to suspend discounting to any member that, in the opinion of the Board, had too many speculative commitments. The power to go more deeply into requests for credit, to inquire into the operations of individual banks, meant a further invasion of business by the federal government and made many bankers wince, although the plan promised to curb speculative credit more adequately. The American Bankers Association objected that this section gave the Board too much arbitrary power, and the Federal Reserve Board itself rejected Section 3 in favor of a weak substitute. The prevailing view seemed to be that political and economic affairs, like church and state, should be kept apart lest they corrupt one another. One general objection to the Glass bill was its allegedly deflationary character; some businessmen thought that credit, speculative or not, should be encouraged in order to pull the country out of the depression.[48]

The anti-speculator Midwest was wary of any increase in Reserve Board powers. The agrarians had long been suspicious of such government agencies as the Interstate Commerce Commission, the Federal Reserve Board, and the Federal Farm Board. Unable to forget the Reserve Board's deflation policy of 1920-1921, they feared that a Board with greater powers would be even less responsive to the regional needs of the farmers. Truly, checking speculation by legislation was not an easy task even in 1932 when the Democrats and progressive Republicans controlled Congress and the havoc of speculative excess could be seen everywhere. That November the voters swept into office Franklin D. Roosevelt and a New Deal Congress. The President-elect was said to favor the Glass bill; indeed, Roosevelt and the Vir-

[48] *Ibid.*, 137:I:961 (August 5, 1933); 135:II:4315 (December 24, 1932); 134:II:2442 (April 2, 1932); 134:I:2261 (March 26, 1932).

ginian were old friends from the Wilson days, and Roosevelt offered Glass an appointment as Secretary of the Treasury—an offer which Glass rejected.[49]

The winter of 1932-1933 was an economic nadir in the history of the United States. Unemployment was over fifteen million, and some prominent banks were forced to close their doors. There was no confidence in Hoover's lame-duck administration and the atmosphere was heavy with claims of conspiracy and zany plans for reform. In New York Thomas W. Lamont, a Morgan partner, deplored the chaos created by forty-nine separate banking systems; noting that failures were four times as frequent among state banks, he urged their absorption into the Federal Reserve System.[50] In North Dakota, legislators considered a resolution calling for secession of the thirty-nine productive states, leaving the nine financial parasites to feed on themselves. Said one advocate: "We will secede carrying with us the star-spangled banner and leave them the stripes which they so richly deserve."[51] Congressman Louis T. McFadden persisted in his attempt to impeach President Hoover, and Norman Vincent Peale, a leading clergyman, called upon guilty bankers and speculators to ask God's forgiveness.[52] Amid this discordant clamor, in a winter of desperate uncertainty, the Glass-Steagall bill, a technical measure of 22,000 words, reached the Senate floor. As predicted, branch banking was the most disputed of many disputed sections. Section 19 authorized branch banks within fifty miles of larger cities, even in the states that prohibited branch banking. Sam G. Bratton of New Mexico, worried over states' rights and realizing that a coalition

[49] *Ibid.*, 136:I:1304 (February 20, 1933); candidate Roosevelt in a banking speech in Columbus in September had promised to keep Reserve System credit away from speculators. *Time* thought this was impractical. 20:10 (November 21, 1932).

[50] *Time*, 20:10 (November 28, 1932).

[51] *The Progressive*, 1:7 (January 21, 1933).

[52] *Time*, 20:7 (December 26, 1932); *ibid.*, 21:46fn. (March 20, 1933).

of anti-branch agrarians and state bank supporters could defeat the section, offered a crucial compromise amendment: branch banking only in states already permitting it, and the national branches to conform to the same rules as state bank branches. These were important concessions—they meant that state legislation could still bar the centralization dreams of the nation's big bankers. The Senate approved Bratton's amendment, 52 to 17. Since branch banking outside city limits was then legal in only nine states, the Bratton amendment in effect limited branch expansion to these nine.[53] But a few Senators were still not satisfied. Huey Pierce Long of Louisiana made his debut in the Senate by filibustering against *any* expansion of branch banking; in fact, this became part of "The Kingfish's" anti-monopoly crusade which aimed to "soak the fat boys." But when Hugo Black tried to ban branch banking expansion entirely, thus closing the nine-state loophole left by the Bratton amendment, his move was defeated, 45 to 17.[54]

The Glass-Steagall bill was approved by the Senate 54 to 9. President Roosevelt signed it in June 1933, and the law was finally on the books although there had been no encouragement from the Federal Reserve Board, the American Bankers Association, or the economists. Senator Glass had been able to retain Section 3 regulating the speculative investments of individual member banks, and security affiliates had been divorced

[53] *Congressional Record,* 72 Cong., 2 sess., v. 76, Pt. 2, 1449. *Ibid.* Unwilling to accept even a little branch banking, Elmer Thomas of Oklahoma joined the Eastern bankers in voting no; *Business Week,* February 1, 1933, 14.

[54] *Commercial & Financial Chronicle,* 136:I:532 (January 25, 1933); The seventeen who favored Black's amendment were: Black (D-Ala.); Blaine (R-Wis.); Capper (R-Kans.); Carey (R-Wyo.); Connally (D-Tex.); Frazier (R-N. D.); McGill (D-Kans.); Norbeck (R-S. D.); Nye (R-N. D.); Patterson (R-Mo.); Reynolds (D-N. C.); Robinson (R-Ind.); Schall (R-Minn.); Sheppard (D-Tex.); Thomas (D-Okla.); Trammell (D-Fla.); and Wheeler (D-Mont.).

from their parent banks. But, to achieve this victory, Glass had had to make concessions. Branch banking, which he favored, had been very seriously circumscribed, and he had to acquiesce in the deposit guarantee of Steagall, a provision he felt was unsound. Nevertheless the act was an important step in insulating the banking system against the kind of speculative orgy that had been so ruinous in 1929.

IV

Tax policy had been a matter of controversy during the 1920s; as the thirties began it was even more of an issue. Agrarian elements, following Populist tradition, insisted that taxes were falling more heavily on real than on personal property, that the tax system was inequitable and that those with large incomes were finding loopholes. The regime of Andrew Mellon in the Treasury Department during the administrations of Coolidge and Hoover, while approved by business, met with hostility in farm areas. Mellon's repeated efforts to lower the tax rates on big incomes—in the belief that confident businessmen would provide prosperity for all—could not evoke any emotion other than anger in regions where prosperity was invisible and the traditions of anti-monopoly, anti-middleman, and pro-inflation had taken root long before. How could Mellon, the Pittsburgh millionaire, understand farm problems?

During the twenties the progressives of both parties pressed for the adoption of publicity of income tax returns. The principle of "pitiless publicity," born in the Progressive Era and triumphant in Wisconsin for some years, was felt to be the remedy for the large speculative profits then being amassed. The progressives had argued that the honest citizen would not be afraid to make public his income from wages, rentals, and dividends; speculators and promoters, on the other hand, might be less daring in their coups if they thought that crusading journalists could discover damaging data and goad the tax authorities into prosecution. Senator LaFollette on many occasions explained to his colleagues the successful operation of Wisconsin's law. But what data and where it should be made available for public-spirited sleuths was the topic of much debate. Most legislators from less homogeneous areas, socially and economically, were wary of the plan; Southerners and Easterners feared the invasion of privacy that would be involved. They argued that business competitors, sensational newspapermen, disenchanted sweethearts, and impecunious relatives could destroy a citizen's business and reputation if income data got into their hands. Many grain traders and others in the business had been grumbling ever since the Grain Futures Administration had required the reporting of large trades. Therefore, despite revelations of tax avoidance by some "big fellows," a coalition of Old Guardsmen and Southern conservatives had defeated the publicity provision in 1926. In 1928, after a progressive success in a Senate with many absentees, the Old Guard had the vote reconsidered and the plan was again defeated.[55] Unlike various other progressive-sponsored tax measures, this reform involved no tax and therefore should not have encountered opposition from regular Democrats who favored a minimum of federal taxation. Yet such was their fear of investigators and demagogues, such was their proud independence, that the Southerners went along with their colleagues from the corporation states in fighting the publicity principle.

As unemployment increased in 1930 and 1931, dissatisfaction with the Hoover Administration also increased. The President's policy was one of economy, an attempt at retrenchment. The administration hoped that

[55] *Congressional Record*, 69 Cong., 1 sess., v. 67, Pt. 4, 3526 (February 8, 1926); 70 Cong., 1 sess., v. 69, Pt. 8, 9082, 9853-9854 (May 25, 1928).

balancing the budget would miraculously turn the business index upward, that sufficient contraction would lead ultimately to expansion as it had always done before. This view had wide support among the economists; the general public also found comfort in the idea of a balanced budget. Were not frugality and industry antidotes for extravagance and indolence? So the Congress began to look about for sources of tax revenue that would not oppress the working classes or discourage business confidence. The most obvious sources were the stock and commodity markets. Why not tax those individuals and practices that had "caused" the depression? Why not utilize the prevalent antipathy toward speculators to enact tax measures that would reach the large profits made in speculation and the large commissions charged by brokers? If laws could be drafted that eliminated or severely curtailed certain types of operations, so much the better; surely the Congress could now see the need for such taxes, thought the reformers; the economic reforms they had urged so consistently but so futilely during the boom might now receive greater attention in a Congress sobered by the prospects of starvation, revolt, and property destruction. But the reformers misjudged the mood of Congress. Senator Glass found the Senate of 1930 indifferent to his plan to tax more heavily securities held less than sixty days, despite statistical evidence showing that the average trader held his stock only twenty-two days.[56]

In 1932, when the House recommended a ¼ per cent tax on stock transfers to replacing the existing two cents per $100 par value, the Senate Finance Committee struck out the provision as "too burdensome." When the tax bill reached the floor of the Senate, however, Clarence C. Dill of Washington, a progressive Demo-

---

[56] During 1917, a fairly active period in market history, stocks were held an average of sixty-seven days. *Operations of the National and Federal Reserve Banking Systems,* 59.

crat, challenged the committee's action. He reminded his colleagues of the startling testimony being given concurrently to the Senate subcommittee investigating stock practices; he reminded them of the billions that speculators had accumulated by fraudulent means during the heyday of prosperity. Speculation had been a neglected source of revenue, but aside from that, said Dill fiercely, the tax should be levied as a deterrent. Why, he asked, was the Senate always so lenient toward the speculative classes? Although the Senate had eliminated the ¼ per cent rate, they had recommended a rate of 4 cents per $100 par, which represented a 100 per cent increase over the existing statute. Senator Reed Smoot of Utah, in charge of steering the tax measure through the Senate, declared that the four-cent rate was adequate for budgetary needs.[57]

But Senator Dill was not easily silenced. He argued that the ¼ per cent rate was much superior because, in contrast to the flat rate, it varied with the price of the security and acted to dampen stock prices that climbed too high. It only equaled the broker's average commission and would not put anyone out of business; moreover it would raise some revenue from those most culpable and would probably reduce gambling. Opponents objected that it would reduce trading volume at a time when sales were sagging. As the vote on the amendment approached, Dill made a concession, halving the rate to ⅛ per cent of the market price; but even after this severe modification, the amendment, embodying the progressive tax principle, was defeated on a roll call vote, 37 to 45. Senator Burton K. Wheeler of Montana then proposed a flat rate of six cents per $100 in place of the

[57] *Congressional Record,* 72 Cong., 1 sess., v. 75, Pt. 10, 11484ff. Dill's tax was much more to the liking of small western mining companies whose stocks sold only in pennies per share. A flat rate of four cents was prohibitive for them; they wanted a graduated rate.

committee recommendation of four cents. This too was defeated, 32 to 47. The four cent rate prevailed.[58]

The anti-speculators then discovered, upon examining the bill closely, that loaned stock was exempted from the tax. Why should short sellers—the great majority of those who borrowed stock, and the particular villains in the public mind at this time—be exempt? David Aiken Reed of Pennsylvania, reputed agent of steel and oil interests in the Keystone state, undertook to explain this seemingly significant exemption: short selling could not be reached without taxing the legitimate lending of stock. Reed told the Senate that a tax on loaned stock would penalize the seller who was more than twenty-four hours from New York City. Such a man was not able to deliver his stock certificates to the broker in New York by 2:15 P.M. the following day as required by exchange rules; consequently he authorized his broker to borrow the necessary securities pending the arrival by mail of the securities he had sold. According to Reed, a person in this situation, although making a legitimate and not a short sale, would be obliged to pay a tax not only on the sale but also on the stock his broker borrowed for him. Investors in the interior of the country, who could not hover over the tickers in New York, would be penalized. Senator Reed Smoot concurred in this interpretation.

But some lawmakers were unwilling to be turned aside by the possibility of double taxation. Blaine and Wheeler urged the passage of any tax that would reach some short selling, and Dill reminded the Senate of recent White House disapproval of bear activities. Wheeler went on to suggest that the crusade against Al Capone and American Communists might better be

[58] *Ibid.*, 11531-11541. As a result of a later House modification, the rate was set at five cents until 1934 when it was to drop to three cents. The five-cent rate was justified as a temporary expedient to aid in balancing the budget. *Ibid.*, 75 Cong., 3 sess., v. 83, Pt. 5, 5030ff.

directed toward market speculators. He accused the Senate of fear and referred to the strong lobbies against any taxes that would hamper the markets. "Every senator will admit in private that speculation caused the 'crash.' Why not put the brokers out of work?" the Montana lawyer asked. After all, Montana miners were unemployed. The Senate then held a roll call vote on whether loaned stock should be exempted from the stock transfer tax. The result was 40 to 37 against the exemption, a narrow victory for the anti-speculators.[59] But in the spring of 1932 the United States Senate was not yet prepared to jeopardize recovery by placing too burdensome a tax on stock transactions. Perhaps the stock market still seemed too closely associated with prosperity—but at least the Senate had blocked one loophole for short sellers.

After his inauguration, President Franklin D. Roosevelt speeded passage of the Federal Securities Act, and Huston Thompson, a New Deal lawyer, enlisted the aid of several of Professor Felix Frankfurter's protégés to draw up the provisions. Thompson, who had served on the Federal Trade Commission, had long advocated a Federal blue sky law and had written the 1932 Democratic plank on this subject.[60] The law required truth and full disclosure in prospectuses and registration statements for new securities sold in interstate commerce. In his message to Congress the President added the dictum "Let the seller beware" to the ancient "caveat emptor," and also noted that state blue sky laws had proved inadequate against interstate stock selling frauds. The Senate Banking and Currency Committee later substantiated this, declaring that $25 million of worthless stock had been sold to American investors in the last ten years.

[59] *Ibid.*, 11486ff.; 11540 (May 30, 1932).

[60] Russell Owen, "The President's Brain-Trust is again Target for Critics," *New York Times,* April 1, 1934, 3:6-8.

The Securities Act, coming in the whirlwind first hundred days of the New Deal, met vociferous but numerically weak opposition. Financiers prefaced their criticism with statements professing to favor its principles; "truth in securities" was a slogan that could not be attacked head-on. The Investment Bankers' Association claimed that the law's stiff penalties and liabilities would discourage investment at a time when stimulus to the economy was desperately needed. But the country, angered by testimony wrung from bankers by the Senate investigating committee, was in a mood to blame the broker-banker community for the depression ills, and the act became law on May 27, 1933.[61] The Federal Securities Act required elaborate registration statements from corporations whose securities were to be sold in interstate commerce, statements which included details of the business. Corporate officers, large stockholders, and those employed as experts were held strictly responsible for misstatements of fact. The act also included regulations on the construction of summarized prospectuses for public consumption. Recovery was made easier than under common law, and the Federal Trade Commission, watchdog of business ethics, was to administer the law.

William O. Douglas, at that time Sterling Professor of law at Yale University, assailed the new act as an anachronism. After identifying the measure as the Federal culmination of state blue sky movements which had begun in the Progressive Era, he challenged the underlying assumptions of the act—that truth in securities was an important or adequate goal. The ideas behind the measure, said Douglas, were based upon a belief that we should return to a less complex, more personal economy where investor, manager, and worker were more intimately associated. The Federal Security Act

[61] *Commercial & Financial Chronicle*, 136:II:2108, 3043, 3272, 3786-3791.

assumed that intricate corporate details could be made intelligible in prospectuses to investors, and that prospective investors would actually analyze them. Douglas thought that complexity would increase, and was dubious about the analytical abilities of "the investor-in-the-street." He predicted failure of the law if it were rigorously enforced and enumerated specific weaknesses stemming from its faulty premises. The severe and politically motivated liability provisions would result, he felt, in widespread subterfuge and a decline in the caliber of men participating in the investment business. The act was punitive rather than preventive; it was not consonant with the basic principles of the New Deal, which called for general planning and increased social control of the economy.

The Yale jurist thus repudiated the Wilson-Brandeis New Freedom which had stressed individual responsibility and a return to small-unit, competitive economy. Instead he reflected the coastal, urban predilection—already encountered, from both professors and bankers —for flexible administrative law more concerned with experience and socio-economic effects than with rational relation to legal precedents. The progressive principle of publicity seemed, to Douglas, not essential to the New Nationalism—Hamilton had triumphed over Jefferson, Wilson, and LaFollette. Subsequent New Deal security legislation reflected this point of view.[62] In the meanwhile financial critics of the Securities Act echoed Douglas. They hammered at the personal liabilities of corporate officers and directors in the hope that Congress would relent and modify these provisions, and they argued that directors should not be held responsible unless wrongful intent could be shown. Brokers also muttered about the lengthy registration forms. They asserted that security issues made under the new act were

---

[62] William O. Douglas, "Protecting the Investor," *Yale Review,* ns 23:521-533 (March 1934).

of no better quality than before, that the public was being lulled by a false sense of security, thinking that the government had guaranteed these shares.[63] Despite this pressure, Congress was reluctant to take up mitigating amendments during 1934. Senator Elmer Thomas of Oklahoma, a leading Democratic inflationist, introduced a bill to modify the liability provisions; this was interpreted to mean that he regarded the act as an obstacle to inflation.[64]

The stock market reacted favorably to the early months of the Roosevelt Administration. The confidence that radiated from the White House quickly made itself felt in stock prices; anticipated repeal of prohibition gave special impetus to liquor and related stocks. Trading increased in the spring, and reached boom proportions in June and July. Then a severe correction, especially in commodities, followed. Dr. Edward Crawford, a dentist, was refuting the belief that professional men were poor speculators; he managed a brief corner in grain and extended himself in all the markets. Erratic prices in stocks and commodities recalled the halcyon days of 1929. But this renaissance of trading got little sympathetic reaction from the government. Congress decided to investigate Dr. Crawford's operations, and New Dealers and old-line Democrats declared that regulation of stock exchanges was needed; the Securities Act was not enough. Legislative sentiment, in the fall of 1933, was crystallizing in favor of exchange regulation.[65]

[63] *Financial World*, 61:5 (January 3, 1934); *New York Times*, January 7, 1934, 11:3.

[64] *New York Times*, February 7, 1934, 27:3; March 23, 1934, 35:5.

[65] *Commercial & Financial Chronicle*, 137:I:729 (July 29, 1933), 3766-3767 (November 25, 1933), 137:II:2727 (October 14, 1933). "Doc Crawford Shakes the Commodity Markets of the World," *Business Week*, August 5, 1933, 20. The Department of Agriculture found that ten to fifteen individuals were primarily responsible for erratic commodity prices. During the Hoover Administration the rule requiring grain speculators to report their trades had been

The *New Republic* thought that the collapse of the New Deal–Repeal stock boom in July was good news for the Roosevelt administration. The market slump was a warning that mere inflation was not the answer to recovery. Wheat speculators had pushed prices too high in anticipation of the Agricultural Adjustment Administration's restrictive policy, so high in fact that some groups were claiming that there was no longer need for crop allotments. Speculation as then practiced, said the magazine, was socially wasteful. Unlike horse racing, moreover, stock gambling hurt even non-participants. Speculators had evolved to a few shrewd traders who could anticipate induced speculative fevers; the rest were excitable, ignorant, and superstitious sheep. The New Deal should be aware that old-fashioned speculation could overpower all attempts to rationalize the economic system, that anarchistic individuals would continue to gamble for profits instead of earning a living at production and distribution. The *New Republic* wanted the elimination of the profit trader; it suggested comprehensive planning and the indirect changing of business motives to reach this end. It advanced investment by the government and cooperative marketing as two means of circumventing the toll of middleman speculators.[66]

By 1934 much data upon which to base a regulatory law had been gathered. There were voluminous Senate hearings on short selling and stock exchange practices; in addition the intelligentsia had made various proposals for reform. Professor William Z. Ripley of Harvard, for example, whose studies of finance and railroad regulation in the twenties had given him prestige in the regu-

---

rescinded in the hope of stimulating prices. On July 20, 1933, the rule was reinstated.

[66] "Regulating the Speculators," *New Republic*, 78:33-34 (February 21, 1934); "Gambling vs. Social Planning," 75:302-303 (August 2, 1933).

latory field, offered his formula in *Scribner's*. He advanced the proposition that stock traders should be divided into two groups—on different footings at the bar of public opinion. The first group was the uninitiated; the second was the experienced, which was in turn subdivided into the scientific analysts and the insiders who had access to information in advance of the public. Ripley believed insiders were particularly culpable in the events of the previous decade: foreknowledge, he held, was not legitimate in an age of separation of management and stockholders. In the old days of small concerns, the shareholders knew what the officers and directors of the company knew, since they were virtually the same persons. But since the rise of the mammoth corporation with thousands of stockholders scattered all over the Union, the close owner-manager relationship had disappeared and the temptation for corporation officers to mulct both the stockholders and the public had greatly increased. Ripley's solution for reducing the insider was the progressive remedy, publicity. He argued that if standard accounting procedures and frequent earnings reports were required, the rumors which gave rise to so much speculation would be lessened. He also wished to extend this publicity to the activities of company officials, and to have them report periodically on their holdings of company stock. To discourage outside money and stabilize call loan rates, Ripley suggested adoption of the British fortnightly settlement of loans to brokers.[67]

The Roosevelt Administration started study of the speculative problem as soon as it took office. John Dickinson, Assistant Secretary of Commerce, was designated to head a special committee to study speculation; Adolph A. Berle, Jr., was a member. The committee

[67] William Z. Ripley, "Speculation; What to do about it," *Scribner's*, 92:193-198 (October 1932). Senator Borah had suggested this plan in 1929, see p. 152 above.

completed its report as 1933 ended, and the findings were forwarded to the Senate Banking and Currency Committee via the Secretary of Commerce, Daniel C. Roper. The report acknowledged that the exchanges presented new problems in federal regulation, because the situation was dynamic and not subject to fixed standards. The committee recommended that only minimums be set by statute. It opposed the licensing of individual brokers or interfering with the system of discipline that had operated through the business conduct committees of the exchanges for some years. The committee recognized the wisdom of graduated fines to supplement the penalty of suspension of an exchange, because the latter was such an extreme move that it might never be used. It took a liberal attitude toward gambling: "we must recognize that the average man has an inherent instinct for gambling in some form or other." No method of combating gambling had been completely successful, and men had probably turned to the stock market because so many other forms of gambling had been outlawed. The Roper Report went on to declare that "if the speculative tendencies of our people could be turned into other channels, this instinct might be satisfied without the far reaching consequences which come from widespread public speculation in the stock market."[68]

During the winter of 1934 financial circles were buzzing about the administration's policy toward speculation. Brokers were generally surprised and encouraged by

[68] *Report of the Committee on Stock Exchange Regulation appointed by the Secretary of Commerce* (Washington, 1934), 15-16. In addition to Dickinson and Berle, other committee members were Arthur H. Dean, James M. Landis, and Henry J. Richardson. Arthur Krock observed that the New Deal Administration seemed to take the attitude that it was better to legalize gambling and derive revenue from it than to see it drain off money illegally. He said some administration men had privately hailed the passage of various state horse racing laws, thinking that racing would shift gamblers away from the stock market. *New York Times,* April 24, 1934, 22:6.

the moderate tone of the committee's report, but on the other hand Adolph A. Berle, Jr., had suggested (in a radio address in New York) that the nation's banks be socialized, and there were hints that radical "brain-trusters" were drafting a vindictive stock exchange bill. Congress and the public had been aroused by extensive short selling in the aircraft stocks during January—it appeared that "insiders" had taken advantage of advance information that the government would not renew its air-mail contracts. The President made it clear that he wanted an exchange regulation bill enacted that spring.

In the meantime the New York Stock Exchange had been busy instituting various reforms. It put customers' men, a group that in 1929 had been eager for commissions but ignorant of stocks, on salaries. The exchange hoped in this way to improve the stability of the occupation and raise it to professional status. The exchange also began to require independent auditing, to increase the reliability of periodic business statements submitted to the market. It required holders of large blocks of stock to sign agreements to lend; this was intended to augment the floating supply and avoid a possible corner. Companies were also restricted in trading in their own stock, and exchange members were required to publicize options and participation in pools. The exchange still had to face charges of monopoly, oligarchy, and secrecy. The Pujo Report of 1913 had stressed the dictatorial powers of exchange committees, and this claim was renewed after the Crash: Senator Costigan of Colorado said that exchange government was so secretive that even many exchange members were in the dark. Investment bankers also demanded a voice in exchange administration.[69]

The stock exchange control measure, introduced in

[69] *New York Times,* January 7, 1934, 28:6, January 30, 27:6, March 2, 29:6, March 27, 1:8, January 2, 28:1, March 3, 19:6, March 20, 31:8, February 27, 34:6, March 8, 29:1.

February, was known as the Fletcher-Rayburn bill. It was a complicated proposal that attempted to outlaw manipulative practices revealed by Congressional investigation, to improve the ethics of brokers and dealers, and to control the credit facilities used by exchange members to carry their many margin customers. As first drafted, the Federal Trade Commission was to administer the act, and was granted great discretionary power. Like the Federal Securities Act, the bill was written by fledgling New Deal lawyers, in this case Thomas Corcoran and Benjamin Cohen, again protégés of Harvard law professor Felix Frankfurter. Their "brain-trust" origin, coupled with their apparent impatience with the parliamentary process, offended a Senate traditionally sensitive about its prerogatives, and Senators resolved to explore the bill fully in debate. Their suspicions were further aroused by the testimony of John Dickinson, chairman of the special speculation committee, that neither he nor any other member of his group had been consulted in the drafting of the Fletcher-Rayburn bill; and the Treasury Department would not endorse the bill *in toto*—it would only comment on specific sections.[70]

Both the administration and Congress seemed to want more teeth in the bill than Wall Street did; in fact, the bill stirred the first real opposition to the New Deal since it had assumed office. The President noted that "a more definite and more highly organized drive is being made against effective legislation for Federal supervision of stock exchanges than against any similar recommendation made by me."[71] Richard Whitney, president of the New York Stock Exchange since 1930, led the attack. The aristocratic financier—a product of

[70] *Time*, 23:I:53 (February 26, 1934); *Wall Street Journal*, March 26, 1934, 1:5; March 22, 1:5; *Commercial & Financial Chronicle*, 138:I:1837 (March 17, 1934).

[71] *Ibid.*, 138:II:2625 (April 21, 1934); *Congressional Record*, 73 Cong., 2 sess., v. 80, 8916.

Groton, Harvard, and Kidder, Peabody—had always been a formidable opponent, especially in committee hearings. He wrote letters to brokers and corporation officials trying to stimulate their opposition to the bill; and to Congress he suggested amendments modifying every section.[72] Whitney told brokers that they had failed miserably in their public relations, that they had failed to get the facts about the exchanges to the general public. Mass meetings to protest the bill were held by brokers and exchange employees under auspices of the wire houses. Fenner and Beane, the world's largest brokerage firm, sent out letters to their clients urging protest against any vindictive legislation. Whitney took the line with the corporations that the Federal Trade Commission was given too much power to snoop into their affairs, and this brought results: 250 New England companies went on record against the bill; so did nineteen from St. Louis. The Dry Goods Industry Committee announced its opposition. Harvard economics professor Seymour Harris thought the bill "untimely,"[73] and James H. Rand, Jr., chairman of the Committee of the Nation, a right-wing inflationist group, backed Whitney in criticizing the interference with exchange operations and the high, rigid margin requirements.[74] Henry I. Harriman of the United States Chamber of Commerce was against the bill. President Michael J. O'Brien of the Chicago Stock Exchange predicted that many companies would delist their securities rather than comply, and that smaller exchanges would thus be eliminated.[75] The vice-president of the National Association of Manufacturers thought the proposed regulation would hurt the

[72] *Time,* 23:I:53 (February 26, 1934).

[73] *New York Times,* February 16, 1934, 27:6, February 15, 27:8, February 19, 27:2, April 15, 11:4, April 1, 7:8, April 6, 35:6-7, March 14, 27:8.

[74] *Time,* 23:II:9 (April 2, 1934).

[75] *Commercial & Financial Chronicle,* 138:I:1837 (March 17, 1934); 1320 (February 24, 1934).

capital supply and therefore impede recovery, and the *Wall Street Journal's* Washington correspondent feared the social control of capital by the Federal Trade Commission.[76]

But not all the critics were financiers or businessmen. From Palm Springs came word that Samuel Untermyer, the stock market regulation crusader of 1912-1914, thought the Fletcher-Rayburn measure too harsh to be effective—it would defeat its own purpose, he said, and Alfred Bernheim of the Twentieth Century Fund agreed. John Dickinson was also doubtful about effects of the bill; he wanted a separate body to administer the law, as his special speculation committee report had recommended. He predicted that a ban on loans on unlisted securities would cause a panicky liquidation with adverse effects on the economy.[77] Under the growing pressure of financial and commercial interests, the bill's advocates made some concessions. In March they presented a revised draft which gave administrative power to the Securities and Exchange Commission, a body especially created for the purpose, instead of the Federal Trade Commission. Credit controls were entrusted to the Federal Reserve Board. The President acquiesced in this change, which was widely interpreted as a victory for the brokers. There were many other modifications, many of which were opposed by counsel Ferdinand Pecora.

Despite the concessions, the discretionary power of the new commission, the margin requirements, and the prohibition of loans on unlisted stocks were sore points on Wall Street, and Richard Whitney kept up his vigorous campaign.[78] In the Senate, Frederick Steiwer, an Oregon Republican, outlined all the arguments against

[76] *Wall Street Journal,* March 13, 1934, 6:5, March 21, 1:5.

[77] *Ibid.,* March 7, 1934, 2:2; *Commercial & Financial Chronicle,* 138:I:1187 (February 9, 1934), 1836 (March 17, 1934).

[78] *New York Times,* April 10, 1934, 33:4, April 18, 29:5, March 13, 37:2, March 28, 33:8.

the bill in a long speech. First, said Steiwer, although the act purported to regulate the exchanges, it actually brought 450,000 firms with no Wall Street connections under the "strangling regulation of a Federal bureau." He suggested that the requirement that companies agree in advance to Commission rules which would be promulgated later was a violation of the constitutional protection against *ex post facto* laws. The blue sky provisions had the effect, he said, of broadening the law beyond mere exchange regulation. Steiwer stressed the unfavorable psychological effect the act would have on business. A state of mind can produce a depression, he observed, whether the law actually hurt companies or not. The disclosures of business details could be used by rivals and would add to business uncertainty. Curiously he blamed Congress for not acting sooner to stop specific market abuses, implying that anti-market sentiment could have been dampened earlier had that been done. And he concluded that it is better not to go far enough than to go too far.

Hugo Black of Alabama and Alben Barkley of Kentucky replied to this attack. Black claimed that the agreement to comply was really superfluous anyway; if regulations were valid, companies had to abide by them. Barkley observed that the public was entitled to more information than the Federal Securities Act provided for, that continuous earnings reports and balance sheets were in the public interest. If truth makes a security unsalable, then so be it, said Barkley, the public interest must come before the protection of corporations.[79]

Toward the end of the debate the margins issue came to a head. Many analysts had emphasized the role which installment buying, especially the margin purchases of stocks, had played in the 1929 collapse. Indeed, easy credit was for many the prime cause of the Crash. Ex-

[79] *Congressional Record*, 73 Cong., 2 sess., v. 78, Pt. 8, 8270ff.

change critics therefore favored very strict credit limitations; they also wanted to end alleged favoritism in dispensing credit to speculators.

V

A move to outlaw margins entirely, however, had not reached the floor of Congress since the Crash. In 1931 rather ludicrous hearings had been held on a measure offered by Senator Heflin to ban margins and set the maximum call loan rate at 8 per cent, and President Whitney of the New York Stock Exchange and General Coxey, the venerable Populist, had disputed the causes and effects of the Crash.[80] After this episode no bill affecting margins came up until 1934.

The Fletcher-Rayburn Bill, after its revision, provided for a margin requirement between 55 and 75 per cent. Power to set rates within this range was given to the Federal Reserve Board, although the remainder of the act was to be administered by the Securities and Exchange Commission. While opponents of this provision were inclined to agree that margins had played a large part in the 1929 debacle, they still felt that the high, somewhat rigid standards for margins would inhibit trading at a time when it should be encouraged, and feared a sudden liquidation when the act went into effect. This was the universal bankers' prejudice against rigid credit requirements. Like J. P. Morgan, they were convinced that credit was a matter of character, that financiers should be free to use their judgment in setting varying credit margins for different individuals in different market situations. A regulatory board, they believed, could not possibly foresee the individual situations that constantly arose in bankers' and brokers' offices.[81]

[80] *Prohibition of Margin Trading,* 10-37.
[81] *New York Times,* February 10, 1934, 8:4; March 5, 6:5. President Roosevelt, in letters to Fletcher and Rayburn urged high margin requirements, *ibid.,* March 27, 1:8.

The reformers, on the other hand, were generally suspicious of credit transactions. The use of "other people's money" by financiers had been a particular sore point since talk of The System and the Money Trust in the heyday of the muckrakers. Although the bill provided for a 55-75 per cent margin requirement, which was higher than the 20-40 per cent rate prevalent during the twenties, it did not satisfy the anti-speculator bloc. They regarded margin purchases of stock as prima facie evidence of speculative intent. Therefore, midway in the Senate debate, Robert J. Bulkley of Ohio, a hard-money man but a Democratic progressive, spearheaded a move for the abolition of margin trading. In a lengthy speech on the floor he declared that the broker-customer relationship was not a natural one, that the loans advanced to customers were on too casual and impersonal a basis. Unlike a banker, the broker never felt it necessary to inquire as to the standing of the borrower because the broker could sell out the customer and get his money. The broker, therefore, had no interest in the soundness of the loan. In normal periods this was fairly satisfactory but the accumulation of margin accounts by people of inadequate resources would ultimately lead, as it had before, to an orgy of liquidation, a panic in which brokers would be unable to sell out their customers fast enough. In contrast, Bulkley pointed to the banker-customer relation, where the banker collected adequate data on the borrower and often knew him personally. If people wanted to buy securities, let them go to their local banks and obtain the funds, as did most other legitimate businessmen. This would ensure safer and saner stock purchases. The Senator quoted from the Senate Stock Exchange Practices Report: "By the development of the margin account, a great many people have been induced to embark upon speculative ventures in which they were doomed to certain loss."

Bulkley went on to the broader aspects of the ques-

tion. The United States, he said, was built upon speculation, but not on the kind the security exchanges represented. There was a difference between the pioneer
inventor and builder, and the man who bought today in
order to sell tomorrow. Whatever differing opinions men
may hold in regard to the ethical, economic, and social
effects of gambling, said the Senator, they all agree that
a man should at least gamble with his own money—
stock margin is the only form of gambling that can be
carried on with the nation's credit. Senate reception of
this speech was naturally mixed. George Norris of Nebraska thought it was magnificent and that Bulkley's
amendment was more important than the whole bill.
Daniel U. Fletcher of Florida, cosponsor of the measure,
stated that he was afraid to eliminate margin trading because it constituted approximately 40 per cent of brokers' business. Alben Barkley of Kentucky quoted the
recent report of the Twentieth Century Fund, which
presented these arguments against the abolition of margins: (1) Speculation would not be reduced because
borrowers would go to the banks; (2) A bootleg market
in funds would start if collateral loans were banned; (3)
People who legitimately needed collateral loans would
be injured; (4) It would be unwise to prohibit security
credit while credit is still permitted in real estate and
commodities; (5) Corporate financing would be im-
peded; and (6) The elimination of speculation would
impede trading. Rather than injure the genuine investors by reducing liquidity, the Senator suggested that
certain restrictions be placed upon solicitation of customers by brokers.[82] Barkley's position was typical of
informed opinion close to the markets. One broker sug-

[82] *Congressional Record,* 73 Cong., 2 sess., v. 78, Pt. 8, 8386-
8396. The Twentieth Century Fund was a nonpartisan research
organization whose chief sponsor was Edward Filene, the Boston
merchant. The Fund had completed a study of the stock market
in January.

gested that the Street would be satisfied with the current margin rates if only 25 per cent margin were required on the reliable shares. Few close to finance favored putting stock markets on a complete cash basis, and the New Deal itself had never made such a drastic proposal.[83]

Bulkley's amendment was defeated by the Senate, 48 to 30. The thirty-vote bloc mustered for this extreme expedient was respectable enough, however, and was interpreted to mean that Congress wanted high margin requirements and would not modify this demand.[84] Thus margins, although stiffened, were still permitted in the new security regulation program. Wall Street's faint hope that the whole Fletcher-Rayburn bill would die in committee was not, of course, realized: the Senate voted 62 to 13 in favor of it. The hold-outs were Northeastern Republicans plus Republican Robert D. Carey of Wyoming and Democrat Thomas P. Gore of Oklahoma.[85] The market accepted this Congressional action with fairly good grace. Many brokers hoped that, as in the Hughes investigation of the insurance business in 1907, Congress' efforts at stock reform would at least restore the public's confidence and thereby stimulate trading. There was some grumbling, however; seats on the Toronto Exchange rose in price, and five small stock exchanges in the United States closed rather than comply with the Exchange Act requirements.[86]

Actually the exchange interests had gained many con-

[83] *Wall Street Journal*, March 12, 1934, 13:3; *New York Times*, March 11, 1934, IV, 4:7; *The Cleveland Plain Dealer* believed Bulkley was taking the wrong approach. May 9, 1934, 8:2.

[84] *Congressional Record*, 73 Cong., 2 sess., v. 78, Pt. 8, 8396; *Commercial & Financial Chronicle*, 138:II:3142 (May 12, 1934). John T. Flynn wrote that the administration threw its weight against the Bulkley amendment, otherwise it would have passed. Flynn, *Security Speculation*, 292.

[85] *Congressional Record*, 73 Cong., 2 sess., v. 78, Pt. 8, 8714 (May 12, 1934).

[86] *New York Times*, January 30, 1934, 27:6; *Time Magazine*, 24:II:55 (August 6, 1934); *Commercial & Financial Chronicle*, 142:II:2590.

cessions since the original bill had been introduced in February. In April Samuel Untermyer, who had earlier complained of the harshness of the bill, warned lawmakers against going to the other extreme and relenting too much, and John T. Flynn, in a book written at the time, was quite critical of Congressional concessions to the brokers.[87] In general, Flynn objected to the retreat from outright prohibitions to ambiguous phrases which left the door open, under certain circumstances, to practices he regarded as bad. Specifically, the prohibition of floor trading (brokers trading for their own accounts, which amounted to 30-40 per cent of all trading) was replaced with wording which left the matter up to the new Commission and even seemed to endorse such trading by brokers if they were off the floor. The original ban on specialists trading for themselves was deleted in favor of permitting such trading under certain conditions. One of the most imporant prohibitions, and one favored by the President, was also sacrificed: instead of requiring the separation of function between broker and underwriter, the bill merely asked that the broker refrain for six months from margin financing of an issue he underwrote. Flynn concluded that the law had been weakened, that Congress was putting its faith in the new Securities and Exchange Commission, and that real reform would depend very largely on the personnel and policies of the Commission.[88] The Securities Exchange Act was a notable victory for those who believed in broad, ambiguous statutes and discretionary administration, a government of men rather than laws.

President Roosevelt's appointments to the SEC were not completely hostile to the financial world. To balance Ferdinand Pecora, the crusading counsel for the Senate

[87] *New York Times*, April 16, 1934, 25:3.
[88] Flynn, *Security Speculation*, 277-300. Flynn had opposed from the outset margin trading and "making a market" for new issues, i.e., "pegging" in order to distribute them.

committee which had investigated the stock market, the President chose Joseph P. Kennedy and made him chairman. Kennedy, a capitalist by occupation and familiar with Wall Street, reassured the business world in an early speech; the SEC, he said, did not view business with suspicion; it aimed to make finance more responsible. This was a rare encouraging word to business from the New Deal, *Time* noted, for many New Dealers had acted as if all boom deals were deliberate snares, all speculation was evil, and moneychangers belonged in Hell.[89]

Between 1934 and 1936 the Securities and Exchange Commission perfected its administration. The Federal Security Act and the Public Utility Holding Company Act were brought under its jurisdiction; these were logical steps. The Federal Reserve Board finally abandoned complicated margin formulae for a flat rate; it revoked the double standard for loans on stock—one for banks, another for brokers. The prohibition of brokers from borrowing from anyone other than a Federal Reserve Bank put credit control more securely in the hands of the Federal Reserve Board. The bootleg loan situation of 1929 could never recur. Along the same line the Federal Reserve Act was altered to strengthen the Board's power in relation to its constituent districts, and the Secretary of the Treasury and the Comptroller of the Currency were dropped as ex-officio members.[90] The latter move was taken because many believed that Andrew Mellon and the Treasury Department had unduly

[89] *Time*, 24:II:55 (August 6, 1934). Other members of Commission were Robert E. Healy, F.T.C. counsel, George C. Mathews of the Wisconsin Utilities Commission, and James M. Landis, formerly a Harvard law professor.

[90] *Commercial & Financial Chronicle*, 142:II:2917-2920 (May 2, 1936), 3417 (May 23, 1936). See also Raymond P. Brandt, "Federal Regulation of Security Exchanges," *Literary Digest*, 117:7 (July 27, 1934), and "New Deal Ends Wall Street Freedom," 117:11 (July 16, 1934).

influenced the Board during the twenties.[91] The total effect of these changes in the security and banking fields
was to insulate the financial structure from the vagaries
of public whim, and entrust Presidential appointees with
the power to promulgate the rules.

Government authorities had not forgotten the commodity speculator. The President wanted regulation of
these markets also, and early in 1934 Secretary of Agriculture Henry A. Wallace advocated an omnibus exchange bill to regulate both stocks and commodities.
The Secretary agreed with grain-state Senators that
there was manipulation and too great a spread in price
between farmer and consumer in commodities, but he
defended hedging as necessary. Congress prevailed on
Wallace, however, and he removed stocks from his bill,
merely offering an elaborate amendment to the 1922
Grain Futures Act that would extend regulation over
any desired commodity. The bill also banned manipulation and bucket shops. The administration had the votes
for passage in the House but found itself blocked in the
Senate, where "Cotton Ed" Smith of South Carolina,
chairman of the Agriculture Committee, was opposed to
it; he wanted more carefully drawn individual bills, especially for his pet, cotton.[92] The result was that Congress adjourned without taking any action on commodities.

Some lawmakers feared that daring traders, driven
from the stock markets by the Exchange Act anti-mani-
pulation provisions, might take refuge in the more lax
commodity pits.[93] Grain belt legislators joined Democrats in pressing harder for Wallace's commodity exchange bill. The courts had held, in a case involving Ar-

[91] Charles Gay, "Stock Market Controls," *Vital Speeches*, 2:68-
71.

[92] *New York Times*, February 13, 1934, 29:7, January 29, 29:7,
February 14, 29:6.

[93] *Commercial & Financial Chronicle*, 138:II:3866 (June 9,
1934).

thur Cutten, the Chicago speculator, that the wording of the 1922 law required that the defendant be engaged in the illegal act at the time he was arrested. It was therefore practically impossible to get convictions for violating this law, as most operators could not be caught in the act of rigging the market. Thomas W. Howell, for example, who cornered July corn in 1931, had escaped punishment for this reason, and the proposed act was designed to close the loophole. In addition it required actual margins of 10 per cent and included mill feeds, rice, butter, eggs, and potatoes in the regulation. Future trading, in a small way, had begun in these products since the 1922 act.[94]

For the first time in many years cotton Senators seemed to be willing to have their product included in a regulatory act. There had been no regulation of cotton exchanges as such; the 1916 Cotton Futures Act merely applied to grading, not to markets, but "Cotton Ed" Smith continued to hold out for separate treatment of cotton and finally proposed a rider seeking to limit cotton trades to 600,000 bales per year per account. This stirred dissent among Southern Democrats and the Roosevelt Administration put great pressure on Smith to withdraw the rider, which some government advisers thought would endanger action on the whole bill. In any event, after some discussion cotton was left out, and the Commodity Exchange Act was signed into law in June, 1936.[95] As usual, Senators and Congressmen from the commercial Northeast were its chief opponents.[96]

As indicated earlier, public discussion immediately after the Crash was concerned largely with scapegoats, the

[94] *Congressional Record*, 74 Cong., 2 sess., v. 80, Pt. 6, 6159ff., 7849ff.

[95] *Commercial & Financial Chronicle*, 142:II:3602 (May 30, 1936).

[96] *Congressional Record*, 74 Cong., 2 sess., v. 80, Pt. 8, 8293 (May 29, 1936). Actually grain markets had been restricted earlier; on March 20, 1934 the President had signed an NRA fair competition code for the industry.

bears and insiders who had presumably brought on the catastrophe. Even the *Post's* veteran cynics, Albert Atwood and Edwin Lefevre, could think of a few remedies for the marketplace. Atwood thought excessive speculation should be curbed; he suggested Senator Glass's remedy, a high tax on stock held for short periods. He also believed that bankers would have to learn to look beyond individual collateral and survey the picture of aggregate collateral, that is, the banker should take a social rather than an individualistic point of view. Thinking of the unpopularity of the Federal Reserve Board curbs and warnings in 1929, Atwood remarked feebly that the public must learn greater respect for the Board.[97] Edwin Lefevre thought the agitation against bears in 1930-1932 was characteristic of bear markets. He suggested that it was particularly vehement in these years because most market players had never experienced a bear market before, and even financial writers for the newspapers were acting as if they had just discovered short selling. The public was blaming the bears when it should have seen that the selling was actually liquidation; there were plenty of reasons for stocks to go down.

Later Lefevre enumerated the reasons for public losses, based upon thirty years of observation in the markets. First, the public itself; its quick money motive which meant tips and overtrading. Second, remediable evils arising from the old trading customs of brokers, and bankers' policies that took advantage of sudden increases in the public's speculative appetite. Third, the brokers' desire to do as much business as possible without regard for their moral obligations—a poor attitude toward customers. In this connection, an ex-financial editor told Lefevre that the banks should not have remained silent while brokers, bankers, and tipsters were predicting great profits. The brokerage profession needs

[97] Albert W. Atwood, "The Future of Stock Speculation," *Saturday Evening Post,* 203:20 (September 13, 1930).

rules against overeager "boosting," he said. The insider had set a poor example. But Lefevre, whose acquaintance in the Street was extremely wide, endorsed no drastic reforms. He quoted Justice Oliver Wendell Holmes, early in the century:

> Speculation is the self-adjustment of society to the probable. Its value is well-known as a means of avoiding or mitigating catastrophes, equalizing prices and providing for periods of want. It is true that the success of the strong induces imitations by the weak, and that incompetent persons bring themselves to ruin by undertaking to speculate in their turn. But legislators and courts generally have recognized that the natural evolutions of a complex society are to be touched only with a very cautious hand, and that such coarse attempts at a remedy for the waste incident to every social function as a simple prohibition and laws to stop its being, are harmful and vain.

Lefevre was inclined to think that the average American preferred to speculate rather than invest; it was part of the American huckster instinct, he said. Neighbors' bragging about winnings was a greater stimulus in America than the brokers and tipsters.[98]

By 1934, however, post-mortems on the Crash had achieved a more academic tone. Adolph C. Miller, a member of the Federal Reserve Board, blamed New York banks for not checking the speculation in 1929; he explained that by tradition the Reserve Board could not initiate policy but could only approve it. When the bankers did not come forward with any restrictive proposals, the Board was so worried that it finally issued its famous warning of February 2, 1929. The lesson, as Miller saw it, was that the Board should have full power

[98] Edwin S. Lefevre, "Blame the Broker," *Saturday Evening Post*, 204:26 (April 9, 1932), Lefevre, "New Bull Market, New Dangers," 208:14-15 (May 2, 1936).

over the national credit and be an independent, disinterested body, unwarped by any particular section of the country. Miller's article was strong evidence that the Reserve System had not freed American finances from New York domination. Professor John H. Williams, Harvard banking expert, also saw the need for centralized credit control, and for a Reserve Board that could initiate its own policy.[99]

Like every occupational group from college professors to relief recipients, bankers and brokers wanted government benefits and talked publicly of raising their standards, but they were hesitant and resentful when they discovered the strings of interference attached to aid and reform. Most financial men acknowledged the need for the Federal Security Act, despite criticism of its liability provisions. The *Financial World,* for example, hailed the act as a long step in the right direction. Louis Guenther, its editor and a veteran exposer of financial frauds, observed that he had advocated these reforms for several years in his magazine.[100] But Roosevelt's exchange regulation plan, in contrast to the Security Act, went too far in day-to-day meddling in the Street's affairs to suit moderate reformers like Guenther who had been close to the Street over the years. Even those who professed to want reform were alienated by the prospect of close control by outsiders; rule by capricious "bureaucrats" and "theorists" proved to be a bogeyman for most market old-timers. Like the financial reformers of the Progressive Era, they still wanted to rely mainly on exhortation of erring bankers and brokers, and gradual improvement through education. Though acknowledging market abuses, they instinctively recoiled from attempts at regulation by hostile outsiders who did not un-

[99] Adolph C. Miller, "Responsibility for Federal Reserve Policies, 1927-1929," *American Economic Review,* 25:442-458 (September 1935); John H. Williams, "The Banking Act of 1935," *American Economic Review,* 26 sup. 95-105 (March 1936).

[100] *Financial World,* 59:27 (April 12, 1933).

derstand the foibles of Wall Street. But by 1936, after the passage of the various New Deal acts, the pattern of solution of the speculative problem was virtually complete. Trading was continuing in most products, but government authorities were enforcing rules that prevented the more obviously fraudulent transactions. Brokers and bankers were learning they could still prosper despite the alleged regulatory handicaps; more than the public, they feared a repetition of 1929. Brokers were so regulated that their interests and those of their clients coincided. President Charles Gay of the New York Stock Exchange believed that the Banking Acts of 1933 and 1935, together with the security legislation, provided comprehensive controls for keeping prices and values in a sound relationship. He said that he saw no danger from radical groups despite prevalent unemployment—they were not unified.[101] Without extensive credit and without aggressive salesmanship, the market was rising in 1935 and 1936; Wall Street believed it was out of the woods.

In April, 1938, an anticlimatic skirmish occurred on the old anti-speculator battlefield. On the advice of the Commodities Exchange Commission, the House recommended repeal of the tax on futures transactions. J. W. T. Duvel, still with the Grain Futures Administration, told Senators that the tax, if any, should be reduced to one cent from the current three cents to relieve the economic burden on scalpers, the in-and-out professionals. This transactions tax had originally been imposed in 1926 at the rate of one cent; in 1932 during the depression it was raised to five cents for two years in an effort to balance the budget. In 1934 the tax reverted to a three-cent rate. The Commission argued that the markets' three hundred scalpers were necessary to the hedging process and their livelihood was being endangered by the tax.

[101] Lefevre, "New Bull Market, New Dangers"; Gay, "Stock Market Controls"; *Commercial & Financial Chronicle,* 142:II:2254 (April 4, 1936).

Government defense of the lowly scalper reawakened the declining wrath of the anti-speculators. Senator Lynn J. Frazier of North Dakota recounted the history of the scalper; he recalled the smooth words of Joseph P. Tumulty, attorney for the exchanges, in fighting the five-cent rate in 1932. The Dakotan sarcastically reminded his colleagues of the testimony of a pit trader, Ryan, who had been forced to seek other employment in the afternoons to supplement his income as a scalper at the Chicago Board of Trade. The Nonpartisan League Senator thought it was "too bad," but wanted scalpers to find jobs more beneficial to the economy. The scalpers were the only ones protesting this tax, he said, it was a boon to actual producers. George Norris of Nebraska echoed Frazier in hoping that the scalpers would be run out of business, and the farm-conscious Arthur Capper agreed that no tax relief should be dispensed to gamblers. But the Senate Finance Committee, impressed by the Agriculture Department experts, moved for repeal; it noted that Canada had found it desirable to repeal a similar tax. On a roll-call vote of the Senate, the welfare of the scalpers was sustained 50-28, and the three-cent futures transaction tax was repealed.

Senator Thomas Connally of Texas, long a foe of speculators, wrote the epitaph of the movement during this tax debate. He declared that he was going to vote for the tax repeal because the clock could not be turned back. He recalled that in 1922 Congress had sanctioned the commodity marketing system by enacting the Capper law, which "supervised" the self-regulation of the futures exchanges; since then the only choice had been to perfect that system, said the salty Texan. He was still ready to vote for outright abolition, but he knew it was politically impossible to achieve.[102] Thus the effort to root out exchange speculation was finally abandoned,

[102] *Congressional Record*, 75 Cong., 3 sess., v. 83, Pt. 5, 5030ff. (April 8, 1938).

long after there was any real hope for such a radical goal. In fact, there had been little chance of complete triumph in 1892; it was too late even then. Commerce had already supplanted agrarianism in the seats of power and the forty-six years of struggle, although tempering the thrust of business, fell far short of its original purpose, the eradication of the middleman.

CHAPTER 7

CONCLUSION

I

*T*HIS study has traced the dominant ideas about speculation from 1892 to 1936 and recorded the legislative successes and failures connected with them. The farmers first attracted national attention when, state action proving ineffective, they sought Congressional legislation eliminating commodity futures. The anti-futures campaign was, of course, a relatively obscure part of the larger Populist program that aimed, by the use of agrarian ideology, to regain some politico-economic power for the farmer. But in 1892 and 1893 the futures exchange interests, although weak politically, were strong in economic resources and legal precedents. Before the houses of Congress could reconcile their differences on the Hatch Anti-Option bill, the session ended and the farmers' revolt subsided. The anti-futures bill never became law. Many Congressmen had been reluctant supporters anyway, voting favorably because of political necessity. Their experience was comparable to that of state legislators pressured by Grangers into voting for railroad commission laws in the 1870s. In 1896 the farmers were lured into the embrace of "free silver." When William Jennings Bryan was soundly defeated championing that "heresy," and prices rose in 1897, many farmers drifted back to their protectionist allies, the Eastern industrial and commercial interests.

Monopoly growth, accelerated by the Spanish-American war, led to fights for various stocks on the exchanges. Market operators, taking advantage of the general faith in American industrial growth, mulcted some of the well-to-do public. Commodity speculators were also active,

258

but somewhat less conspicuous, in the McKinley-Roosevelt prosperity. This was the era of the financial brawler, of corners, squeezes, and bucket shops. It was a time when bright New England boys, lacking formal training but adept in Yankee pecuniary skills, learned how to read the ticker tapes in brokers' offices and bucket shops. In a few decades these individuals won and lost many fortunes.

In the states where they still had some power after 1900, the agrarian anti-speculators continued to react by passing punitive anti-futures and anti-gambling laws. Congressional opponents frustrated their national measures—the Scott and Clarke amendments—and the White House was indifferent. Acting alone, this faction —predominantly Bryan Democrats—was not strong enough in national politics. But the "financial reformers," including many muckraking journalists, did have some success in improving ethics in the market place. The respectable citizens of the Hughes Committee in 1909 were responsible for ameliorative changes in the market rules between 1909 and 1913. The committee, however, distrusted Western "demagogic" solutions and favored self-regulation over governmental controls; exchange spokesmen often cited the committee findings to stave off more radical reform.

The financial reformers also had a tempering effect on the more perceptive agrarian and progressive anti-speculators in Congress. Curiously it was the combined efforts of agrarians and financial reformers, acting from different motives, that produced results in this period. Agrarian wrath at stock promoters and Wall Street in general closed most bucket shops and got state blue sky laws on the books; the financial reformers cheerfully cooperated in eliminating their shop competitors and worked to shift the emphasis of the blue sky laws away from Wall Street and regulation and toward local swindlers. The Cotton Futures Act (1914 and 1916) and Grain Standard Act

(1914) were also passed by this coalition. Again agrarian prejudice combined with the financial reformers' desire to reduce fraud and perfect the market mechanism. Both factions settled for honest grading and a minimum of federal apparatus.

The progressives began to differentiate themselves from the other anti-speculators in 1910. They urged a comprehensive view of speculation: grain, cotton, listed securities, watered railroad stock, and local stock promotions were all subject to non-productive activities and constituted a threat to economic democracy. They believed that state, and especially federal, regulation in the speculative field was feasible and desirable.

Although national regulation of railroads and food and drugs had recently been established, neither the other anti-speculators nor the Congress was ready for regulation of the markets. Senator Cummins' proposal of 1913 was ignored. A year later the Owen stock exchange regulation bill foundered, apparently getting no encouragement from President Wilson or administration Democrats. The only triumph of the progressives before the outbreak of World War I was a minor one: the 1911 blue sky law in Kansas. This law, including regulation as well as anti-fraud provisions, was adopted by a number of states, thanks to agrarian support. But "the Kansas Idea" was considerably emasculated by Wall Street standpatters and financial reformers who gained exemptions from regulation for all listed securities.

Most Americans, but especially the agrarians and progressives, were aroused by speculation in foodstuffs after the United States entered the war. But despite agrarian extremism, market machinery was maintained and regulation won out over prohibition. Progressives hoped many of the wartime regulatory rules would be retained when the war was over. Because the price of wheat was fixed but raw cotton escaped control—thanks to the combined pressure of Southern standpatters and agrarians—

the 1918 Congressional election campaigns turned on the Republican charge that Democrats had favored cotton growers over wheat growers during the war. This deepened the division between Southern and Midwestern anti-speculators.

After the war, financial reformers were notable chiefly for their anti-fraud campaign against swindlers selling dubious stocks in exchange for Liberty Bonds. The progressives won their first major victory in the Grain Futures Act of 1922. The emergence of the American Farm Bureau Federation, a powerful pressure group of commerce-oriented farmers, reinforced the middle-of-the-road attitude which won out in the act's provisions. The Futures Act, together with other achievements of the Farm Bloc, tended to link the farmers to the prevailing distributive order. It is significant that this victory came during an agricultural depression and applied only to grain. The progressives still lacked power against Eastern stock market interests, and Southern standpatters and agrarians again united in resisting the inclusion of cotton, claiming the 1916 grading act was sufficient.

World War I accelerated change. Social mobility increased and new strata of "men on the make" found, in the exchanges, tools for capitalizing on the "suckers" drawn into the financial orbit by urban growth and the wide sale of Liberty Bonds. The answer to this invasion of the ambitious had already been supplied by the financial reformers. They continued to suggest private restrictions for the commodity and security markets that would keep "lambs" away from the shearers and keep trading orderly and profitable. Such rules had no chance of success during this fluid period, however; they could too easily be portrayed in an unfavorable light, as contrary to American democratic ideals. The country was moving toward wider and wider public participation in many realms. The traditional "stake in society" idea of the Founding Fathers was to be implemented by giving the people something to preserve, rather than by restricting participation to those who already held adequate stakes. In the face of Bolshevism abroad and labor unrest at home, it seemed clear that wider participation in investment by the public would increase social stability and would diffuse the interests of the have-nots. That this process moved too quickly is obvious from the events of 1929. This change could have been controlled and made more orderly, but it is hard to see any result other than ultimate diffusion of stock ownership.

The general periodicals usually struck cautious notes when discussing speculation, but their advice apparently had little effect when primal greed was thoroughly aroused. They constantly warned against fraud and offered banal moral tales to illustrate the pitfalls of the exchanges. But the effect of these was dampened by the journalistic tendency to emphasize the personal, to stimulate the reader to emulation by glamorized accounts of the powerful protagonists of the Street. The reader may well have been confused or irritated by stories of gambling folly mixed with adulation, hardly concealed, of successful speculators. The lay reader of 1929, not a close observer of economic conditions, probably could not tell, from the puerile advice given him in most periodicals, whether the nation was approaching a speculative climax or not; only observations by a few market habitués contained enough evidence to persuade the thoughtful reader. It is likely that admonitions not to speculate, to investigate before investing, and so forth, generated relatively little attention as long as the magazine at the same time defended the market structure itself. The mere knowledge of the existence of these markets and the few large fortunes made in them was probably enough to offset the impact of the warnings. If the magazines had taken a firm position in favor of federal regulation of the exchanges—a completely unrealistic supposition in view of the orientation of magazine advertisers—market reforms might have been considerably hastened. But this is pure conjecture. The fact remains that most magazines defended the markets and tried to explain their functions to the public—a slower and more difficult process than the recruiting of "investors" by ambitious customers' men.

The market frenzy was primarily the result of indigestion—the failure to assimilate new social elements rapidly enough; the play of these irrational elements accentuated accumulation of capital at the top of the economic pyramid. The critical period was 1927-1928; at this point the doors could have been closed and the assimilation could probably have taken place with only a recession instead of the Great Depression. But the traditional deference of the Federal Reserve Board toward the New York Federal Reserve Bank was important in explaining the Board's slowness in acting for the public interest. Financial reformers rather than progressives completely dominated the scene and their leadership was inadequate. By 1929 the irrational elements were too large, and they had spread their contagious New Era philosophy into too many high councils. Some progressives like Senator Couzens not only correctly described the situation, but castigated the leaders who had contributed to it.

Looking at the 1929 Crash itself, it is easy to see it as the inevitable result of postwar economic policy, namely the high tariff and the failure to pass on to the worker the fruits of increased productivity. If, however, the President and his cabinet had been less amenable, or the Federal Reserve Board more detached, the impact of the "readjustment" would have been very much lessened. The presence of novices in the market, both as customers and lenders, indicated clearly what the denouement would be; only the date of the collapse was uncertain. The key to the situation was not the stream of corporate earnings reports nor the general business indexes; until late 1929 they were rather contradictory, and only hind-sight perceived a downward trend. The key was brokers' loans. When in 1929 amateurs invaded the lending field and supplied funds to brokers while bankers withdrew, the climax was approaching. Stock prices had been pushed up to levels where they were discounting twenty years' growth. Those doing the pushing were neophytes lacking the independence of mind that comes from personal analysis of the economic facts. The chief lend-ers in the latter stages were companies and businessmen beguiled by high call-loan rates and their liquidity, and these lenders, without the bankers' discipline and re-sponsibility, naturally took flight at the first sign of collapse.

Each faction of anti-speculators reacted to the onset of the Great Depression differently; cooperation was at first minimal. There was not to be a real consensus until 1934 when Roosevelt's New Deal was well under way. The philosophy of the financial reformers had proved disas-trously inadequate in the 1920s. Yet even in 1930 they claimed market evils were being corrected by the ex-changes. And of course the Crash and depression had taken care of one financial reformer complaint: there were no more lambs; they had been sheared and re-moved. Still, reform should be postponed until business confidence was restored and the gold lured out of the mattresses. To aid recovery they urged expanded branch banking, again pointing to the excess of incompetent rural banks as a factor in the Crash. In 1930 these argu-ments had a certain plausibility. In the months after the collapse, the agrarians reacted paranoiacally, searching for the Wall Street bears who had perpetrated this crime against the virtuous yeomanry. Rumors of Soviet grain dealings and domestic communism rekindled xenophobia, and General Jacob Coxey and John Simpson revived Populist nostrums in their testimony before Congressional committees. After making an embarassing foray against

Hoover's Federal Farm Board, the agrarians went on to attack successfully the expansion of branch banking. In this they attracted support from Midwest progressives, although branch banking was destined to grow in the long run.

The progressives, caught between attacking agrarians and defending financial reformers, could make little headway. Although they alone had retained their objectivity in the frenetic pre-Crash days, afterward they were embarrassed by the agrarians, largely Southern Democrats, whose partisan attacks fell on them as Republicans. Senator Black's efforts to end the Federal Farm Board forced them to defend it, although they had all along thought the Board inadequate to the situation. Even the election of Franklin Roosevelt and a New Deal Congress did not mean an immediate victory for market regulation. First, the blue sky plank in the Democratic plank had to be fulfilled. The resulting Federal Securities Act really reflected the viewpoint of the agrarian-financial reformer coalition which had won the state blue sky laws of the 1910s, rather than the aims of progressives in 1933. Noting the obsolescence of the Truth-in-Securities idea— the bankruptcy of the publicity approach—William O. Douglas was bold enough to label the new act reactionary.

The Glass-Steagall Banking Act of 1933 was also much less than a progressive measure. Like the Federal Reserve Act of 1913 it was designed to improve, Senator Glass's bill was a compromise to please all three anti-speculator factions. For the progressives the Federal Reserve Board was given new power to look into the speculative commitments of individual banks; the agrarians were promised a guarantee of bank deposits. The financial reformers were to get the green light for expanded branch banking. The agrarians balked and, joined by many progressives, threw out branch banking, but still the Glass-Steagall Banking Act was multidirectional in its philosophy. But the New Deal finally produced truly progressive legislation in the Fletcher-Rayburn bill of 1934. This bill, which established the Securities Exchange Commission, was the first major advance made since progressives put grain exchanges under control in 1922. The success of the bill was due to the cooperation of all segments of the anti-speculators. Only a handful of determined standpatters in the financial hubs dared to resist stock exchange regulation and their attempt to stir up grass roots opposition was an absolute failure.

Thus the New Deal succeeded in partially insulating the credit structure of the nation from the public's tides of optimism and pessimism. This was achieved by centralizing power, specifically by reducing the self-regulation to which the exchanges had been accustomed, and by increasing the power of the Federal Reserve Board in relation to its constituent districts. Branch banking, stimulated by rural bank failures between 1921 and 1933, continued to spread despite agrarian opposition and state barriers, thereby concentrating funds in populous centers and projecting big bank policies into smaller communities. The persons entrusted with the administrative functions were undoubtedly further insulated from the currents of business thought by academic training and the apparent failure of business leadership in the previous decade. Changes in both structure and personnel went far in the direction of assuring greater stability in the marketplace, for there were some speculators, brokers, and bankers who were either bankrupt or under prosecution for the excesses of the twenties.

While the SEC Act and its companion measure, the Commodity Exchange Act of 1936, seemed to accomplish everything the progressives desired, it is too much to say that this was a triumph for the Norrises, Norbecks, and LaFollettes. The mood of the Roosevelt Administration proved to be more pragmatic than moralistic.

General social planning, rather than emphasis on personal guilt or credit manipulation, was the New Deal keystone. Thus the remaining anti-speculators were as uneasy with bureaucratic power and moral diffidence in the thirties as they were with the selfish materialism of the twenties.

II

The sectional character of anti-speculation in its various forms has been evident throughout this study. It was early discovered that Congressional attitudes on this subject followed a definite pattern—a pattern which did not materially change from 1892 to the days of the New Deal. Senate votes between 1892 and 1936 revealed the hard core of anti-speculator sentiment. This core—more appropriately, this axis—consisted of the Great Plains states: the Dakotas, Nebraska, Kansas, Oklahoma, and Texas. The viewpoint of this anti-speculator tier naturally impinged on adjacent areas where similar politico-economic conditions prevailed. In Wisconsin, Minnesota, Iowa, Missouri, Arkansas, Louisiana, Montana, Colorado, New Mexico, Utah, Idaho, and Washington some kinship was evident. The tier formed an important Senate bloc on speculation questions but was only a subgroup on the more general farm issues; the Farm Bloc of 1921-1922 and the McNary-Haugenites represented a more widely dispersed constituency. The anti-speculator tier was rural and populated by growers of staple crops: spring wheat, winter wheat, cotton, oats, and corn. The region's grievances since Populist days had centered on the marketing of crops, and struggles with the railroads, elevator companies, banks, and boards of trade were predicated on the assumption that the producer received too little of the retail price and the middleman too much for less important services.

At least in the matter of anti-speculator sentiment, Walter P. Webb seems to be correct: the Great Plains have been different.[1] The terrain required fungible crops, and these were subject to the whims of speculators. The aridity hardened "character," discouraged industry, and retarded population concentration with its accompanying specialization of occupation. From these conditions and the people subjected to them comes a suggestive recipe for progressivism: 1) Take Yankee and Southern moralism, perpetuated and intensified by this environment; 2) add a pinch of "frontier democracy," i.e., a virile socialism of the kind one finds among males working together in isolation in mine, orchard, ranch, forest, ship, and battlefield, and 3) leaven with the pro-bureaucratic communalism of German, Scandinavian, and Slavic immigrants settling in the region. The result is progressivism, moralistic, still individualistic, but with a disposition for state controls, a position more practical than the discreet reformism of the Eastern upper middle class but not so anti-bureaucratic and nihilistic as that of dirt farmers from the Old South.[2]

Since World War II the anti-speculator tier has been somewhat modified. The rural population continues to decline, but on the other hand, some aircraft industries have moved inland to Wichita and Tulsa to avoid air attack, an embryo garment trade has emerged in Dallas, and Houston has important space industry contracts. Oil has loomed large not only in Oklahoma and Texas, but

[1] Walter P. Webb, *The Great Plains* (Boston, 1931).

[2] The politico-economic notions of this region as a whole, and historical links between its Populism of the 1890s and the attitudes of mid-twentieth century have not been satisfactorily explored, but the subject has become controversial. See Carl F. Kraenzel, *The Great Plains in Transition* (Norman, 1955), Ch. 17, "The Minority Status of the People"; Victor C. Ferkiss, "Populist Influences on American Fascism," *Western Political Quarterly*, X:350-373 (June 1957); Daniel Bell, ed., *The New American Right* (New York, 1955); C. Vann Woodward, "The Populist Heritage and the Intellectual," *The American Scholar*, XXVIII:55-72 (1959); Nathan Glazer, *The Social Basis of American Communism* (New York, 1961), 14-16; Norman Pollack, *The Populist Response to Industrialism* (Cambridge, Mass., 1962); Walter Nugent, *The Tolerant Populists* (Chicago, 1963).

even in North Dakota's Williston Basin. With commercial and speculative gains accruing to the region's leaders, cultural inferiority is no longer manifested in attacks on urban speculators; instead it is shown in a bumptious nationalism to shame Chicago and New York, and a vigorous anti-communism to frighten Moscow and Peking.

III

The bloc in the Senate, a few reform-minded bankers, and a handful of articulate proletarians—a small minority—constituted the anti-speculators through five decades. Their chief targets were the grains, cotton, stocks, and railroads; significantly, trading in coffee, cocoa, rubber, tin, and other products was not seriously challenged. Congress does not despise the speculator; neither do the American people. The traits of the speculator comprise an inseparable part of American middle-class culture. The occasions when speculation becomes thoroughly disengaged from the productive base and simply siphons off wealth are slow to be recognized, and only temporarily modify the popular attitude. If the speculators seem to be conspicuously different in culture, then great dissatisfaction occurs, but in the United States these cultural differences are less wide than elsewhere and the effect of the mass media is to reduce and conceal them. What then has been the outcome of the cry against speculation, coming first from the growers, then from disillusioned investors, and finally from the public after the Crash? How has the situation changed since the Gay Nineties?

The result has been a complicated compromise, but one that slightly favors the anti-speculators. The anti-fraud and regulatory acts have squeezed reluctant concessions from the broker-banker fraternity. Reports of all kinds are now available to protect the public against fraud, but the principle of publicity has not proved to be the panacea that Theodore Roosevelt and Robert La-

Follette had hoped. There are credit controls to check bootleg loans and keep margins respectable; the old manipulative tricks have been virtually eliminated. These measures and the financial world's adjustment to them have made it possible for the present investor or speculator to approach an "even shake" in the marketplace. In the 1960s reform continues in the burgeoning periphery of over-the-counter securities and mutual funds. On the other hand the farmers, originally the most vociferous opponents of speculation, have been placated with government insurance, subsidy, and encouragement of cooperative marketing. Promises of parity assuaged old feelings. Significantly, since the farmers have come to rely on organization rather than ideology, their political power has soared in spite of their sharp decline in numbers.

The anti-speculators' extreme demands have not been granted. There are still commodity speculators, scalpers, and short sellers in stock. The futures contract is as important as ever and its use has spread to additional products; there are more markets and brokers. Wide fluctuations, based on a problematic future but unwarranted by current data, still occur, and foresight is still well rewarded. Nor has gambling in its grosser forms diminished; it has increased with urbanism. The types who haunted bucket shops looking for quick wealth early in the century, and later contributed so much to market instability in the twenties, are now venting their gambling urges elsewhere. The lean depression years caused some states to fall back on gambling, a sure but regressive source of revenue. In the mining and ranching regions of the West gambling had been tolerated as a vestige of frontier days; Nevada legalized it in 1931, although it had always been there, even after being outlawed in 1910. Horse racing was only temporarily blocked by the Progressive Era reformers; it revived under the stimulus of the depression and the Totalisator, which made pari-mutuel wagering feasible. The "sport of kings" flourished in industrial, ranch, and resort areas and by the 1960s was being conducted in over half the states and attracting over fifty million spectators annually. Illicit horsebooks, football pools, slot machines, and numbers games have provided supplementary outlets. The more flamboyant speculators did not disappear but were simply eased out of the nation's stock and commodity markets.

On the positive side, America's solution of the speculation question has been characteristic. Instead of trying to ban speculators *in toto*, it has sought to inform everyone as to the ways of speculation while tightening regulations on neophytes. The policy has been to reduce the inequalities in the practice of speculation by making available to everyone the basic knowledge of the speculator, to create autonomous judgments that nevertheless adhere to certain common principles. To this end our laws do not banish participation in economic fluctuation but seek on one hand to limit excessive trading and on the other to convince traders that it is worthwhile to use empirical data. Of course an influx of persons not acclimated to the tradition could upset the equilibrium, if not assimilated fast enough, but with 1929 in mind, most brokers have tried to encourage their customers to assume their own risks, make decisions, and acquaint themselves with the data. Presumably today's investors are better informed and less susceptible to panic.

Above all, the concern of economists themselves has shifted from micro-to macro-economics; since 1929 they have concentrated more and more on the national and international situation. Therefore it seems quite unlikely that the general economic conditions antecedent to 1929 will recur. That is to say, the advice of academic economists will carry more weight in the future, and idle funds will not be available for speculation in the exchanges in the amount they were in the late twenties.

APPENDIX

SENATE VOTING RECORD OF THE

ANTI-SPECULATOR TIER

	Percentage in		
	Tier	*East*	*Nation*
1. For: A Prohibitive Tax on Commodity Futures: (Hatch bill, Jan. 31, 1893)	77.7	40.0	58.0
2. For: A Tax on Bucket Shops: (Amendment to tariff, July 8, 1909)	63.6	7.1	43.7
3. For: A Tax on Future Contracts and the Short Sales of Stocks: (Amendment to tariff, Sept. 6, 1913)	57.2	22.2	31.0
4. For: The closing of exchanges if trading becomes excessive: (Thomas amendment to Food Control Act, June 2, 1917)	33.3	0	30.7
5. Against: Abolition of Inheritance Tax: (tax bill amendment, Feb. 12, 1926)	81.8	0	36.5
6. For: A Prohibitive Tax on Commodity Futures: (Caraway bill, May 10, 1928)	70.0	5.9	33.8
7. For: A 1/20% Tax on Call Loans: (Amendment to tax bill, May 23, 1928)	80.0	6.7	29.0
8. For: Making Income Tax Returns Public: (Amendment to tax bill, May 25, 1928)	75.0	0	28.7
9. For: Prohibiting Futures Trading: (2nd Caraway bill, Feb. 14, 1929)	90.0	0	36.5
10. For: Ending Futures Trading by the Farm Board: (Black amendment to the Offices bill, Feb. 9, 1931)	33.3	7.1	32.1

	Percentage in		
	Tier	*East*	*Nation*
11. For: Raising Stock Transfer Tax to 1/8%: (Dill amendment to the tax bill, May 30, 1932)	90.9	0	45.1
12. Against: Exempting Loaned Stock from Transfer Tax: (Amendment to tax bill, May 30, 1932)	100.0	0	51.9
13. For: Strictly limiting the Expansion of Branch Banking: (Black amendment to Glass-Steagall bill, Jan. 25, 1933)	81.8	0	27.4
14. Against: Passage of the Glass-Steagall bill: (Jan. 25, 1933)	70.0	0	14.3
15. For: A Ban on the Margin Purchases of Stocks: (Bulkley amendment to SEC bill, May 9, 1934)	72.7	5.9	38.5
16. For: Federal Regulation of Stock Exchanges: (May 12, 1934)	90.9	43.8	82.6
17. For: Expanding Commodity Exchange Regulation: (May 29, 1936)	100.0	15.0	79.5
18. Against: Repealing the Tax on Grain Futures: (April 8, 1938)	91.7	15.8	35.9
46 Year Average:	75.6	9.4	40.8

BIBLIOGRAPHY

BIBLIOGRAPHY

COLLECTIONS:

Minnesota Historical Society: Knute Nelson Papers
Missouri Historical Society: Merchants Exchange Collection
Wisconsin State Historical Society: McCormick Collection

GOVERNMENT DOCUMENTS:

DEBATES:

Congressional Record, 1892-1936.

HEARINGS:

Fictitious Dealing in Agricultural Products, Hearings before the Committee on Agriculture. United States House of Representatives. 52 Cong., 2 Sess. (Washington, 1892), 337 pp.
Options and Futures, Hearings before the Committee on the Judiciary. United States Senate. 63 Cong., 2 Sess. (Washington, 1892), 324 pp.
Money Trust Investigation, Hearings before a subcommittee of the Committee on Banking & Currency. United States House of Representatives. 62 Cong., 3 Sess. (Washington, 1913), 3 vols.
Stock Exchange Regulation, Hearings before the Committee on Banking & Currency. United States Senate. 63 Cong., 2 Sess. (Washington, 1914), 943 pp.
Food Production, Consumption, and Distribution, Hearings before the Committee on Agriculture. United States House of Representatives. 65 Cong., 1 Sess. (Washington, 1917), 538 pp.
Future Trading, Hearings before the Committee on Agriculture. United States House of Representatives. 66 Cong., 3 Sess. (Washington, 1921), 1070 pp.
Grain Futures Act, Hearings before the Committee on Agriculture. United States House of Representatives. 67 Cong., 2 Sess. (Washington, 1922), 84 pp.
Blue Sky Bill, Hearings before the Committee on Foreign & Interstate Commerce. United States House of Representatives. 67 Cong., 2 Sess. (Washington, 1922), 120 pp.
Options and Futures, Hearings before the Committee on

Agriculture & Forestry. United States Senate. 69 Cong., 1 Sess. (Washington, 1926), 193 pp.

Grain Futures Act Amendment, Hearings before the Committee on Agriculture on H.R. 11952. United States House of Representatives. 70 Cong., 1 Sess. (Washington, 1928), 41 pp.

Brokers' Loans, Hearings before the Committee on Banking & Currency. United States Senate. 70 Cong., 1 Sess. (Washington, 1928), 96 pp.

Prohibiting Trading on Margins on the New York Stock Exchange, Hearings before the Committee on the Judiciary. United States Senate. 71 Cong., 3 Sess. (Washington, 1931), 43 pp.

Operation of the National and Federal Reserve Banking Systems, Hearings before the Committee on Banking & Currency. United States Senate. 71 Cong., 3 Sess. (Washington, 1931), 1085 pp.

Commodity Short Selling, Hearings before the Committee on Agriculture. United States House of Representatives. 72 Cong., 1 Sess. (Washington, 1932), 421 pp.

To Abolish the Federal Farm Board and Secure to the Farmer Cost of Production, Hearings before the Committee on Agriculture & Forestry. United States Senate. 72 Cong., 1 Sess. (Washington, 1932), 77 pp.

Stock Exchange Practices, Hearings before the Committee on Banking & Currency. United States Senate. 72, 73, and 74 Cong. (Washington, 1932-1934), 11 vols.

REPORTS:

Report 787. Subcommittee on Agricultural Depression (Washington, 1895)

"Report of the Hughes Committee," *Public Papers of Charles Evans Hughes* (Albany, 1910), Appendix I

Report 1593. Committee on Banking & Currency. United States House of Representatives. 62 Cong., 3 Sess., February 28, 1913 (Money Trust Investigation)

Report 1580. Committee on Rules. United States House of Representatives. 64 Cong., 3 Sess., February 27, 1917 (The "Leak" Investigation)

Report on the Grain Trade, the Federal Trade Commission (Washington, 1920-1926), 7 vols.

Report on H.R. 34. Committee on Foreign & Interstate Commerce. United States House of Representatives. 69 Cong., 1 Sess., December 22, 1925

Report 584. Committee on Banking & Currency. United States Senate. 72 Cong., 1 Sess., April 22, 1932 (The Glass-Steagall bill)
Report of the Committee on Stock Exchange Regulation appointed by the Secretary of Commerce (Washington, 1934)

NEWSPAPERS:

Barron's, 1927-1929
Commercial & Financial Chronicle, 1892-1936
Duluth Labor World, 1928-1929
Industrial Worker, 1926-1930
Labor, 1928-1930
McCormick Collection
New York Times, 1912-1936
San Francisco Chronicle
Wall Street Journal, 1928-1929, 1933-1935

PERIODICALS:

Agricultural History
American Economic Review
American Federationist
American Magazine
Annals of the American Academy of Political and Social Sciences, 1911 and 1931
Arena, 1892-1909
Atlantic Monthly, 1892-1936
Bankers' Magazine
Business Week, 1929-1936
Christian Century
Collier's, 1892-1936
Congressional Digest
Cosmopolitan
Current History, 1914-1936
Current Opinion
Everybody's Magazine
Financial World
Forbes'
Forum, 1892-1936
Harper's, 1892-1936
Harper's Weekly, 1892-1916
Harvard Business Review
Independent, 1892-1928
LaFollette's Magazine
Literary Digest, 1892-1936

Magazine of Wall Street, 1924-1929
Munsey's Magazine, 1892-1929
Nation, 1892-1936
New Republic, 1914-1936
Newsweek, 1933-1936
North American Review, 1892-1936
Outlook, 1893-1935
Progressive, 1918-1936
Review of Reviews, 1892-1936
Saturday Evening Post, 1897-1936
Scribner's Magazine, 1892-1936
Time Magazine, 1923-1936
World's Work, 1900-1932
Yale Review, 1892-1936

BOOKS

Adler, Selig, *The Isolationist Impulse,* New York, 1957
Allen, Frederick L., *Lords of Creation,* New York, 1934
——————, *Only Yesterday,* New York, 1931
Ashby, Forrest Bee, *The Economic Effect of Blue Sky Laws,* Philadelphia, 1926
Baer, Julius Bernard, and Saxon, Olin Glenn, *Commodity Exchanges and Futures Trading: Principles and Operating Methods,* New York, 1949
Barnard, Harry, *Independent Man: the Life of Senator James Couzens,* New York, 1958
Barron, Clarence W., *More They Told Barron,* New York, 1931
Beard, Charles A., *America in Midpassage,* New York, 1939
Bell, Daniel, ed., *The New American Right,* New York, 1955
Benedict, Murray R., *Farm Policies of the United States, 1790-1950,* New York, 1953
Bernheim, Alfred L., and Margaret G. Schneider, *The Security Markets,* New York, 1935
Boyle, James E., *Speculation and the Chicago Board of Trade,* New York, 1921
Brace, Harrison H., *The Value of Organized Speculation,* Boston, 1913
Brandeis, Louis D., *Other People's Money and How Bankers Use It,* New York, 1914
Brinton, Job W., *Wheat and Politics,* Minneapolis, 1931
Burdick, Usher L., *The History of the Farmers' Political Action in North Dakota,* Baltimore, 1944
Capper, Arthur, *The Agricultural Bloc,* New York, 1922

278

Chapman, John W. and Westerfield, Ray B., *Branch Banking: its Historical and Theoretical Position in America and Abroad,* New York, 1942

Clark, Evans, ed., *Security Market Control,* New York, 1934

Clews, Henry, *Fifty Years in Wall Street,* New York, 1908

Cochran, Thomas C. and Miller, William, *The Age of Enterprise, A Social History of Industrial America,* New York, 1942

————, *The American Business System, 1900-1955,* Cambridge, Mass., 1957

Crissey, Forrest, *Alexander Legge, 1866-1933,* Chicago, 1936

Daniels, Josephus, *The Wilson Era: The Years of War & After,* Chapel Hill, 1946.

Dewey, T. Henry, *Legislation Against Speculation and Gambling in Futures,* New York, 1905

Dice, Charles A., *New Levels in the Stock Market,* New York, 1929

Dorfman, Joseph, *The Economic Mind in American Civilization, 1918-1933,* New York, 1959

Douglas, William O., *Democracy and Finance,* New Haven, 1940

Draper, Theodore, *The Roots of American Communism,* New York, 1957

Dreiser, Theodore, *The Financier,* New York, 1912

————, *The Titan,* New York, 1914

Edelman, Jacob M., *Security Regulation in the Forty-Eight States,* Washington, 1942

Emery, Henry C., *Speculation on the Stock and Produce Markets,* New York, 1896

Everitt, James A., *The Third Power,* Indianapolis, 1905

Faulkner, Harold U., *The Decline of Laissez-Faire, 1897-1917,* New York, 1951

————, *From Versailles to the New Deal,* New York, 1950

Fisher, Irving, *The Stock Market Crash—and After,* New York, 1930

Fite, Gilbert C., *George N. Peek and the Fight for Farm Parity,* Norman, Okla., 1954

————, *Peter Norbeck: Prairie Statesman,* Columbia, Mo., 1948

Flynn, John T., *Stock Speculation,* New York, 1934

Frank, John P., *Mr. Justice Black—The Man and his Opinions,* New York, 1949

Frederick, Justus G., *Common Stocks and the Average Man,* New York, 1930

Freidel, Frank, *Franklin D. Roosevelt: The Triumph*, Boston, 1956

Fusfeld, Daniel R., *The Economic Thought of Franklin D. Roosevelt and the Origins of the New Deal*, New York, 1956

Galbraith, John K., *The Great Crash, 1929*, New York, 1955

Garraty, John A., *Right Hand Man: The Life of George W. Perkins*, New York, 1960

Glass, Carter, *Adventures in Constructive Finance*, Garden City, 1927

Goldman, Eric F., *Rendezvous with Destiny*, New York, 1952

Graham, Benjamin, *The Intelligent Investor*, New York, 1954

Grantham, Dewey W., Jr., *Hoke Smith and the Politics of the New South*, Baton Rouge, 1958

Haney, Lewis H., and Logan, Lyman S., and Gavens, Henry S., *Brokers' Loans*, New York, 1932

Hardy, Charles O., and Owens, Richard N., *Interest Rates and Stock Speculation*, New York, 1926

Harris, Seymour E., *Twenty Years of Federal Reserve Policy*, Cambridge, 1933

Hicks, John D., *The Populist Revolt*, Minneapolis, 1931

————, *The Republican Ascendancy, 1921-1933*, New York, 1959

Hill, John, Jr., *Gold Bricks of Stock Speculation*, Chicago, 1904

Hirst, Frances W., *Wall Street and Lombard Street*, New York, 1931

Hoffman, George W., *Future Trading upon the Organized Commodity Markets in the United States*, Philadelphia, 1932

Hofstadter, Richard, *The Age of Reform: from Bryan to FDR*, New York, 1955

Hoover, Herbert C., *The Memoirs of Herbert Hoover*, New York, 1952

Kazin, Alfred, *On Native Ground*, New York, 1942

Key, Vladimir O., Jr., *Southern Politics*, New York, 1949

Kraenzel, Carl F., *The Great Plains in Transition*, Norman, Okla., 1955

Lawrence, Joseph S., *Wall Street and Washington*, Princeton, 1929

Lawson, Thomas L., *Frenzied Finance*, New York, 1905

Lefevre, Edwin S., *Reminiscences of a Stock-Operator*, Garden City, 1923

Leuchtenberg, William E., *The Perils of Prosperity, 1914-1932*, Chicago, 1958

Link, Arthur S., *Woodrow Wilson and the Progressive Era*, New York, 1954

———, *Woodrow Wilson: the New Freedom*, New York, 1956

Lipset, Seymour M., *Agrarian Socialism*, Berkeley, 1950

Lynd, Robert S., and Helen M., *Middletown: A Study in Contemporary American Culture*, New York, 1929

MacCauley, Fred R., *Short Selling on the New York Stock Exchange*, New York, 1951

MacKay, Kenneth C., *The Progressive Movement in 1924*, New York, 1947

Mayer, Martin, *Wall Street—Men and Money*, New York, 1959

McConnell, Grant, *The Decline of Agrarian Democracy*, Berkeley, 1953

McCune, Wesley, *The Farm Bloc*, Garden City, 1943

Meeker, James E., *Short Selling*, New York, 1932

Mitchell, Broadus, *The Depression Decade: From the New Era through the New Deal*, New York, 1947

Morlan, Robert L., *Political Prairie Fire: The Nonpartisan League, 1915-1922*, Minneapolis, 1955

Mowry, George E., *The Era of Theodore Roosevelt, 1900-1912*, New York, 1958

———, *Theodore Roosevelt and the Progressive Movement*, Madison, 1946

Neprash, Jerry M., *The Brookhart Campaigns in Iowa, 1920 and 1926*, New York, 1932

Nichols, Jeanette P., *Twentieth Century United States: A History*, New York, 1943

Norris, Frank, *The Pit*, Chicago, 1903

Nugent, Walter T. K., *The Tolerant Populists; Kansas Populism and Nativism*, Chicago, 1963

Nye, Russel B., *Midwestern Progressive Politics*, East Lansing, Mich., 1951

Palmer, James E., Jr., *Carter Glass, Unreconstructed Rebel*, Roanoke, 1938

Pecora, Ferdinand, *Wall Street under Oath*, New York, 1939

Peterson, H. C., and Fite, Gilbert C., *Opponents of the War, 1917-1918*, Madison, Wis., 1957

Pollack, Norman, *The Populist Response to Industrial America*, Cambridge, Mass., 1962

Prothro, James W., *The Dollar Decade: Business Ideas in the 1920s,* Baton Rouge, La., 1954

Rauch, Basil, *The History of the New Deal,* New York, 1944

Reed, Harold L., *Federal Reserve Policy, 1921-1930,* New York, 1930

Reed, Robert R. and Washburn, Lester H., *Blue Sky Laws,* New York, 1921

Regier, Cornelius C., *The Era of the Muckrakers,* Chapel Hill, N. C., 1932

Riesman, David, with Nathan Glazer and Reuel Denney, *The Lonely Crowd: A Study in Changing American Character,* New Haven, 1950

Ripley, William Z., *Main Street and Wall Street,* Boston, 1927

Roosevelt, Franklin D., *Looking Forward,* New York, 1933

Sakolski, Aaron M., *The Great American Land Bubble,* New York, 1932

Salman, David L., *Confessions of a Customers' Man,* New York, 1932

Saloutos, Theodore, *Farmer Movements in the South, 1865-1933,* Berkeley, 1960

———— and Hicks, John D., *Agricultural Discontent in the Middle West, 1900-1939,* Madison, Wis., 1951

Schlesinger, Arthur M., Jr., *The Age of Roosevelt: Crisis of the Old Order,* Boston, 1957

Schonberg, James S., *The Grain Trade; How It Works,* New York, 1956

Shannon, Fred A., *The Farmers' Last Frontier, 1865-1897,* New York, 1945

Slosson, Preston W., *The Great Crusade and After, 1914-1928,* New York, 1928

Smith, Rixley and Beasley, Norman, *Carter Glass; A Biography,* New York, 1939

Socolofsky, Homer E., *Arthur Capper,* Lawrence, Kansas, 1962

Sparling, Earl, *Mystery Men of Wall Street,* New York, 1930

Soule, George H., *Prosperity Decade: from War to Depression, 1917-1929,* New York, 1947

Stock Market Control, Twentieth Century Fund, New York, 1934

Surface, Frank M., *The Grain Trade during the War . . . ,* New York, 1928

Tucker, Ray and Barkley, Frederic, *Sons of the Wild Jackass,* Boston, 1932

BIBLIOGRAPHY

Van Antwerp, William C., *The Stock Exchange from Within,* Garden City, 1913

Warburg, Paul M., *The Federal Reserve System,* New York, 1930, 2 vols.

Webb, Walter P., *The Great Plains,* Boston, 1931

Wendt, Paul F., *The Classification and Financial Experience of the Customers of a Typical New York Stock Exchange Firm from 1933 to 1938,* Marysville, Tenn., 1941

Wiebe, Robert H., *Businessmen and Reform: a Study of the Progressive Movement,* Cambridge, Mass., 1962

Willis, Henry P., *The Federal Reserve System,* New York, 1923

Woodward, C. Vann, *Origins of the New South, 1877-1913,* Baton Rouge, 1951

Wyckoff, Richard D., *Wall Street Ventures and Adventures,* New York, 1930

INDEX

agrarians, 4, 17, 27, 30, 34, 35, 38, 48, 73, 74, 177; achievements, 1914–24, 103, 104; and anti-speculation, 259; and Banking Act of 1933, 265–66; and branch banking, 265; and commodity futures, 258; defined, 4; and Farm Board, 219; and Federal Reserve Board, 224; and Federal Securities Act, 265; and financial reformers in Progressive Era, 259–60; and futures trading, 131; and short selling, 57; Southern, 81; and speculation in small towns, 111; at state level, 37; and tax policy, 227; and Wall street bears, 264

Agricultural Marketing Act (1929), 211

Albany Argus, 77

Aldrich, Sen. Nelson W. (R.I.), 42, 73; and Aldrich-Vreeland bill, 220

American Agriculturalist, 6

American Bankers Association, 224, 226

American Farm Bureau Federation, 104; and commodity regulation, 88; and Grain Futures Act, 261

American Federation of Labor, and 1929 Crash, 173–75

American Magazine, 166

Anderson, Sydney, 201–2

Andrews, Stephen Pearl, 120

anti-fraud legislation, 30, 37, 40, 51, 63, 65n, 67–74, 232–35, 243, 259–60, 261, 265, 269

anti-monopoly, 4, 30, 31, 38, 52, 61, 216, 226, 227; and Farm Board, 217

anti-speculation, 71, 74, 269, 270; and grain and hog merchants, 6; and sales/ production ratio, 8; and call loan tax vote, 143n; and retention of stock transfer tax, 144-46, 232; and Farm Board, 214–17; and Fletcher-Rayburn margin requirements, 245; and scalpers, 256; sectional nature of, 267–69

anti-speculator tier, 23, 42n, 267–69; and anti-futures bill, 130; Senate voting record of, 272–73; vote on stock transfer tax, 145n

Aron, Harold G., 207

Atlantic Monthly, 155, 182

Atwood, Albert W., 156, 180; and stock market conditions, 99, 101, 170; and manipulation, 103; and stock promotion, 103; and post-Crash speculation, 252

automobile stocks, profits in, 183

Bacon, Sen. Augustus O. (Ga.), and anti-bucket shop amendment, 42, 73

Baer, John M., 86

Baker, George F., 199–200

Bankers' Panic of 1907, 38, 42, 67, 73, 74n, 220

banking, 38; reforms proposed, 51, 73; criticism of small banks, 190–91. *See also* branch banking

Banking Act of 1933, 265. *See also* Glass-Steagall bill

Barkley, Sen. Alben (Ky.), opposes LaFollette resolution, 141n; defends stock exchange

Commercial and Financial
Chronicle, 16, 45, 167
Commodity Exchange Act, 251,
255, 266
commodity trading, 3–24, 210–
19, 229; and speculative competence, 110–11; and short
selling, 195; investigation of,
199; attempted corner in, 235
communism, 18–19, 182n, 198,
231
Conant, Charles A., 31; view
on speculative competence,
106
Connally, Sen. Thomas (Tex.),
opposes branch banking, 22;
and speculation, 256–57
Congressional election of 1918,
86, 261
Consolidated Stock Exchange,
60, 65
Content, Harry, 55
Coolidge, Calvin, 132, 133,
144, 154, 189; and stock
market, 187
Cooperative Marketing Act
(1922), 94, 129
Copeland, Sen. Royal S. (N.Y.),
attacks capital gains tax, 190;
defends speculation, 190; and
"super-bankers," 198
Corcoran, Thomas, author of
Fletcher-Rayburn exchange
bill, 240
Corey, Lewis, see Louis C.
Fraina
Costigan, Sen. Edward P.
(Colo.), supports branch
banking, 221n; attacks exchange secrecy, 239
cotton, 18, 23, 26, 112, 201,
219, 259–60, 269; and futures
contracts, 43–45; grading, 47,
66; proposed price controls,
85–86, 260–61; and speculative competence, 114; proposed tax on futures, 129–30;
and Farm Board, 211, 215
Cotton Futures Act (1914), 66,

92, 104–5, 129, 251, 259
Couzens, Sen. James (Mich.),
143–44, 154, 216; and Federal Reserve Board, 152–53;
and the Crash, 152–53, 263;
progressivism of, 153n; supports branch banking, 221n
Coxey, Jacob S., 244, 264; and
financial conspiracy, 197
Crawford, Sen. Coe I. (S.D.),
59; and central banking, 222
Crawford, Dr. Edward, and
commodity speculation, 235
Cromwell, Chester T., discusses
amateurs, 180–81
Cromwell, Seymour L., defends
stock exchanges, 164; and
participation in the market,
179–80; and employee stock
plans, 179–80
Cudahy, John, 17
Cummins, Sen. Albert Baird
(Ia.), 45, 89, 137, 260; his
proposed amendment to the
Underwood-Simmons Tariff,
46, 47, 65; and central banking, 222; Senate vote on
amendment, 272
Curb Exchange, 35, 166; and
fraudulent stock, 96
Curtis, William Buckingham,
25–26
Cutten, Arthur, W., 37, 250–51;
defends speculation, 163;
criticizes Farm Board, 203,
212; opposes regulation of
exchanges, 203

Daniel, Sen. John W. (Va), 18
Davis, John W., 132
deflation of 1920–21, 87–88,
104; and land speculation,
140
Democratic party, and anti-
futures bill, 18; and cotton,
46–47, 261; and exchange
regulation, 60, 63; platform
of 1932, 72; and "peace
scare" of 1916, 76; and Food

Middletown, 155
Milburn, John G., 56
Miller, Adolph C., and 1929
Crash, 253–54
millers, 7, 8, 11, 12, 14, 15, 16,
24; and Food Control bill,
81–82
mining and oil interests, 67, 71,
73
Mitchell, Sen. John H. (Ore.),
20
"Money Trust," 52, 108, 197
Morgan, J. P., 53, 192, 244
Morgan, House of, 189n, 197,
198, 225
Moses, Sen. George (N.H.),
128
muckraking, 29, 35, 38, 58,
259; magazines, 27
Munsey's, 30, 64
Myrick, Herbert, 6

Nation, 52, 64, 161, 180
National Association of Manu-
facturers, opposes stock ex-
change regulation, 241–42
National Association of Security
Commissioners, 71
National City Bank of New
York, 94
Nearing, Scott, 176
Nelson, Sen. Knute (Minn.),
58, 61; and Food Control bill,
81–83
Newark News, 83
New England Homestead, 6
New Orleans Cotton Exchange,
201
New Orleans Item, 83
New Republic, 181; and specu-
lation, 171–72, 236
New York Evening Mail, 58
New York Evening Post, 31
New York Federal Reserve
Bank, 223, 263; and redis-
count rate, 134
*New York Journal of Com-
merce,* 58, 59, 60, 136
New York Post, 59

New York Stock Exchange, *see*
stock exchange
New York Sun, 34, 45, 83, 84
New York Times, 52, 58; reaction to LaFollette resolution,
142
New York Tribune, 60, 83
New York World, 59, 77
newspapers, 6, 38, 157; defend
market practices, 16; oppose
speculation, 16, 17; and
gambling, 25; and Lawson,
34; and cotton futures, 45;
purchasable news columns,
49, 205; and "peace scare" of
1916, 76–78; reaction to Food
Control bill, 83–84; and La-
Follette resolution, 142; and
Reserve Board warning, 149n
Nonpartisan League, 78, 217,
219
Norbeck, Sen. Peter (S.D.),
and dangers of speculation,
141; and tax on call loans,
143; and Farm Board, 216
Norris, Frank, 36
Norris, Sen. George W. (Neb.),
46, 127, 246; and Farm
Board, 216; and central banking, 222; and tax on scalpers,
256
North American Review, 31,
161
Northwest Miller, 16
Noyes, Alexander D., 31
Nye, Sen. Gerald P. (N.D.)
opposes branch banking, 222

O'Brien, Michael J., opposes
stock exchange regulation, 241
O'Conner, James, defends speculation, 189–90
odd-lots, increased trading in,
166–67
options, 14, 15, 239; opposition
to, 66; proposed ban on, 202
"other people's money," 33, 34,
52
Outlook, 52, 95, 98, 179; and